Decadent daughters and monstrous mothers

Manchester University Press

Decadent daughters and monstrous mothers

Angela Carter and European Gothic

REBECCA MUNFORD

Manchester University Press

Manchester and New York

*distributed in the United States exclusively
by Palgrave Macmillan*

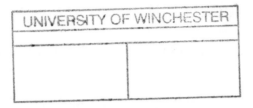

Copyright © Rebecca Munford 2013

The right of Rebecca Munford to be identified as the author of this work has been asserted by her in accordance with the Copyright, Designs and Patents Act 1988.

Published by Manchester University Press
Oxford Road, Manchester M13 9NR, UK
and Room 400, 175 Fifth Avenue, New York, NY 10010, USA
www.manchesteruniversitypress.co.uk

Distributed in the United States exclusively by
Palgrave Macmillan, 175 Fifth Avenue, New York,
NY 10010, USA

Distributed in Canada exclusively by
UBC Press, University of British Columbia, 2029 West Mall,
Vancouver, BC, Canada V6T 1Z2

British Library Cataloguing-in-Publication Data
A catalogue record for this book is available from the British Library

Library of Congress Cataloging-in-Publication Data applied for

ISBN   978 0 7190 7671 8 hardback

First published 2013

The publisher has no responsibility for the persistence or accuracy of URLs for any external or third-party internet websites referred to in this book, and does not guarantee that any content on such websites is, or will remain, accurate or appropriate.

Typeset
by Carnegie Book Production, Lancaster
Printed in Great Britain
by TJ International Ltd

I do think that detaching the worm from the rose
and displaying it is a useful social function.

Angela Carter

Contents

Preface

There is a lot of dust in Angela Carter's fiction. It is 'curded thickly on the heaped junk' in Honeybuzzard and Morris's shop in her first novel, *Shadow Dance* (1966), and covers the 'banal apparatus of despair' in Joseph Harker's room in *Several Perceptions* (1968). A layer of dust lurks under Melanie's bed in *The Magic Toyshop* (1967) and clings to the heavy curtains and jumble of furniture in Lee and Annabel's room in *Love* (1971). It creeps across the cobwebby surfaces of the Mayor's office and the Doctor's laboratory in *The Infernal Desire Machines of Doctor Hoffman* (1972). Blooms of dust also obscure the honesty of the mirrors into which the prostitutes in Ma Nelson's brothel gaze in *Nights at the Circus* (1984), and powder the mouldering 'Museum of dust' inhabited by Dora and Nora in *Wise Children* (1991).

Littered with allusions, quotations and references drawn from a diverse range of cultural spheres, Carter's fictions are full of second-hand furnishings. Worn with use, they bear the ghostly traces of departed texts and objects. At once fetid and fecund, the dust that pervades and invades their interiors gives form to a series of refigured surfaces and transformed textures. A quintessentially Gothic matter, dust tells the story of bodies and things; it is an uncanny register of time, signifying the lingering presence of the past in the present. In its verb form, Carolyn Steedman points out, 'dust' possesses a curious semantic circuitousness: it 'bifurcates in meaning, performs an action of perfect circularity, and arrives to denote its very opposite. If you "dust" you can remove something, or you can put something there' (2001: 160). To dust, then, means at once to *dust away* something old (decaying matter) and to *dust with* something new (powdered matter).

Decadent Daughters and Monstrous Mothers is a book about the dialectical processes of composition and decomposition in Carter's work. In its simultaneous insistence on the significance of matter and the deconstructive gestures afforded by its comminution, dust provides an apt (if somewhat grubby) lens through which to view Carter's intertextual strategies. In particular, it emblematises the tension between her textual extravagancies and her self-declared 'absolute and committed materialism' — her firm belief 'that *this* world is all that there is, and in order to question the nature of reality one must move from a strongly grounded base in what constitutes material reality' ('NFL' 70). The idea and substance of dust illuminates a notion of Gothic intertextuality in which the literary particle jostles alongside the particularity of historical context.

Exploring the ways in which Carter's work speaks to broader discussions about the Gothic and its representations, this book is especially concerned with analysing her textual engagements with a male-authored strand of European Gothic — a dirty lineage that can be mapped from the Marquis de Sade's obsession with desecration and defilement to surrealism's violent dreams of abjection. Spending most of its time in the cobwebby and musty interiors of Carter's fiction, it will also breathe in the dust of the archive. The literary reflections, notes and false starts scattered through Carter's literary journals and manuscripts, recently acquired by the British Library, are brought to light here to offer new ways of thinking about her textual practices, and her use of European Gothic as an aesthetic mode. In what follows, I do not seek to blow the dust away from Carter's writings. Rather, I explore how that dust — in its jumbled, fragmented and obfuscating traces — makes visible new readings of her work.

Acknowledgements

There are many people who have inspired my research and helped me to finish this book. I would like to thank the librarians at the Arts and Social Studies Library at Cardiff University and the British Library. Jamie Andrews provided invaluable help with the Angela Carter Papers. I gratefully acknowledge the financial support I received from the School of English, Communication and Philosophy at Cardiff University for research trips to visit this archive. Many thanks too to the staff at Manchester University Press, especially Kim Walker for her patience, and John Banks for his scrupulous copy-editing.

This book has been enriched by the conversation, advice and timely suggestions of a number of friends and colleagues. I am indebted to Mary Orr for the intellectual guidance she offered me when I was a doctoral student in the French department at the University of Exeter, where I first started to work on Angela Carter. Opportunities to present my work at conferences and research seminars have helped me to develop my thinking about Carter and European Gothic. The 'Angela Carter: A Critical Exploration' conference at the University of Northampton provided a particularly stimulating environment in which to work through my ideas about chess and surrealism. Thanks also to Anke Bernau, Anastasia Valassopoulos, Daniela Caselli, Paul Young, Paul Crosthwaite, Irene Morra, Carl Phelpstead, Julia Thomas, Anthony Mandal, Katie Garner and Sarah Gamble, with whom I have discussed my research at various times and in various places. It has been a pleasure to puzzle over *Love*, *The Passion of New Eve* and *The Sadeian Woman* with

Acknowledgements

students in my MA classes on 'Gothic and Gender' and 'Women's Writing Since 1970' at Cardiff University (Rhys Tranter provided some particularly illuminating chess-related insights). I am especially grateful to Neil Badmington, Claire Connolly, Rob Gossedge, Tomos Owen and Melanie Waters for their incisive comments on parts of the draft manuscript, and to Helen Vassallo for her translations of Baudelaire. A particular debt of gratitude is owed to Stephen Knight for his seemingly boundless intellectual generosity and attention to hyphens.

Lastly, my love and gratitude go to Roberta Munford, Alan Munford, Katherine Munford, Bob Boyce and Tom Melson. And to Tomos, who always has my deepest thanks and admiration.

I would like to thank Susannah Clapp, Angela Carter's Literary Executor, and Deborah Rogers, agent to the Estate of Angela Carter, for granting permission to quote from unpublished materials held in the Angela Carter Papers at the British Library. I am also grateful to the Estate of Angela Carter c/o Rogers, Coleridge & White Ltd, 20 Powis Mews, London W11 1JN for permission to use copyright material from *Shadow Dance*, © 1966 Angela Carter; *The Sadeian Woman: An Exercise in Cultural History*, © 1979 Angela Carter; *The Bloody Chamber and Other Stories*, © 1979 Angela Carter; and *Black Venus*, © 1985 Angela Carter.

An earlier version of some of the material in Chapter 2 appeared in 'Re-presenting Charles Baudelaire/Re-presencing Jeanne Duval: Transformations of the Muse in Angela Carter's "Black Venus"', *Forum for Modern Language Studies*, 40.1 (2004): 1–13. I am grateful to the journal and Oxford University Press for permission to include this material here.

List of abbreviations

'A'   'Afterword' to *Fireworks*
'AW'   'The Alchemy of the Word' (from *Shaking a Leg*)
'BC'   'The Bloody Chamber' (from *The Bloody Chamber and Other Stories*)
'BV'   'Black Venus' (from *Black Venus*)
'CP'   'The Cabinet of Edgar Allan Poe' (from *Black Venus*)
'GB'   'Georges Bataille: *Story of the Eye*' (from *Shaking a Leg*)
HV   *Heroes and Villains*
IDM   *The Infernal Desire Machines of Doctor Hoffman*
L   *Love*
'LHL'   'The Lady of the House of Love' (from *The Bloody Chamber and Other Stories*)
'LLP'   'The Loves of Lady Purple' (from *Fireworks*)
MT   *The Magic Toyshop*
NC   *Nights at the Circus*
'NFL'   'Notes from the Front Line'
'NGM'   'Notes on the Gothic Mode'
PNE   *The Passion of New Eve*
'P'   'Preface' to *Come unto These Yellow Sands* (from *The Curious Room*)
'SB'   'Sleeping Beauty' (translation from *The Fairy Tales of Charles Perrault*)
'SC'   'The Snow Child' (from *The Bloody Chamber and Other Stories*)
SD   *Shadow Dance*
SP   *Several Perceptions*
SW   *The Sadeian Woman: An Exercise in Cultural History*
'TTB'   'Through a Text Backwards: The Resurrection of the House of Usher' (from *Shaking a Leg*)
V   *Vampirella* (from *The Curious Room*)
WC   *Wise Children*

A note on translation

Although most of the primary French texts have been read in the original language, I have used translations, except where Angela Carter is working directly with the French language texts (most notably with Charles Baudelaire's *Les Fleurs du mal*). In these instances, I have provided translations in the notes.

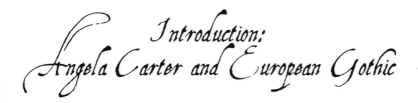

Introduction: Angela Carter and European Gothic

> All art, of any kind, is part of politics – it either expresses or
> criticizes an ideology.
>
> (Angela Carter, 'Notes on the Gothic Mode')

LITERARY VAMPIRISM

Angela Carter's writing is fascinated by the macabre and the erotic, the
dissolute and the grotesque. Inhabited by vamps and vampires, dandies
and decadents, sadistic puppet-masters and disconsolate masochists,
her textual landscapes conjure images of desire and deviance which
have at once captivated and disquieted readers. One of the most
exercising aspects of Carter's work is that it eludes easy categori-
sations and unambiguous classifications. Yet, from the spectacles of
suffering femininity and highly stylised displays of cruelty in her
early novels to the representations of theatricality, illegitimacy and
disguise in her later fiction, Gothic appurtenances and acts produce
some of the most compelling and unsettling effects of Carter's work.
Her writing, with its flamboyant cast of characters, is predisposed to
performance and adornment, to duplicity and disguise. Lorna Sage
fittingly describes how Carter's fictions 'prowl around on the fringes
of the proper English novel like dream-monsters – nasty, erotic,
brilliant creations that feed off cultural crisis' (1977: 51). Vampiric,
menacing and sly, they are conspicuously Gothic creations, built, like

Frankenstein's creature, from the dusty vestiges of previous literary and cultural forms.

The voluptuous textures of Carter's prose have, however, been cast in direct conflict with her feminist politics. In an interview with Carter, John Haffenden asks whether 'the highly stylized and decorative apparatus' of her novels 'might appear to be disengaged from the social and historical realities' she wishes to illuminate in them (Haffenden, 1985: 85).[1] Christina Britzolakis similarly maintains that

> [f]or a certain purist tradition of Marxism, as much as for liberal humanist criticism, Carter is a deeply embarrassing figure, adopting as she does a postmodern aesthetic which, it has been argued, privileges style over substance, eroticizes the fragment and parasitically colludes with consumer capitalism. (1995: 460)

Foregrounding the tension between the aesthetic and the political which frequently marks Carter criticism, Britzolakis posits Carter's literary scavenging as parasitic and predatory; the vampire, one of Carter's preferred motifs, becomes a metaphor for her textual practice.

Of particular concern for some readers of Carter's work is her stylistic investment in male-authored representations of self-sacrificing femininity and sexual violence in her novels of the 1960s and 1970s, what Elaine Jordan describes as the 'apparent contradiction between Carter's feminist "line" and her exploitation of a dangerous reactionary fascination – heterosexual desire in thrall to soft pornography and sado-masochism' (1992: 123). It is not surprising, then, that in the 1980s Carter was taken to task for ostensibly colluding with – even glamorising – male-authored, fetishistic definitions of female sexuality. Robert Clark, in a now infamous essay that appeared in *Women's Studies*, argues that Carter's 'writing is often a feminism in male chauvinist drag'; its 'transvestite style', he elaborates, reveals a 'primary allegiance' to a postmodern aesthetics that 'precludes an affirmative feminism founded in referential commitment to women's historical and organic being' (1987: 158–9). For Clark, the 'brilliant and choice lexicon' and 'incantatory rhythms and tantalizing literariness' of Carter's writing are 'strategies that bind the reader poetically' and 'put the reason to sleep' (1987: 158–9). Carter is positioned as a spellbound Gothic daughter perpetuating the trappings and enchantments of a paternal literary inheritance.

Decadent Daughters and Monstrous Mothers argues that European Gothic is vital to illuminating and understanding the tension between politics and aesthetics in Carter's work. It shows how a more concerted focus on Carter's European literary inheritance sheds light on her particular and perverse engagements with androcentric literary and cultural frameworks. There is evidence of Carter's foraging in what she describes as 'the lumber room of the Western European imagination' (Kenyon, 1992: 29) in both her published work and unpublished notes and reading journals, which are peppered throughout with allusions to European literature – from Auguste Villiers de L'Isle-Adam and André Breton to Charles Baudelaire and Georges Bataille. Particularly apparent is her attraction to the eloquence and excess of the French tradition. In response to a question about 'Gothic' prose styles posed by Sage, Carter attributes the 'polish' of her own writing to her acquaintance with the French language (1977: 55), and describes the immense influence of French literature on the development of her literary sensibility:

> we had this very good French teacher, and we did *Les Fleurs du Mal* and *Phèdre*, and the minute I read Racine, I knew that it moved me much more savagely than Shakespeare [...]. Anyway at this point I was completely lost to the English tradition. Anyone who has had a stiff injection of Rimbaud at eighteen isn't going to be able to cope terribly well with Philip Larkin, I'm afraid. [...] Later the surrealists had the same effect. (Sage, 1977: 54)

Carter's work is also engaged with, and forms part of, a tradition of European intellectual thought that is marked by Gothic preoccupations. She cites Bataille as a 'grand old surrealist fellow-traveller and sexual *philosophe*' ('GB' 68), but she also embarks upon intellectual journeys with Sigmund Freud, Michel Foucault and Roland Barthes, amongst others.

Carter's engagement with and emulation of French Gothic prose styles in particular has been at the heart of some of the most cutting criticisms levelled at her work. Owing to her attraction to what Britzolakis describes as 'the rhetoric and iconography of a prominent, largely male-authored strand of European literary history, which runs from the mid-nineteenth century through Baudelaire, Poe, Sade, much of French Symbolism, the Decadent writing of the *fin de siècle* and Surrealism' (1995: 466), Carter's fictions have often been censured for their complicity with a sadistic and fetishistic erotic register. It is precisely to this European lineage that this book turns in its examination of the fraught relationship between Carter's sexual and textual politics. *Decadent Daughters and Monstrous Mothers* returns to Carter's fiction to re-read it alongside its European intertexts, and in light of new insights into her literary and translational practices afforded by access to archival material. It locates Carter's treatment of male-authored, often misogynistic, Gothic forms as part of a feminist engagement with the genre, albeit one that does not always fit comfortably into Anglo-American definitions of the 'female Gothic' – or the 'monster's mother,' as Ellen Moers describes it (1974a). Writing as a decadent daughter does not, however, mean that Carter is necessarily a daddy's girl.

'NOTES ON THE GOTHIC MODE'

In the 'Afterword' to the first edition of *Fireworks* (1974), a collection of short stories written during the time she spent in Japan, Carter declares that 'we live in Gothic times' ('A' 460). This statement has been interpreted as an expression of the affinities between 'gothicism and postmodernism' (Becker, 1999: 7; see also Neumeier, 1996: 141).[2] That Carter's fiction shares the Gothic's fascination with 'objects and practices that are constructed as negative, irrational, immoral and fantastic' (Botting, 1996: 2) has in turn been understood as evidence of her postmodernist aesthetic. Cristina Bacchilega, for example, positions *The Bloody Chamber and Other Stories* (1979) as a collection of postmodern fairy tales, while Linda Hutcheon claims 'Black Venus' (1985) and *Nights at the Circus* (1984) as exemplars of postmodernist parody (see Bacchilega 1997; Hutcheon 1989).3 Certainly, Carter's writing deploys techniques of parody, citation and appropriation that resemble postmodernist tools of deconstruction; it also engages in a relentless interrogation of essentialist definitions of gender and sexuality that calls into question Enlightenment notions of identity and the totalising effect of grand narratives. However, Carter's positioning as a postmodern writer is less than straightforward. Her fiction is very much concerned with deconstructing the ways in which patriarchal structures of knowledge and power work to marginalise and alienate women, but it also insists upon the historical meanings attached to cultural images and, as Carter puts it in 'Notes from the Front Line' (1983), the need 'for women to write fiction *as* women – it is part of the slow process of decolonialising our language and our basic habits of thought' ('NFL' 75; emphasis in original).

Reading her work as 'fundamentally anti-postmodern,' Aidan Day suggests that Carter is not at odds with 'postmodernism as defined simply by formal textual features such as pastiche, intertextuality, or reflexiveness' but, rather, a notion of 'postmodernism as defined also in a more philosophical sense [...] because the relativising impulse of such postmodernism threatens to undermine the grounds of a liberal-rationalist, specifically feminist politics' (1998: 12). Day's reservations about the 'relativising impulse' of postmodernism chime with Carter's firm belief 'that *this* world is all that there is, and in order to question the nature of reality one must move from a strongly grounded base in what constitutes material reality' ('NFL' 70; emphasis in original). Nevertheless, his suggestion that the 'fantastic elements in Carter's fiction do not anarchically disrupt established orders' but are 'entirely under conscious, rational control' (1998: 7) is rather more difficult to accord with the unruly subversions and disruptions that characterise her fictions. Patricia Waugh more effectively analyses the political stakes of Carter's aesthetic practice, identifying her as a writer who has 'been influenced by post-structuralist theory and postmodernist experiment' but who refuses the 'impersonality' central to their theoretical refusal of the subject. As Waugh suggests, a 'conception of self which involves the possibility of historical agency and integration of ego is necessary for effective operation in the world and must be experienced before its conceptual basis can be theoretically deconstructed' (1989: 30). *Decadent Daughters and Monstrous Mothers* develops such insights into the vexed question of Carter's textual practices through the dusty lens of the Gothic. Forever 'caught in the act' of representation (Punter, 1998: 2), the Gothic provides an apt way of rethinking the conflict between Carter's aesthetic extravagancies and experimentation and her feminist politics. Throwing the subject into crisis, but refusing to relinquish the body, the Gothic brings to the fore the tension between textuality and materialism that haunts her fiction.

Although Carter's fiction is often positioned as part of a broader Gothic current in contemporary women's writing, and in spite of multiple references to and glosses of its Gothic aspects, there has not yet been a sustained analysis of its engagement with and contribution to the development of literary Gothic forms (strangely, references to work on Carter's Gothicism are in excess of actual work on her Gothic aesthetic). Critics have tended to isolate specific texts or clusters of texts rather than explore Gothic patterns across Carter's oeuvre. Linden Peach, for example, argues that Carter's early work is influenced by a 'Euro-American Gothic' tradition and is particularly indebted to some of the key features of American Gothic outlined by Leslie Fiedler in his seminal study *Love and Death in the American Novel*. Peach's readings of Carter's Gothic engagements produce some suggestive discussions of American Gothic influences on Carter's early work (for example, Herman Melville and Edgar Allan Poe),[4] but they confine Carter's Gothicism to her early novels, placing her later works in relation to music, the circus and theatre.[5] Moreover, Peach positions Carter's writing more generally as 'anticipating the late twentieth and twenty-first-century concept of the post-Gothic', which he goes on to describe as 'a place beyond Gothic, in which it is then possible to engage with Gothic in a kind of ludic play' (2009: 23).[6] Peach's approach acknowledges recent shifts in thinking about genre and gender, in particular the critical reverberations of 'post-feminism'. However, it neither takes account of the ways in which the Gothic is already engaged in self-conscious processes of re-examination, transformation and contradiction, nor acknowledges the genre's extant capacity for uncertainty and ambivalence — a quality that is at the heart of Carter's conceptualisation of the genre.

In the 'Afterword' to *Fireworks*, Carter very specifically identifies the genre's capacity for ambiguity and contradiction, and for dismantling the boundaries between 'high' and 'low' cultural forms. Describing her fondness for the tales of Edgar Allan Poe and E. T. A. Hoffmann in particular, she proposes that Gothic writing 'grandly ignores the value systems of our institutions; it deals entirely with the profane. [...] Its style will tend to be ornate, unnatural — and thus operates against the perennial human desire to believe the word as fact' ('A' 459). Crucially, she suggests that Gothic 'retains a singular moral function — that of provoking unease' ('A' 459). The 'Afterword' to *Fireworks* has become the most common point of reference for discussions of Gothicism in Carter's work. I want to broaden this starting point by turning to a surprisingly little-known essay called 'Notes on the Gothic Mode' (1975). 'Notes on the Gothic Mode' was written especially for *The Iowa Review* in 1975 and appeared as part of a special section, entitled 'The Angela Carter Show: An Introduction'. Edited by Robert Coover, the special section showcased Carter's work in its rich variety. Alongside 'Notes on the Gothic Mode' appeared: 'Master' and 'Reflections', from the then recently published *Fireworks*; an early version of 'The Lady of the House of Love' (also written especially for *The Iowa Review*); and two poems, 'Liede' and 'The Named Thing', a grotesque exposition of the Gothic relationship between 'image' and 'thing'. Positioned in the midst of this array of stories and poems, all of which touch on Gothic themes and topoi, 'Notes on the Gothic Mode' sets out a fuller analysis of the nature and potential of the Gothic aesthetic, and provides new insights into Carter's thinking about the genre, including the significance of its European dimensions.

Carter begins this essay by reflecting on the critical move to categorise her early work as part of a broader 'Gothic' project. She tentatively attributes this impulse to the 'clap and sweat and pustules and necrophily' in *Shadow Dance* (1966), which led British reviewers to liken the novel to the work of 'Southern Gothic' writers, such as Tennessee Williams and Truman Capote. Her Gothic credentials, she proposes, were confirmed with the publication of *The Magic Toyshop* (1967): 'from then on there was no holding them: I could be conveniently categorized as "Gothic" and thus outside the mainstream' ('NGM' 132).[7] She goes on to describe her subsequent decision to write *Heroes and Villains* (1969), 'a truly Gothic novel, full of dread and glamour and passion', at around the time she 'began to read the surrealists' ('NGM' 132). What is striking here is Carter's conceptualisation of the Gothic as a European, rather than a specifically Anglo-American, tradition – one that accommodates later avant-garde genres, such as surrealism, in its lineage. Working with the Gothic, Carter argues, gave her a 'wonderful sense of freedom' because of 'the pictorial, expository nature of Gothic imagery, its ambivalence, and the rhetorical, non-naturalistic use of language' ('NGM' 133). European Gothic is formulated as a mode of excess: ornate and unnatural, its revelatory power lies in its proclivity for disguise and embellishment.

While Carter's 'Notes on the Gothic Mode' restates a sense of the Gothic's unnatural and adorned style as a cause of unease, or disquiet, it goes further in placing the imaginative freedoms afforded by the genre in the context of both critique and transformation.[8] Precisely because of 'its holocausts, its stereotyped characterization, its ghosts, its concentration on inner life, its rhetorical and conventionalized prose style', Carter argues, Gothic writing cannot 'pretend to be an imitation of nature; so it cannot disseminate false knowledge of the world' ('NGM' 133). There is an insistence in this essay that '[a]ll art is part of politics – it either expresses or criticizes an ideology'. Moreover, Carter suggests, as a kind of 'fiction absolutely self-conscious of itself as a different form of human experience than reality (that is, not a logbook of events)', the Gothic can 'help to transform reality itself' ('NGM' 133).[9] What emerges here, then, is a notion of the Gothic that is not at odds with political commitment but, rather, which has the prospect of political critique and change at its very core.

The conceptualisation of the Gothic that Carter sets out in 'Notes on the Gothic Mode' extends beyond Southern Gothic and the Byronic heroism from which she ironically distances herself at the beginning of the essay to envisage the genre as part of a distinctly European aesthetic. It emerges in the dread and passion of surrealism, and surfaces 'unexpectedly in writers with a tendency to hysteria', such as Dickens and Dostoevsky ('NGM' 133). It is present too in aspects of Naturalism, which, Carter adds, 'need not affirm the status quo, but when it doesn't, as in Zola, when it becomes a form of heightened realism, it's amazing how Gothic it gets'. She also identifies this Gothic mode in the 'formal abstraction' of Lewis Carroll's writing and the absurdly truthful meaninglessness of Kazimir Malevich's Suprematist art. Above all, Carter suggests, this Gothic aesthetic inhabits the Marquis de Sade's edict that 'Art is the perpetual immoral subversion of the established order' ('NGM' 133). The political edge and edginess of the Gothic resides in its ability to contest the status quo. This is an aesthetic that is fully aware of its status as 'non-being' and thus does not have pretensions to a 'human, tactile immediacy'; at the same time, it recognises the 'concrete existence' of verbal structures because 'if something does not exist, it cannot possess any qualities at all' ('NGM' 133). Thus, Carter's 'Notes on the Gothic Mode' is much more that an inventory of Gothic practitioners and effects. It articulates a politics of representation – one that combines deconstructive strategies with a commitment to materiality. 'Contradictions', after all, Carter writes in the closing line of the essay, 'are the only things that make any sense' ('NGM' 134).

PATERNAL BLOODLINES
AND THE 'MONSTER'S MOTHER'

The history of the Gothic has been written many times over and it is not my intention to rehearse that history here.[10] Rather, in what follows, I foreground a particular European Gothic bloodline that can be traced through Carter's oeuvre. From its beginnings, the Gothic has been preoccupied with origins, inheritance and the relationship between familial and societal structures. Published in 1764, Horace Walpole's *The Castle of Otranto* is widely accepted as the first Gothic novel and, to borrow Carter's words, set 'in train a great vogue for tales of unease' ('TTB' 484). Walpole's novel puts in place some of the key themes and motifs that continue to be associated with the genre in its subsequent manifestations, most notably the Gothic castle as a site for anxieties about inheritance and bloodline, as well as the location of the incestuous and murderous desires of a brutal patriarch. But more than this, suggests Anne Williams, Walpole's novel fulfils Gothic criticism's 'own powerful myth of origins' by furnishing the genre with a literary father (1995: 8).

The publication of David Punter's *The Literature of Terror: A History of Gothic Fictions from 1765 to the Present Day* in 1980 heralded a new era in Gothic criticism, one that saw profuse and diverse moves to expand understandings of the genre beyond the canon of established writers associated with the Gothic 'heyday' (e.g. Horace Walpole, Ann Radcliffe, Matthew Lewis, Mary Shelley and Charles Maturin, etc.) and the 'shopping list approach to a definition of Gothic Romance' that dominated early criticism (DeLamotte, 1989: 5). In turn, Gothic criticism has responded readily to the genre's overtures as 'a Surrealist or revolutionary nihilist, an eerily prescient prophet of psychoanalysis, deconstruction, and the miseries of the modern world' (Williams, 1995: 8). At the same time, the emergence of the Gothic novel in the latter decades of the eighteenth century has signalled its historical importance as a genre that yields insights into emergent formations of the modern subject (see Miles, 2002: 2). Representing a 'darker undercurrent to the literary tradition itself' (Botting, 1996: 15), Gothic signifies the shadowy underside of Enlightenment values by blurring the boundaries demarcating reason and emotion, reality and fantasy, the natural and the supernatural, past and present.

Nevertheless, although the Gothic is characterised by boundary-crossings and exchanges, critical debates about the genre have retained a conspicuously Anglophone bias. *Decadent Daughters and Monstrous Mothers* belongs to a current in recent Gothic scholarship that seeks to challenge what Avril Horner describes as the 'tyranny of Anglo-American narratives of the Gothic' by foregrounding the voracious character of the genre as 'a vampire-like phenomenon that thrives on the blood of others' (2002: 1).[11] After all, the Gothic is not, Daniel Hall points out, 'simply a one nation affair, not simply a "genre anglais"' (2005: 45); its evolution has been determined by reciprocal processes of translation and adaptation, with Gothic motifs as prevalent in German and French texts of the 1790s as in English ones.[12] My reading of Carter's Gothic engagements similarly envisages European Gothic as a series of transactions and transfusions. It is concerned especially with the ways in which Carter's fiction preys upon and feeds off an aggressively masculinist lineage of European Gothic writers – from the infernal eroticism of the Marquis de Sade and Charles Baudelaire to the violent excesses of Decadence and French surrealism, and the uncanny imaginings of psychoanalysis.

The Gothic has since its beginnings suggested an apposite space for women writers to contest and re-imagine the social scripts of femininity and female sexuality fictionalised by the Gothic castle as a site of paternal power. Identifying the innovations of writers such as Clara Reeve, Sophia Lee, Ann Radcliffe, Joanna Baillie, Charlotte Dacre and Mary Shelley, E. J. Clery argues that Gothic literature in the late eighteenth and early nineteenth centuries 'sees women writers at their most pushy and argumentative' (2000: 3). Nevertheless, Carter's fascination with the sexual and textual violence of male-authored scripts of femininity means that her fiction rests uneasily with prevailing accounts of the 'female Gothic'. Coined by Ellen Moers in two articles she wrote for the *New York Review of Books* in 1974 – 'Female Gothic: The Monster's Mother' and 'Female Gothic: Monsters, Goblins, Freaks' – the 'female Gothic' has secured a lasting, if not unshakeable, hold in critical discussions of the genre.[13] The 'female Gothic', Moers proposes, is 'easily defined': it is 'the work that women writers have done in the literary mode that, since the eighteenth century, we have called the Gothic' (1978: 90). The validity of the 'female Gothic' has been vigorously explored, contested and debated, especially in light of poststructuralist challenges to the stability of gender categories.[14] Nevertheless, it played a vital role in centring female subjectivity in critical accounts of the genre, paving the way for a flurry of critical studies addressing the Gothic's potential (and limitations) as a mode of feminist contestation and critique.[15]

In Moers's genealogy of the female Gothic, Radcliffe is accorded the place of literary foremother for firmly setting 'the Gothic in one of the ways it would go for ever after: a novel in which the central figure is a young woman who is simultaneously persecuted victim and courageous heroine' (Moers, 1978: 91). Radcliffe is thus positioned as founding a Gothic paradigm – or, even, as Michel Foucault discusses, making 'possible the appearance of the Gothic horror novel at the beginning of the nineteenth century' (Foucault, 1991: 114). In 'Through a Text Backwards: The Resurrection of the House of Usher' (1988), Carter similarly points to Radcliffe's *The Mysteries of Udolpho* (1794) as establishing, along with Walpole's *The Castle of Otranto*, the 'architecture of anxiety' as a 'literary convention' ('TTB' 484). But Radcliffe's Gothic diverges very significantly from that of Walpole by bringing to the fore the subjectivity of the victimised woman. The enduring importance of her contribution to the Gothic's exploration of female subjectivity and empowerment was established in her second novel, *A Sicilian Romance* (1790). Here Julia de Mazzini is imprisoned within the family castle by her father who is forcing her into an arranged marriage. Haunted by mysterious noises emanating from beneath the castle, she eventually discovers her incarcerated mother Louisa, who has been presumed dead for years. Radcliffe's novel thus sets in place the female Gothic's exploration of the daughter's flight from the threat of male violence, alongside her search for an absent mother.

Subject to the violent and bullying advances of villainous men – from La Motte in *The Romance of the Forest* (1791) to Montoni in *The Mysteries of Udolpho* – Radcliffe's imperilled Gothic heroines embody virtue in distress. Imaginative and intrepid, they embark upon journeys of self-discovery, spurred on by strange discoveries, ghostly imaginings and their encounters with sublime landscapes – Ellena, in *The Italian* (1797), for example, loses 'consciousness of her prison' by allowing herself to travel imaginatively through the 'grandeur' of the landscape she beholds outside of it (Radcliffe, 1998a: 90).[16] However, while recognising the pioneering contribution Radcliffe made in using the Gothic as a language for the expression of female desire in the late eighteenth century, critics have argued that the possibilities of establishing new definitions of female sexuality are undercut by her novels' impulse towards marriage and the re-domestication of the virtuous woman within the bourgeois family.[17] Cynthia Griffin Wolff suggests that while it is 'important to recognize and acknowledge' this heritage, 'it is even more important now to move on and invent other, less mutilating conventions for the rendering of feminine sexual desire' (1983: 223).

Carter makes only fleeting allusions to Radcliffe in her discussions of and notes on the Gothic – referring to her very briefly as a 'contemporary of Sade' in an unpublished essay on the Marquis (BL Add MS88899/1/84). Turning away from the monster's mother, she foregrounds instead an altogether more monstrous paternal literary inheritance – one that makes the 'mutilating conventions' of sexual representation a source of both horror and enthralment. In *Art of Darkness*, Williams argues that male Gothic plot and narrative conventions 'focus on female suffering, positioning the audience as voyeurs who, though sympathetic, may take pleasure in victimization. Such situations are intimately related to its delight in sexual frankness and perversity, its proximity to the "pornographic"' (1995: 104–5). For example, the threat of sexual violence that structures Radcliffe's narratives is recast in Matthew Lewis's *The Monk* (1796) to even more horrifying ends.[18] Deviating from Radcliffe's use of the 'supernatural explained', *The Monk* heightens the theatrical effects of Gothicism to lay bare the supernatural and the daemonic as horrible realities. Actualising the sexual menace only threatened in Radcliffe's Gothic novels, it transforms the idea of virtue in distress into an image of erotic fascination for the fiery gaze of the monk, Ambrosio.[19]

It is no wonder, then, that the Marquis de Sade declares Lewis's novel as 'superior in all respects to the strange flights of Mrs Radcliffe's brilliant imagination' (Sade, 1966: 109). Analysing the proliferation of the English Gothic in the last decade of the eighteenth century, Sade writes in 'Reflections on the Novel' (1800) that 'these new novels in which sorcery and phantasmagoria constitute practically the entire merit' are

> the inevitable result of the revolutionary shocks which all of Europe has suffered. For anyone familiar with the full range of misfortunes wherewith evildoers can beset mankind, the novel became as

difficult to write as monotonous to read. [...] Thus, to compose works of interest, one had to call upon the aid of hell itself, and to find in the world of make-believe things wherewith one was fully familiar merely by delving into man's daily life in this age of iron. (1966: 108–9)

Although, in the same essay, Sade, who was incarcerated in the Bastille at the time of the French Revolution, denies his authorship of *Justine* (1966: 116), his novel also enters hellish domains. The hellish realm of Sade's fiction is not, however, in the 'world of make-believe things' but firmly grounded in the social realities of the material world. *Justine, ou les Malheurs de la vertu* (1791), translated as *Justine, or Good Conduct Well Chastised*, is infamous for its portrayal of the polymorphous sadisms inflicted upon the vulnerable and 'virginal' Gothic heroine within specifically choreographed Gothic geographies. In the Sadeian Gothic, the castle becomes an elaborate setting for an erotic display of female victimisation and suffering that lays bare the power relationships and economic relations outside it.

The Marquis de Sade is perhaps the most significant – and certainly the most notorious – of Carter's literary influences. Although Sade's work provides an explicit focus for *The Sadeian Woman: An Exercise in Cultural History* (1979), Sadeian impulses and influences resonate through much of Carter's fiction – from her Gothic reworking of fairy tales in *The Bloody Chamber and Other Stories* to the quotation from Sade that mysteriously appears in Desiderio's pocket in *The Infernal Desire Machines of Doctor Hoffman* (1972). Carter's unpublished reading journals and notebooks are similarly shot through with commentary on and translated lines from Sade's work. In an interview with Janet Watt, Carter describes how she discovered Sade's complete works in a second-hand bookshop while she was living in Tokyo in the early 1970s, and that she 'fell on them with "shrill shrieks of glee" and no more complicated intention than a "quick thrill"' (Watt, 1979: 54; qtd in Benedikz, 2002: 9n16). Yet, in spite of these glib initial comments, Sade clearly provides a critical touchstone for Carter as a major theorist of the relationship between sexuality and power. Although his shadows can be felt in her early fictions – in the savage but highly stylised violence of Honeybuzzard in *Shadow Dance*, for example – Sade's infernal aesthetic can be traced through Carter's writing of the 1970s and beyond.

In an unpublished essay, Carter maps a direct line between Sade and Poe, drawing a particular connection between *Les 120 Journées de Sodom*, which was published posthumously in 1935 and translated as *The 120 Days of Sodom*, and 'The Masque of the Red Death' (1842) (BL Add MS88899/1/84). So remarked upon is the influence of British Gothic and German Romanticism on Poe's writing that it has become a critical commonplace to consider his work as belonging to both a European and an American tradition. In *The Literature of Terror*, Punter describes the breadth and range of Poe's contribution to the development of Gothic forms 'in terms not of themes but of structure and tone, in the evolution of a variety of symbolist terror in which he has never been surpassed, but which seems in most ways more European than American' (1996a: 177). Poe, Punter proposes, invented something very particular in the Gothic short story; he developed a mode which is driven not simply by narrative but by 'spiralling intensification' (1996a: 177) – an effect that is exemplified by the use of symbolism in 'The Fall of the House of Usher' (1839). According to Punter, this 'vampire story', with its concerns about the 'problem of the blood-line' and aristocratic degeneracy, stands as a kind of hinge in a European Gothic lineage: 'Poe's story points both forward and back: back to Walpole and Radcliffe, forward to another whole constellation of Gothic at the end of the nineteenth century, exemplified particularly in [Oscar] Wilde and in Bram Stoker' (1996a: 180). While Punter appositely foregrounds his pivotal position in a British Gothic tradition, Poe's aesthetic of perversity might be similarly located in a European, and specifically French, tradition – one that looks back to the excruciating mechanics of Sade's sexual schema and forward to the morbid fantasies of femininity that mark French Symbolism, Decadence and surrealism.[20]

Carter similarly reads Poe backwards and forwards. In 'Through a Text Backwards: The Resurrection of the House of Usher' (first published in *Metaphores* in 1988), she analyses the over-determined effects of 'Poe's voluptuous tales of terror' ('TTB' 482) by playing 'The

Fall of the House of Usher' backwards. What she finds there is an image of deathly femininity in a 'half-sleeping state, neither fully dead nor fully alive' – Madeline Usher with the face of a vampire ('TTB' 488, 489). Speaking of her 'familial attachment' to Poe, Carter tells Les Bedford: 'I've used him a lot decoratively, but never structurally. I don't know if that makes sense. [...] I've used a lot of the imagery from Poe. I say I've used it, I've used it as a starting point for imagery of my own' (Bedford, 1977). Certainly, references to Poe and his work are integral to the decor of Carter's fictions. The early novels and their male protagonists in particular betray the influence of his Gothic theatre. For example, Buzz in *Love* (1971) 'emerge[s] from a doorway folded in the wings of a black cape like Poe's raven named Nevermore' (*L* 69), while in *Several Perceptions* (1968) Joseph Harker (whose name locates him in the tradition of Bram Stoker's vampire hunter) tells Mrs Boulder that he 'used to be very fond of Edgar Allan Poe' (*SP* 115) – a comment that reflects his morbid fascination with the maternal muse.

If Poe's writing bears the influence of a European Gothic tradition, it exerts an immeasurable, almost numinous, influence on its later inflections – from Baudelaire's naming of Poe as an intercessor with God (1989: 61) to André Breton's identification of him as 'Surrealist in adventure' in his 1924 'Manifesto of Surrealism' (1972: 27). It is Baudelaire, another of Carter's primary literary forebears, who reanimated Poe for the French tradition, translating five volumes of his work between 1848 and his death in 1867.[21] In his essay 'Edgar Allan Poe: His Life and Works', Baudelaire stated his admiration for the 'high-strung fantasy' of Poe's expression and his depiction of 'luminous and ailing' women (1995a: 91). Baudelaire himself has a strangely underdeveloped presence in the footnotes of Gothic history. Yet, as Catherine Lanone suggests, he is a significant figure in the redemption of the Gothic 'in a new era of doubt and darkening political prospects' as 'that advocate of modernity enamoured with satanic rebellion, who chose as poetical objects skeletons, prostitutes and the depth of the abyss' (2002: 74).[22] Baudelaire's Gothic gaze turns outwards, away from the crumbling castle, with its ailing bloodline, to the labyrinthine space of the modern city. While the aristocratic villain finds form in the figure of the dandy, and the romantic outcast in the figure of the *flâneur*, the prostitute provides an image of infernal femininity.

Baudelaire, like a *flâneur*, travels around the pages of Carter's published texts and her unpublished reading journals. Quotations from his poetry and prose poems – usually directly from the French, but sometimes translated by Carter – litter her notes. Baudelaire's influence is also present in the characterisation of the dandyish male protagonists of her early work – most notably Honeybuzzard and Joseph Harker – as well as the female prostitutes and performers in her later fiction, particularly Leilah in *The Passion of New Eve* (1977), Fevvers in *Nights at the Circus*, the Chance sisters in *Wise Children* (1991) and Jeanne Duval in 'Black Venus'. In an interview with John Mortimer, Carter proclaims that reading *Les Fleurs du mal* (*Flowers of Evil*) (1857 and 1861), was so exciting that she 'really got the feeling of being scalped' (1984: 45). If Carter 'uses' Poe as a starting point for her own Gothic compositions, this encounter with Baudelaire, with its Medusan intimations of decapitation, betrays an altogether more dangerous relation to one of her most mesmeric and persistent literary forebears. It is not always clear if Carter is 'using' Poe and Baudelaire, or if she is being used by her literary forefathers, as they transform her into their decadent daughter.

A self-declared inheritor of Sade's aesthetics of evil – 'Il faut toujours en revenir à de Sade, c'est-à-dire à l'homme naturel, pour expliquer le mal'[23] (qtd in Ward Jouve, 1980: 31) – Baudelaire also represents a 'model' for the decadent movement (Birkett, 1986: 21). For, as Jennifer Birkett proposes, although Baudelaire shared with Sade 'the cult of self-conscious evil', it was he who placed 'the origins of evil in Nature rather than man, and, most of all, in the women who for him are Nature's chief representatives. Juliette is an exception in the Sadean world, while Baudelaire's poetry is dominated by the *femme fatale* and her innocent victims' (1986: 22). This Gothic imagining of femininity anticipates the vilification of nature and idealisation of artificiality in the decadent Gothic of the *fin de siècle* – in, for example, J.-K. Huysmans's *À rebours* (*Against Nature*) (1884) – as well as the sadistic violence and Gothic symbolism of Villiers de L'Isle-Adam's, *Contes Cruels* (*Cruel Tales*)

(1883) and *L'Ève future* (*Future Eve*) (1886). It prefigures too the repertoire of images of the *femme fatale* in such texts as Arthur Machen's *The Great God Pan* (1894), Oscar Wilde's *Salome* (1894), Richard Marsh's *The Beetle* (1897) and Bram Stoker's *Dracula* (1897), as well as French Symbolist poetry and painting.

The fetishistic modes of femininity that characterise this European Gothic bloodline are given reinvigorated form in surrealism's erotic imagination. French surrealists, such as André Breton and Louis Aragon, expressed their interest in the Gothic as a mode of initiating new ways of seeing and challenging socially constructed definitions of desire. Breton claims the Gothic as one of surrealism's most 'outstanding' antecedents, naming Walpole, Radcliffe, Lewis and Maturin as 'the chief representatives of the Gothic novel' (1978: 84). Brought to the attention of the surrealists by Guillaume Apollinaire, Sade was also celebrated by Breton as 'Surrealist in Sadism' (1972: 27) and embraced for the redefinition of sexuality promised by his atheistic agenda. Sade, wrote Breton in the 'Second Manifesto of Surrealism' (1930), represented a revolutionary desire 'to try to make the human mind get rid of its chains' (1972: 186). Surrealist notions of the 'marvellous' also have an affinity with the Freudian uncanny, which is similarly concerned with estrangement, defamiliarisation and the opposition between animacy and inanimacy.[24] In 'The Alchemy of the Word' (1978) Carter describes surrealism as 'not an artistic movement but a theory of knowledge [...] derived from a synthesis of Freud and Hegel' ('AW' 508). Surrealist art, she continues, is 'in the deepest sense, philosophical – that is, art created in the terms of certain premises about reality; and also an art that is itself a series of adventures in, or propositions and expositions of, this surrealist philosophy' ('AW' 508). The revolutionary power of surrealist art lies in its insistence on 'dragging sex and politics into everything' ('AW' 508) and its violent assault on everyday reality. Not just a theory of knowledge, however, surrealism is also 'a way of life; of living on the edge of the senses; of perpetual outrage and scandal; the destruction of the churches, of the prisons, of the armies, of the brothels' ('AW' 508–9). Placing profanation at its intellectual centre, surrealism is an heir of Sade's edict, eulogised by Carter in 'Notes on the Gothic Mode', that 'Art is the perpetual immoral subversion of the established order' ('NGM' 133).

Still, if surrealism proposed – or demanded – the 'liberation of the human spirit as both the ends and the means of art' ('AW' 509), its notion of liberation was limited to the male subject. Male surrealists, writes Rudolf E. Kuenzli,

> did not see woman as a subject, but as a projection, an object of their own dreams of femininity. [...] Women are to the male Surrealists, as in the longstanding traditions of patriarchy, servants, helpers in the forms of child muse, virgin, *femme-enfant*, angel, celestial creature who is their salvation, or erotic object, model, doll – or she may be the threat of castration in the forms of the ubiquitous praying mantis and other devouring female animals. (Kuenzli, 1991: 18–19)

In 'The Alchemy of the Word', Carter similarly concedes that if surrealist beauty is 'put at the service of liberty', this is a liberty to which women – who are positioned as 'the source of all mystery, beauty, and otherness' ('AW' 512) – are denied access. She claims in the same essay that, in the end, she had to 'give up' the surrealists when she realised that surrealist art did not recognise that 'she had her own rights to liberty and love and vision as an autonomous being, not as a projected image' ('AW' 512).

Carter's vexed relation to surrealism has recently been given a new inflection by Anna Watz, who has brought to light Carter's translation of Xavière Gauthier's *Surréalisme et sexualité* (1971). In a landmark article, Watz reveals that Carter was contracted to translate Gauthier's pioneering feminist analysis of surrealist poetry and painting by a small independent publishing house, Calder and Boyars, in 1972. Although she completed the translation, a copy of which is now held at the British Library, Carter withdrew the manuscript after it received a cutting critical review from an editor at the American publishing house, Basic Books (Watz, 2010: 105). Nevertheless, as Watz's analysis conveys, the presence of this work in Carter's oeuvre does not only develop understandings of her role as a translator of French but also illuminates the ambivalent influence of surrealism on her work (2010: 110). In a letter to Marion Boyars, Carter likens Gauthier's book, which she describes as 'a piece of feminist aesthetic polemic', to de Beauvoir's *The Second Sex* in its construction of 'a minute inventory of the myths of the "eternal feminine"' (BL Add MS88899/1/83). Carter highlights, then, the importance of Gauthier's work in unveiling the pernicious myths of femininity that refuse women subjectivity – at the very moment that they claim to expand definitions of the subject. Gauthier's text provides an apt paradigm for thinking through Carter's aesthetic allegiance to surrealism in so far as, to borrow Susan Rubin Suleiman's words, it '*pose[s] as a problem* the subject position of male artists in relation to the objects of their representations, women' (1990: 19; emphasis in original).

In *Subversive Intent*, Suleiman examines the gender politics of avant-garde aesthetics by foregrounding the intersections between male avant-garde writing and 1970s (French) feminism in its transgressive mode. Both movements, she proposes, link 'artistic experimentation and a critique of outmoded artistic practices with an ideological critique of bourgeois thought and a desire for social change' (1990: 12). Such a combination of formal experimentation and ideological critique distinguishes Carter's work. In 'Notes from the Front Line', Carter writes that the summer of 1968 marked a defining moment in the development of her feminist consciousness – 'when, truly, it felt like Year One, that all that was holy was in the process of being profaned and we were attempting to grapple with the real relations between human beings' ('NFL' 70). Taking a dual pleasure in profanation and cultural reappraisal, one that is firmly grounded in a feminist politics, Carter's writing evinces what Suleiman identifies as a 'double allegiance' – 'on the one hand, to the formal experiments and some of the cultural aspirations of the male avant-gardes; on the other hand, to the feminist critique of dominant sexual ideologies, including those of the very same avant-gardes (1990: 162–3). It is with this notion of a 'double allegiance' in mind that *Decadent Daughters and Monstrous Mothers* analyses Carter's feminist dialogues with a male-authored – and often misogynist – bloodline of European Gothic.

Introduction

FEMINISM IN THE GOTHIC HOUSE OF FICTION

My analysis of European Gothic's topographical and representational territories engages, in the course of its travels, with aspects of French feminist theory, in particular the work of Luce Irigaray and Julia Kristeva, that operate in this field of Gothic signification. In this respect, *Decadent Daughters and Monstrous Mothers* not only situates Carter as part of a European Gothic tradition but theoretically aligns her with what Jane Gallop, in her book on Sade, describes as France's '"deconstructive" feminism, daughter of antihumanism' (1981: 3). To illuminate Carter's at times shadowy, even shady, feminist politics, this reading of her European Gothic encounters visits her texts thematically rather than chronologically. This is not to ignore the internal patterns of her oeuvre but, instead, to read outside of their grooves. *Decadent Daughters and Monstrous Mothers* does not attempt to construct a totalising argument about Carter's Gothic engagements – should such an endeavour be either possible or desirable. Rather, it revisits some of the most contentious and exercising aspects of Carter's writing through the lens of European Gothic.

In the chapters that follow, I explore the ways in which Carter's texts prey upon the sexual and textual borders of a male-authored strand of European Gothic that renders femininity in its most spectacular modes. Chapter 1, 'Sleeping Beauty and the Sadeian Gothic', addresses Carter's textual engagements with the 'monstrous and daunting cultural edifice' that is the Marquis de Sade (*SW* 37), placing a close analysis of Sade's *Justine* in dialogue with *The Sadeian Woman*, *The Infernal Desire Machines of Doctor Hoffman* and *The Bloody Chamber*. Foregrounding the Gothic castle as the site of paternal power, it traces European Gothic links with the fairy tale, focusing in particular on the figure of Sleeping Beauty as an exemplification of the virginal female body that becomes a site of erotic enthralment and bloody violence in the pornographic scenarios of the Sadeian Gothic.

Chapter 2, 'Poe, Baudelaire and the decomposing muse', shifts the focus from material to aesthetic enclosures. Positioning Poe and Baudelaire as inheritors and renovators of Sade's aesthetics of perversity, it explores, with reference to 'The Cabinet of Edgar Allan Poe' and 'Black Venus', how the deathly female body becomes a precondition for Gothic composition. Similarly concerned with the female muse, Chapter 3, 'Dolls, dreams and mad queens', enters the territories of surrealism and psychoanalysis, via E. T. A. Hoffmann's Gothic influence, to explore constructions of automated femininity as a reassertion of male creative power and autonomy. Investigating *The Magic Toyshop* and 'The Loves of Lady Purple' (1974) as dialogues with the Freudian uncanny and the precarious power of the toy-maker, it moves on to interrogate surrealist inventions of 'woman' as doll, mannequin and chess queen in *Shadow Dance* and *Love*.

The fourth chapter, 'Daddy's girls and the Gothic fiction of maternity', returns to the figure that haunts the Gothic and its representations: the absent mother. 'Gothic-marked narratives', suggests Susan Wolstenholme, 'always point to the space where the absent mother might be' (1993: 151). While the male bloodline of European Gothic mapped here evinces a macabre fascination with the monstrous mother, feminist criticism has re-inscribed the mother–daughter relationship in the female Gothic, often codifying the Gothic heroine's journey of self-discovery within the labyrinthine spaces of the Gothic castle as an encounter with a spectral maternal presence. But does dramatising anxieties about female sexual identity as a 'conflict with the all-powerful, devouring mother' (Fleenor, 1983: 16) condemn the Gothic mother to the recesses of the Gothic castle? Returning to the Marquis de Sade, the literary forefather of Carter's Gothicism, this chapter analyses the matriphobic death sentences that structure European Gothic writing. *The Sadeian Woman* and *The Passion of New Eve* provide a focal point for thinking through Carter's treatment of 'mother' as a 'figure of speech', while 'The Bloody Chamber' and *Nights at the Circus* invite a reading of the mother's return to the Gothic text. By mapping representations of the mother–daughter relationship, the chapter concludes by asking whether Carter's transgressions and rebellions privilege the subjectivity of the decadent daughter and turn the Gothic mother into nothing but dust.

There is no doubt that Carter's fiction sits uneasily in relation to both dominant Gothic conventions and feminist discourse, especially as they converge through the 'female Gothic'. Sage writes in *Women in the House of Fiction* that, in its unravelling of the 'romance of exclusion', Carter's writing occupies 'an oblique and sometimes mocking relation to the kind of model of female fantasy deployed by Gilbert and Gubar in *The Madwoman in the Attic* – where fantasy is a matter of writing against the patriarchal grain' (1992: 168). The trouble with Carter, then, is that she often appears to be writing against the feminist grain. In so doing, she contests an Anglo-American feminist assumption that 'the "Gothic" women' are not just 'cunning subversives' but are 'also *virtuous* because they didn't construct their prison' (Sage, 1992: 168; emphasis in original).[25] Feeding off a European Gothic bloodline, Carter builds instead new scenarios from its imprisoning fantasies of self-sacrificing and monstrous femininity – the sexual violence in her early novels in particular suggests a closer alignment with the unflinching brutality of the Marquis de Sade's Gothic theatre than with Ann Radcliffe's Gothic of sensibility. Nevertheless, *Decadent Daughters and Monstrous Mothers* argues that Carter's most troublesome engagements with her European Gothic forefathers are unexpectedly those which are most vital to a consideration of her feminist politics. If, as Michelle A. Massé argues, feminism 'insists that we cannot look away from the body or face of a woman in pain' (1992: 3), then Carter's Gothic aesthetic is an unequivocally feminist one.

NOTES

1 Elsewhere in the interview, Haffenden puts it to Carter that: 'It is understandable, I suppose, that someone could approach the fantastic and exotic surface of your fictions and not be able to bridge the gap to the central point that your theatricality is meant to heighten real social attitudes and myths of femininity' (1985: 91).

2 This 'Afterword' did not appear in the 1987 edition of the collection.

3 For further discussions of Carter's postmodernism see Michael (1996); Müller (1997); Benedikz (2002); and Pitchford (2002).

4 Although Peach points out that these American writers were much influenced by German Romanticism, he does not go on to elaborate on specific examples or the implications of this influence in detail.

5 Peach is not alone in sketching this chronological delineation. For example, David Punter includes *Heroes and Villains* and *Love* as representations of 'modern Gothic' in his groundbreaking study *The Literature of Terror* (1996b: 139–43), but in a separate article reads *Nights at the Circus* within the contexts of magical realism (Punter, 1991).

6 The second edition of Peach's book shifts its critical emphasis from 'Euro-American Gothic' (see Peach, 1998) to 'post-Gothic'.

7 In a later interview with Les Bedford for Sheffield University Television in 1977, Carter echoes these views, expressing a greater level of disgruntlement at the 'Gothic tag' imposed upon her writing by reviewers of her early novels: 'I was, and am, a great pedant, and I knew perfectly well what a Gothic novel was. I knew it was all owls and ivy and male passions and Byronic heroes who were probably damned, and I knew I wasn't writing them. Even though some of my heroes were quite emphatically damned, they weren't damned in the Byronic fashion, and that was why, when I set about writing my fourth novel, I very consciously chose the Gothic mode, with owls and ivy and ruins and a breathtakingly Byronic hero' (Bedford, 1977). I am grateful to Sarah Gamble for providing me with a transcript of this television interview.

8 Part of the 'Afterword' from *Fireworks* is reproduced, in slightly re-worked form, towards the end of this essay.

9 A similar sentiment is expressed by Carter in a letter to Elaine Jordan in which she describes how *Heroes and Villains* redeploys the form of the 'pastiche Gothic novel [...] as a vehicle for discussion of certain ideas about liberty – it was my contribution to May, '68 actually' (BL Add MS88899/1/84). The letter is undated, but its discussion of some of the criticisms levelled at *The Bloody Chamber* (and a reference to the novel having been written twenty years earlier) dates it in the 1980s.

10 For a more general overview of English Gothic see, for example, Lévy (1968); Punter (1996a and 1996b); Botting (1996); and Kilgour (1999). For an overview of French and German Gothics see Hall (2005), and on French Gothic see Killen (1967).

11 Aspects of European Gothic have also been illuminated in works by Cornwell (1990); Davenport-Hines (1998); Punter (2000); and, more recently, Horner and Zlosnik (2008). Horner and Zlosnik suggest that the prevalence of Anglo-American narratives of the Gothic might, at least partially, be attributed to the nationally determined critical operations of the 'Gothic' as a category of genre. They point out that the French critical

tradition 'has engaged in a continuing debate about *le roman noir* and *la littérature fantastique*, but has not acknowledged "Gothic" as a valid literary term, reserving it instead for architecture' (2008: 2).

12 Hall is borrowing Maurice Lévy's term (see Lévy, 1984: 5–13). Terry Hale similarly argues that 'the English gothic genre was by no means the only example of a popular aesthetic of horror in late eighteenth- and early nineteenth-century Europe' and foregrounds the important connections between the development of the Gothic novel in Britain, the *roman noir* and *roman frénétique* in France, and the *Schauerroman* in Germany (2002: 63).

13 The 'female Gothic' subsequently provided the focus for one of the chapters in Moers's seminal work of second-wave feminist literary criticism, *Literary Women* (1976).

14 The relationship between gender and genre suggested by Moers's 'female Gothic' has been variously adjusted and re-imagined as 'Gothic Feminism' (Hoeveler, 1998), 'the feminine Gothic' (Becker, 1999), the 'lesbian Gothic' (Palmer, 1999) and, most recently, the 'postfeminist Gothic' (Brabon and Genz, 2007). For further analysis and modifications of the 'female Gothic' see Miles (1994), Smith and Wallace (2004) and Wallace and Smith (2009).

15 According to Robert Miles, 'a recurring family of narratives began to emerge as a common description of the female Gothic plot [...]: a heroine caught between a pastoral haven and a threatening castle, sometimes in flight from a sinister patriarchal figure, sometimes in search of an absent mother, and, often, both together (that is to say, we encounter variations on Ann Radcliffe's *A Sicilian Romance*)' (Miles, 1994: 131). See, for example, Fleenor (1983); Kahane (1985); DeLamotte (1989); Wolstenholme (1993); and Becker (1999).

16 For further discussion of Radcliffe's work see Miles (1995).

17 James Watt argues that Radcliffe's heroines may 'indulge in the natural sublimity of mountain landscapes as a temporarily empowering release from actuality' but 'this form of elevated individualism remains potentially at odds with the organic and family-oriented community that is celebrated by moralizing closure' (1999: 104).

18 Lewis wrote in a letter to his mother that *Udolpho* was 'one of the most interesting Books that ever have been [...] I confess that it struck me, and as He is the Villain of the tale, I did not feel much flattered by the likeness' (qtd in Kilgour, 1999: 142). The figure of the Satanic monk

Schedoni in Radcliffe's *The Italian* can in turn be read as a response to the polymorphous sadisms of *The Monk*.

19 For a discussion of Carter's work in the context of Radcliffe's and Lewis's Gothic innovations see Duncker (1996).

20 David Galloway, for example, posits that 'Poe's relationship to the European romantic tradition – to Coleridge and De Quincey, to Byron, Keats and Shelley, to the Gothic traditions of Germany and the critical theories of Schlegel – is more immediately recognizable than any other American tradition, and his work marks him not simply as a precursor to the Symbolist school in France, but as a direct and major influence on Baudelaire, Mallarmé, Verlaine and Rimbaud' (1986: 12).

21 In a letter to Paul Verlaine, Baudelaire wrote that 'Edgar Poe, who isn't much in America, *must* become a great man in France – at least that is what I want' (qtd in Quinn, 1957: 9; emphasis in original).

22 Lanone suggests that Baudelaire's *flâneur* re-works the tormented, nomadic Gothic hero of Charles Maturin's *Melmoth the Wanderer* (1820) as 'the epitome of the romantic outcast' (2002: 74).

23 'One must always come back to de Sade, that is to say to natural man, to explain evil' (my translation).

24 Hal Foster suggests that the uncanny 'is not merely contemporaneous with surrealism, developed by Freud from concerns shared by the movement, but also indicative of many of its activities' (1993: xvii). It is the 'principle of order that clarifies the disorder of surrealism' (1993: xviii).

25 As I have argued elsewhere, the criticisms levelled at Carter's feminist credentials seem to rest on particular assumptions about the role and responsibility of the 'woman author' and the inimical position Carter occupies in relation to dominant models of second-wave Anglo-American feminist literary criticism (see Munford, 2006: 3–5).

1

Sleeping Beauty and the Sadeian Gothic

The storytellers have not realised that the Sleeping Beauty would have awoken covered in a thick layer of dust; nor have they envisaged the sinister spiders' webs that would have been torn apart at the first movement of her red tresses.

(Georges Bataille, 'Dust')

To be the *object* of desire is to be defined in the passive case.

To exist in the passive case is to die in the passive case – that is, to be killed.

This is the moral of the fairy tale about the perfect woman.

(Angela Carter, *The Sadeian Woman*)

DESECRATING THE FEMINIST TEMPLE

'The satanic marquis, the ghastly figure with eyes like burning coals and a heart like a gigantic torture chamber', is the most troubling and absorbing of Carter's literary forebears. This Miltonic description of the Marquis de Sade appears as part of an unpublished fragment in Carter's manuscripts (BL Add MS88899/1/84). In it she positions Sade as father of a Gothic mode that is at once political and appalling, foregrounding his imaginative legacy in the work of Edgar Allan Poe but signalling his wider influence on the unrestrained recesses of the European literary imagination. Carter's most sustained dialogue with Sade structures *The*

Decadent daughters and monstrous mothers

Sadeian Woman: An Exercise in Cultural History. Published in 1979, this text is frequently acknowledged as representing what Sally Keenan describes as a 'watershed moment in [Carter's] thinking about feminism, a moment when her fictional narratives become increasingly bound up with theoretical considerations' (1997: 134). Through an exploration of three of his most famous works – *Justine, ou les Malheurs de la vertu* (1791), *L'Histoire de Juliette* (1797) and *La Philosophie dans le boudoir* (1795) – Carter asks whether Sade 'put pornography in the service of women, or, perhaps, allowed it to be invaded by an ideology not inimical to women' (*SW* 37). In so doing, she investigates the possibility of Sade's status as a 'moral pornographer' who 'uses pornographic material as part of the acceptance of the logic of a world of absolute sexual licence for all the genders, and projects a model of the way such a world might work' (*SW* 19). Such a pornographer, she provocatively suggests, would not necessarily be 'the enemy of women' (*SW* 20).

Commissioned by the then newly founded Virago Press, *The Sadeian Woman* was positioned quite explicitly as a 'feminist' publication. However, if it was Carter's 'feminist book', it was, as Sage argues, one 'also aimed against a certain sisterhood. Other writers during these years were constructing women's traditions; it's characteristic of Carter that she was setting out to identify and demolish one' (Sage, 1994b: 12). In a more recent broadcast for BBC Radio 4, Carmen Callil, the founder of Virago Press, similarly recalls Carter saying that the publication of *The Sadeian Woman* would 'shock the sisters' (*In the Company of Poets*, 2011). It is no wonder, then, that Carter's work was received with some enmity. Just as scholars such as Mary Ellmann, Elaine Showalter, Barbara Smith, and Sandra Gilbert and Susan Gubar were developing critical paradigms grounded in the recovery of female literary traditions, so Carter was turning to the Marquis de Sade, the eighteenth-century pornographer and architect of female suffering, to uncover a model of sexual freedom that demystified the cult of victimisation that she perceived in the work of certain women writers and feminist literary critics.

That Carter took Sade seriously as a theorist of sexual politics notoriously affronted some feminist readers, especially in the context of the pornography debates of the late 1970s and early 1980s in the US and the UK.[1] Some of the most loudly voiced responses to *The Sadeian Woman* were unequivocally hostile, accusing Carter of wantonly elevating Sade from the position of 'multiple rapist and murderer' to that of 'artist and writing subject' (Kappeler, 1986: 134). In *The Pornography of Representation*, Susanne Kappeler argues that, in offering an analysis of the textual machinations of the Sadeian pornographic scenario, 'Carter, the potential feminist critic, has withdrawn into the literary sanctuary, has become literary critic' (1986: 134). Sharing Kappeler's disquiet about the ideological efficacy of literary criticism, Andrea Dworkin famously censures *The Sadeian Woman* as a 'pseudofeminist literary essay' and accuses Carter of entering 'the realm of literary affectation heretofore reserved for the boys' (1981: 84–5). For Kappeler and Dworkin, Carter's engagement with the 'literariness' of the Sadeian pornograph in some way delimits the possibilities of her feminist critique.[2] In other words, both install an opposition between the aesthetic and the political (or representations and acts) that allows them to place Carter's analysis of Sade's work firmly within the masculine realm of 'literary affectation'.

Dworkin in particular denounces Carter as part of a broader condemnation of the ways in which female suffering and victimisation are erased in critical accounts of Sade's work that focus on the structural and generic aspects of his writing. This is an offence epitomised, for both Dworkin and Kappeler, by Roland Barthes's *Sade, Fourier, Loyola* – a work that Carter includes in the bibliography for *The Sadeian Woman*.[3] However, as I explore here, Carter is concerned neither with deifying nor with demonising the 'divine Marquis'. Rather, like Simone de Beauvoir in the playfully titled 'Must We Burn Sade?' (1951–52), she refuses to make of him either a 'villain' or an 'idol' and, instead, is concerned with bringing him 'back at last to earth, among us' (Beauvoir, 1966: 4). Underlying her dramatic evocation of the 'ghastly figure' of the Satanic Marquis as a literary forefather is a serious feminist investigation of his contribution as a theorist of sexuality and power – one that does not rest upon a separation of aesthetics and politics, or material reality and representation. Rather, Carter's analysis of Sade's work resides in the Gothic space of 'contradiction' she establishes in 'Notes on the Gothic Mode'.[4]

Decadent daughters and monstrous mothers

Although *The Sadeian Woman* represents an important contribution to feminist discussions of pornography, it also sheds light on the development of Carter's textual strategies, especially with regard to the relationship between gender and genre. Here Carter uses two Sadeian women, the suffering Justine and the sexually aggressive Juliette, to explore the ostensibly dichotomous positions of the female victim and the female aggressor within a history of Gothic representation and discourse. Although the 'Gothic' is not addressed directly, its forms and operations are at play throughout the text (in, for example, its deployment of images of enclosure and entrapment, and its articulation of the deathly forces of sexualised power). Furthermore, Carter's unpublished notebooks and manuscripts for *The Sadeian Woman* portray both Sade and his work in explicitly Gothic terms. His novels, for example, are described as 'immensely long, immensely pornographic, immensely if bizarrely erudite' and as a blend of 'the Gothic tale and the moral fable' (BL Add MS88899/1/84). This chapter is concerned, in part, with bodying forth – or awakening – the spectral presence of the Gothic in *The Sadeian Woman* to realign its political and aesthetic matters. To that end it explores the Gothic as a site for the intersection of Sadeian and feminist discourses of female victimisation.

The figure of Sleeping Beauty, as an embodiment of virtuous and victimised femininity in the Sadeian Gothic, provides a focus for this discussion. According to Hélène Cixous, Sleeping Beauty represents an archetypal image of female passivity that is reiterated throughout Western representation: 'Beauties slept in their woods, waiting for princes to come and wake them up. In their beds, in their glass coffins, in their childhood forests like dead women. Beautiful, but passive; hence desirable: all mystery emanates from them' (1996: 66; see also 1981: 43). A dormant subject on the brink of womanhood, Sleeping Beauty is an exemplary Gothic daughter, whose body is subject to the disciplinary practices fictionalised by the Gothic castle as a locus of paternal power. Most often interpreted as marking the sexual awakening of an adolescent girl on the threshold of womanhood or the onset of menstruation (see Bettelheim, 1991: 232), 'Sleeping Beauty' is an inevitably bloody tale. Revisiting the traditional fairy tale, I consider how the architectural thresholds of the fairy tale castle work to keep the daughter 'in her place' in the father's house. Moving on to Sade's Gothic, I explore how the passive female body becomes a source of erotic and deathly enthralment, subject to the bloody 'prick' of male punishment and violation without end.[5] While Carter confronts the deadly boundaries of the Sadeian body/corpus in *The Sadeian Woman*, Sadeian inflections of 'Sleeping Beauty' reappear through her fiction, most strikingly in *The Infernal Desire Machines of Doctor Hoffman* and *The Bloody Chamber*. These Gothic re-imaginings of Sleeping Beauty do not return to find her immaculate, supine body in the 'glass coffin' described by Cixous. Rather, they visit her deathly and decomposing body in the dusty, mouldering space envisaged by Georges Bataille.

THE PATERNAL PRICK

Although Carter is best known for her re-imagining of traditional fairy tales in *The Bloody Chamber*, she was also an accomplished translator. Her translation of Charles Perrault's *Histoire ou Contes du temps passé* (1697) as *The Fairy Tales of Charles Perrault* appeared in 1977 and was followed by a second illustrated collection, *Sleeping Beauty and Other Favourite Fairy Tales* (1982), which includes two tales by Jeanne-Marie Le Prince de Beaumont. Although Perrault's 'Sleeping Beauty and the Wood' (1697) and the Grimm Brothers' 'Little Briar Rose' (1812) are the most enduring versions of 'Sleeping Beauty', both are, to varying degrees, censored reworkings of Giambattista Basile's 'Sun, Moon and Talia', a tale of necrophilia and cannibalism, collected in *The Pentamerone* (1634–36). In Basile's story, the young and beautiful Talia is gazing out of her window when she sees an old woman spinning outside. She beckons the woman inside and attempts to handle the thread herself, upon which she catches a splinter of flax under her fingernail and, as foretold by the wise men summoned by her father at her birth, falls dead to the ground. Talia's distraught father lays out his daughter's body 'on a velvet throne under a daïs of brocade; and closing the doors, being desirous to forget all and to drive from his memory his great misfortune, he abandoned for ever the house wherein he had suffered so great a loss' (Basile, n.d.: 373). It is, therefore, at the moment of her bleeding – of the first 'prick' – that the abandoned daughter is immobilised within the father's house. Another king, passing by the palace and finding it empty, goes inside to explore, where he discovers the unconscious, and seemingly 'enchanted', beautiful body of Talia: 'Crying aloud, he beheld her charms and felt his blood course hotly through his veins. He lifted her in his arms and carried her to a bed, where he gathered the first fruits of love' (Basile, n.d.: 374). In Basile's version, then, the sleeping woman is explicitly presented as the victim of a necrophilic violation. Although the king returns to his own kingdom and his wife and forgets all about the encounter, Talia (still in her somnolent state) gives birth to two children – Sun and Moon. When one of the babies accidentally suckles Talia's finger, rather than her breast, the splinter is removed and she awakes. Accordingly, the first part of Basile's tale lays bare the sacrifice of the daughter, and the eroticisation of her passivity, that underlies this cultural narrative of adolescent femininity.[6]

In the unpublished notes for her translation of Perrault's 'Sleeping Beauty in the Wood', Carter links the story directly to the 'older, literary versions of the tale, in Basile's "Pentamerone" and the prose romance, "Perceforest"', which includes a similar violation of a sleeping woman (BL Add MS88899/1/82).[7] While Perrault leaves out the princess's conception during sleep, he makes two significant additions to the contextual situation of the Sleeping Beauty – both of which are paramount in Carter's Sadeian re-workings of the fairy tale. The first of these is the detail of the one-hundred-year sleep as the sentence of immobility imposed upon the daughter; the second crucial adaptation is the addition of the thorny hedge, 'so thick that neither man nor beast could penetrate it', that grows up around the castle when the princess falls into her somnolent state and makes the castle (and the female body) impregnable ('SB' 20). This hedge opens only briefly to allow the prince who is destined to 'have' the princess to enter the castle one hundred years later and wake her up. As in Basile's story, it is the aesthetic staging of the recumbent female body – hovering on the boundary of life and death – that arouses the prince's desire:

At last he arrived in a room that was entirely covered in gilding and, there on a bed with the curtains drawn back so that he could see her clearly, lay a princess about fifteen or sixteen years old and she was so lovely that she seemed, almost, to shine. The prince approached her trembling, and fell on his knees before her.

The enchantment was over; the princess woke. She gazed at him so tenderly you would not have thought it was the first time she had ever seen him. ('SB' 21)[8]

Resplendent in her passivity and perfection, the Sleeping Beauty is cast here as a divine and untouched body, her radiant exterior linking her to the Virgin Mary who, as Carter remarks in her unpublished notes on Sleeping Beauty, 'conceives with neither sin nor pleasure' (BL Add MS88899/1/34).[9] Perrault's rendering of 'Sleeping Beauty' thus calls attention to the spectacle of the virtuous and virginal female body cast in relation to a series of corporeal and topographical thresholds. Encased at the centre of the narrative's Chinese-box configurations (within the bedchamber, within the castle, within the hedge, within the forest), the deathly female body is located as the mysterious secret locked away at the centre of the Gothic castle.

The spectacle of the virginal female body within highly choreographed Gothic geographies becomes a more explicit source of erotic enthralment in male Gothic reiterations of the 'Sleeping Beauty' narrative, and especially in Sade's depiction of Justine, where the simplistic boundaries demarcating fairy tale space proliferate into a claustrophobic Gothic excess.[10] Barthes suggests that there is a 'relentlessness' about the Sadeian enclosure which both works 'to isolate, to shelter vice from the world's punitive attempts' and also 'forms the basis of a social autarchy' with its own economy, morality and language (1976: 16–17). For both Barthes and Carter, the model of the Sadeian site is the Castle at Silling in *The 120 Days of Sodom* in which the libertines shut themselves away for four months of violent debauchery.

This château is hermetically isolated from the world by a series of obstacles that recall those found in certain fairy tales: a village of woodcutter-smugglers (who allow no one to pass), a steep mountain, a dizzy precipice which can be crossed only by a bridge (which the libertines destroy once they are inside), a thirty-foot wall, a deep moat, a door which is walled up as soon as they entered, and lastly, a frightful lot of snow. (Barthes, 1976: 15–16)

Echoing Barthes's reading, Carter argues that, brought to this 'utterly impregnable' castle, the libertines' victims have already been 'erased from the world and now live, their own ghosts although they are not dead, only awaiting death' (*SW* 139–40).[11] This alignment of the topographical and the corporeal border points to the Sadeian text as a space of abjection where the subject is suspended in a position of perpetual danger. A morbid inversion of the womb space, the Sadeian Gothic castle buries its subjects alive.

A similarly persistent system of enclosure dominates *Justine*, which provides the focus for the first chapter of Carter's *The Sadeian Woman*. *Justine* is obsessively concerned with acts of opening and closing and with crossing thresholds – both topographical and corporeal. That the novel was published in three separate versions suggests that the figure of suffering femininity represented by Justine was an especial preoccupation for Sade. While differing in their formal aspects and thematic emphases, all three editions of the novel spotlight Justine's 'virginal' beauty and her imperilled virtue, alongside her naive investment in that virtue. The first version, *Les Infortunes de la vertu* (translated as *The Misfortunes of Virtue*), was written in 1787 while Sade was imprisoned in the Bastille and, in turn, morphed into the more excessive (in terms of length and atrocity) text of 1791, *Justine, ou les Malheurs de la vertu*. Although this edition also deploys a first-person narration, it is nonetheless embellished with more vivid and prolonged descriptions of sexual brutality and suffering, as well as a more intricate stage set for its spectacular displays of violence. The yet more cruel and violent final version, *La Nouvelle Justine, ou les malheurs de la vertu, suivi de l'Histoire de Juliette, sa soeur* (the narrative of Justine's abominable sister), included amongst its ten volumes one hundred obscene engravings and was published in 1797. It is the second edition of *Justine* that is of interest here because of its amplified Gothic architecture – of dungeons, underground passageways, seraglios, concealed torture chambers and sepulchres (see Wright, 2002: 41). But it is also, as her reading journals and notebooks reveal, this edition that Carter was using while working on *The Sadeian Woman* and *The Bloody Chamber*.[12]

Although the violent pornography of Sade's text is superficially at a far remove from the sanitised versions of 'Sleeping Beauty' disseminated in contemporary fairy tale anthologies, *Justine* capitalises on its Gothic undercurrents by relentlessly re-casting the suffering virgin heroine within increasingly macabre and impassable enclosures. Justine is, from the very early stages of the text, portrayed as possessing a 'pensive and melancholy character' and 'endowed with a surprising sensibility' (Sade, 1965: 459). Her positioning as a fairy-tale maiden is heightened by the emphasis placed on how her diffident disposition marks her apart from her wicked sister, the brunette Juliette:

> for all the artifice, wiles, coquetry one noticed in the features of the one, there were proportionate amounts of modesty, decency, and timidity to be admired in the other; a virginal air, large blue eyes very soulful and appealing, a dazzling fair skin, a supple and resilient body, a touching voice, teeth of ivory and the loveliest blond hair.
> (Sade, 1965: 459)

The 'sketch' offered by the narrator foregrounds the importance of the visual in the characterisation of Justine, whose 'virginal air' is directly linked to her physical beauty.[13] In Sade's text, Justine's blonde hair, timidity and virginal air align her with the Virgin Mary – and position the text in an immediately antagonistic relation to Catholic discourses of the body. For, in a parodic articulation of the cult of suffering, it is precisely Justine's 'supple and resilient' body that will become the blank canvas across which the violent scripts of her libertine aggressors will be carved out again and again in blood.

If Sade's novel is, at least partly, indebted to the fairy tale's topography, it amplifies its structures. According to Carter, Justine is

> the heroine of a black inverted-fairy tale and its subject is the misfortunes of unfreedom [...]. The recurring images of the novel

are the road, the place of flight and hence of momentary safety; the forest, the place of rape; and the fortress, the place of confinement and pain. (*SW* 39)

Justine travels through a series of menacing and dangerous spaces in which she is assailed and brutalised. The Gothic motif of the threshold assumes a central importance in terms of both the boundaries demarcating the 'relentless' architectural enclosures in the novel and the 'threshold' position of the adolescent women who suffers such brutal punishments in Sade's pornographic regime. For example, in a Gothic inversion of 'Sleeping Beauty', the atheist surgeon Rodin locks his fifteen-year-old daughter Rosalie in a cellar with the intention of performing a dissection of her 'vaginal canal' and 'hymeneal membrane' after she has died a painful and cruel death to 'obtain a complete analysis of a so highly interesting part'. According to his conspirator Rombeau, it is essential to find a young girl for the surgical procedure because 'after the age of puberty [...] the menstrual discharge rupture[s] the hymen' (Sade, 1965: 551). Rosalie's escape is prevented when she is seized by Rodin 'the instant she crossed the threshold of the door beyond which, a few steps away, lay deliverance' (Sade, 1965: 555). Tied back to the bed, the potentially menstrual body is viciously disciplined and made to bleed instead the blood of paternal violation.

In 'Frenchwomen, Stop Trying' (the title of which echoes and dialogues with Sade's political pamphlet, 'Yet Another Effort, Frenchmen, if You Would Become Republicans'), Luce Irigaray argues that the initiation of the female subject in the pornographic scene is a violent and bloody one because the 'libertine loves blood. At least the blood that flows according to his own techniques. For whatever form his libertinage may take, however he may flout all (?) prohibitions, *menstrual blood generally remains taboo*' (1985b: 200; emphasis in original). In Sade's *Justine*, the flow of menstrual blood is repeatedly occluded as the virginal (intact) state of the adolescent body is perpetually renewed and re-written. For, in 'phallic fantasy', argues Jane Gallop,

the solid-closed-virginal body is opened with violence; and blood flows. The fluid here signifies defloration, wound as proof of

penetration, breaking and entering, property damage [...]. In
sadistic science there is no place for menstrual blood, for the latter
marks woman as woman (virgin or not) with no need of man's tools.
(1982: 83)

Subject to a violent gaze that is by turns that of the Enlightened surgeon
and the Gothic butcher (the Sadeian text discloses their proximity),
Rosalie's body is forced open and made to bleed. It is when the
adolescent girl is on the threshold between girlhood and womanhood
that phallic power (the 'prick') must be re-emphasised with utmost
brutality. Disavowing the subjectivity of the menstrual daughter, the
flow of blood in Rodin's surgery guarantees the supremacy of the male
'prick': the exercise and reassertion of male power.

Reading (or re-opening) the Sadeian wound, Carter similarly places
it in a psychoanalytic context (the annotations on Sade's primary texts
that fill her notebooks for *The Sadeian Woman* are interspersed throughout
with notes on Freud's *Introductory Lectures on Psychoanalysis*). Carter argues
that the 'whippings, the beatings, the gougings, the stabbings of erotic
violence' that mark the Sadeian pornograph 'reawaken the memory of
the social fiction of the female wound, the bleeding scar left by her
castration, which is a psychic fiction as deeply at the heart of Western
culture as the myth of Oedipus' (*SW* 23). It is this myth, she proposes,
'that transforms women from human beings into wounded creatures
who were born to bleed' (*SW* 23). Sadeian violence, she suggests, makes
visible the social and cultural structures of power that subjugate and
mutilate the female subject.

One of the most poignant examples of Sade's re-casting of the
'Sleeping Beauty' scenario, and disciplining of female sexuality, takes
place at the Saint Mary-in-the-Wood monastery. This intricate stage set
is described by Carter as 'the novel's longest set-piece, a microcosm in
which a small group of privileged men operate a system of government
by terror upon a seraglio of kidnapped women' (*SW* 42). As indicated
by its name, the Benedictine monastery brings to the fore the Virgin
Mary as the pre-eminent figure of female chastity, humility and virtue.
Here the thorny issue of Justine's virtue is geographically reconfigured

by the architecture of the Saint Mary-in-the-Wood monastery that outwardly promises a place of refuge from the rape and violation she has previously suffered at the hands of Saint-Florent in the forest. Throughout *Justine*, the thorn motif, which is set in play from the novel's opening philosophical reflection on the individual's journey 'along life's thorny way' (Sade, 1965: 457), marks the boundaries between inside and outside, virtue and vice, and intactness and rupture.

During her time in prison after a wrongful conviction, Justine is implored by Dubois, one of a series of surrogate mothers whom she encounters on her journey, to 'renounce the practice of virtue which [...] is the courting of disaster' (Sade, 1965: 480) and to pursue the more profitable way of crime. Justine, however, claims that 'whatever be the thorns of virtue' she prefers them 'unhesitatingly and always to the perilous favors which are crime's accompaniment' (Sade, 1965: 481). It is, however, her pursuit of these thorns that leads her to the Benedictine monastery which, like so many Sadeian constructions, is cast in extreme isolation and, like Perrault's castle, is surrounded by thorny hedges. As Justine recounts:

> at last I perceive several hedges and soon afterward the monastery; [...] dense tracts of forest surround the house on all sides [...] a gardener's cabin nestled against the monastery's walls; it was there one applied before entering. [...] I advised him that religious duty had drawn me to this holy refuge and that I would be well repaid for all the trouble I had experienced to get to it were I able to kneel an instant before the feet of the miraculous Virgin and the saintly ecclesiastics in whose house the divine image was preserved. The gardener rings and I penetrate into the monastery. (Sade, 1965: 560–1)

In a reversal of the 'Sleeping Beauty' paradigm it is Justine who 'penetrates' the threshold of the Gothic castle in the hope of seeking the 'divine' image of the Virgin. Far from laying herself at the feet of the munificent Virgin Mother, however, she soon finds herself back in the position of subjugated daughter, submitting to the brutal desires of four depraved Fathers.

Justine's inevitable subjection to the 'prick' (as a symbol of phallic power) is represented in relation to her crossing over the various thresholds in the monastery. She may have gained access to the monastery's walls, but there is prospect of neither rescue nor escape for the women who are brutalised within them. As Dom Sévérino instructs Justine, shoving her 'forward over the threshold' into the illuminated room where the other monks are gathered, the 'impenetrable asylum' has never been invaded by an outsider: 'the monastery could be taken, searched, sacked, and burned, and this retreat would still be perfectly safe from discovery: we are in an isolated outbuilding, as good as buried within the six walls of incredible thickness surrounding us entirely' (Sade, 1965: 567). Like Perrault's castle, the Benedictine monastery is an 'impregnable retreat' (Sade, 1965: 580), fortified to keep its prisoners inside and potential interlopers out. The language of containment and penetration used to describe the Saint Mary-in-the-Wood monastery is echoed in the vocabulary of besiegement and invasion deployed in the text's pornography. However, while the borders isolating the castle from the outside world are 'impenetrable' and 'impregnable', the female body is assailed, infiltrated and burst open ('the chastened flesh yields, the gate cedes, the ram bursts through (Sade, 1965: 569)). It becomes the 'blood-spattered altar' (Sade, 1965: 570) at which the licentious monks 'sacrifice' their blasphemous offerings. The women prisoners are in turn buried alive within the walls of the Gothic edifice. Like ghostly automata performing their parts in the monks' mechanical, orgiastic spectacles, their subjectivity is gradually eroded through their suffering.

The women imprisoned within the multiple boundaries of the monastery are ordered very specifically by age and task. Reading this episode in *The Sadeian Woman*, Carter proposes that their 'sexual function [...] is a thorough negation of their existence as human beings' (*SW* 43). As is the case elsewhere in Sade's oeuvre, the most violent humiliations and punishments are levelled at the (potentially) reproductive female body, with pregnancy a cause for particular humiliation and cruelty (Sadeian treatments of the maternal will be examined more fully in Chapter 4). The unruly female body is relentlessly disciplined as it is brought under the order of the monks. Amongst the various transgressions committed by the girls and women in the Saint Mary-in-the-Wood monastery – for example, having untidy hair or wearing inappropriate dress – menstruating without 'prior notice of incapacitation' and pregnancy (confirmed by a surgeon) are punished with whippings (Sade, 1965: 581). When the women and girls (the youngest of whom is ten years old) are assembled in a particularly elaborate orgiastic tableau, a thirty-six-year-old pregnant woman is positioned above them in a sacrilegious imitation of the Virgin Mother. Perched on an eight-foot-high pedestal she is forced to stand on one leg and keep the other in the air until her strength fails her and she falls down on the mattresses 'garnished three feet deep with thorns, spines, holly'. When she finally tumbles, her body is pricked all over and the 'villains, wild with lust, one last time step forward to lavish upon her body their ferocity's abominable homage' (Sade, 1965: 574). Viciously removed from her pedestal, the sacred mother figure is subject to a violent desacralisation. Through this hyperbolic staging of the social scripts of femininity, Sade's text does not just puncture Justine's devotion to the Virgin Mary, as an embodiment of female virtue; it also launches an unrestrained assault on a wider culture of Mariolatry.

Brutal, violent and bloody, Sade's Gothic inflections of the 'Sleeping Beauty' paradigm of passive and virtuous femininity reveal, through horrific hyperbole, the limits – and dangers – of mystifying female virtue, suffering and the sanctity of motherhood (a mystification that is exemplified by the Catholic Church). Justine locates her virtue in her body and, more precisely, her virginity and thus the body that wants to stay closed is opened, infiltrated and plundered. As long as she remains cloaked in 'the thorns of virtue' she will suffer the fate of the passive Sleeping Beauty, forever subject to the 'prick' within the parameters of a sadistic male Gothic imaginary. Furthermore, although Justine wishes to enter the monastery in order to submit to the munificence of the Virgin Mary and restore her virtue, she takes up a dual position as virgin and whore for the sadistic monks. As Dom Séverino announces to his cruel accomplices: 'allow me to present you with one of the veritable wonders of the world, a Lucretia who simultaneously carries upon her shoulder the mark stigmatizing girls who are of evil repute, and, in her conscience, all the candor, all the naïveté of a virgin' (Sade, 1965: 564).[14] In Sade's Gothic landscape, the virgin and the whore belong to the same topography. The Sadeian pornograph thus strips back the social and economic operations of power which distribute female sexual identity across the Madonna/whore binary. Or, as Sarah Henstra puts it, the 'distortions and repetitions' of the Sadeian orgy reflect 'society in the buff' (1999: 103).

THE SADEIAN WOMAN AND THE SUFFERING DAUGHTER

In *The Sadeian Woman,* Carter interrogates the phallic economy of the Sadeian imaginary and its implications for an understanding of the complex and mobile relationship between social structures and the body. Bringing into focus the potential of genre as an analytical tool, she argues that 'Sade describes the condition of women in the genre of the pornography of sexual violence' (*SW* 26) because sexual relations 'render explicit the nature of social relations in the society in which they take place and, if described explicitly, will form a critique of those relations, even if that is not and never has been the intention of the pornographer' (*SW* 20). Sade, she suggests, uses this peculiarly Gothic mode to magnify the relationship between social and sexual power structures. By describing 'a society and a system of social relations *in extremis*' (*SW* 23), his pornography functions to both reveal and analyse the cultural conditions of gender and sexuality – in particular those structures that mystify femininity and, therefore, place women outside of history. Carter's interest in Sade as a potential 'moral pornographer' (the term that enraged the text's first detractors) lies in his use of pornography to describe 'sexual relations in the context of an unfree society as the expression of pure tyranny' (*SW* 24). Sade, like Carter, is in the 'demythologising business' ('NFL' 70).

In this respect, *The Sadeian Woman* is not an endorsement of sexual terrorism but, rather, an exploration of the potential of literary terrorism as a 'praxis of destruction and sacrilege' (*SW* 26). The target of this sacrilegious destruction is the suffering and tormented daughter, exemplified by Justine who, by embracing her victimisation, has become

> the prototype of two centuries of women who find the world was not, as they had been promised, made for them and who do not have, because they have not been given, the existential tools to remake the world for themselves [...] a woman with no place in the world, no status, the core of whose resistance has been eaten away by self-pity. (*SW* 57)

This is a narrative, Carter suggests, that finds its form in the masochistic poses of the Gothic heroine – in Justine's adoption of 'the cringe as a means of self-defence' (*SW* 47) – as well as the mystification and mythologisation of female virtue and victimhood which haunts strands of 1970s radical feminist discourse.[15] In this respect, the provocation in *The Sadeian Woman* is not, Keenan argues, Carter's 'supposed validation of pornography, but her employment of [Sade's] work to expose her female readers to their own complicity with the fictional representations of themselves as mythic archetypes' (1997: 138). Like Beauvoir, who asks 'why is it that women do not dispute male sovereignty?' (1988: 18), Carter is concerned with challenging a willingness to take up the role of man's vassal (and vessel) by demythologising virtue and virginity as 'the precious jewel of the ruling classes, token and guarantor of their property rights' (Keenan, 1997: 138). For Carter, Sade is an important figure for feminist thinking because his all-permeating atheism means that he 'treats the facts of female sexuality not as a moral dilemma but as a political reality' (*SW* 27).

Carter's insistence on sexuality as a historical rather than an eternal or timeless entity is best illustrated by her statement that 'our flesh arrives to us out of history, like everything else does. We may believe we fuck stripped of social artifice; in bed, we even feel we touch the bedrock of human nature. But we are deceived. Flesh is not an irreducible human universal' (*SW* 9). *The Sadeian Woman*'s attempts to demystify woman's lack of a place in the world resonates with Foucault's argument, in *The Will to Knowledge: The History of Sexuality*, that 'deployments of power are directly connected to the body – to bodies, functions, physiological processes, sensations, and pleasures' and that 'the biological and the historical are not consecutive to one another, [...] but are bound together in an increasingly complex fashion in accordance with the development of modern technologies of power that take life as their objective' (Foucault, 1998: 151–2).[16] *The Sadeian Woman* shares with Foucault's study an investigation of the history of bodies 'and the manner in which what is most material and most vital in them has been invested' (Foucault, 1990: 152).

For both Carter and Foucault, Sade, the 'eighteenth-century lecher' (*SW* 11), represents a key shift in thinking about sexuality. In *Madness and Civilization*, Foucault attributes to Sade (who spent a large portion of his life in prison)

> one of the greatest conversions of Western Imagination: unreason transformed into delirium of the heart, madness of desire, the insane dialogue of love and death in the limitless presumption of appetite. Sadism appears at the very moment that unreason, confined for over a century and reduced to silence, reappears, no longer as an image of the world, no longer as a *figura*, but as language and desire.
> (Foucault, 2001: 199)

For Foucault, it is no accident that this untangling of the Enlightenment's mingling of madmen and criminals in a notion of abstract 'unreason' emerged from a 'fortress of confinement' (2001: 198) – or that Sade's work is 'dominated by the images of the Fortress, the Cell, the Cellar, the Convent, the inaccessible Island', which form 'the natural habitat of unreason' (2001: 199). However, while Carter too identifies the 'monstrous and daunting cultural edifice' that is Sade as a transitional figure in modern theories of sexuality and the body, *The Sadeian Woman* inflects its investigation of his contribution to debates about the erotic body with an explicit feminist politics. Her treatment of 'the Sadeian woman' focalises those mystifications of sexuality that exile women to the habitats of unreason.[17]

Carter's interest in Sade lies not only in his demystification of female suffering but also in his ability to imagine alternative models of female sexuality that resist the mechanisms of power and knowledge that bring the idea of the suffering woman into being. She is fascinated by Sade's incitement to women 'to fuck as actively as they are able' so that they will 'be able to fuck their way into history and, in doing so, change it' (*SW* 27). Hence, if Justine is the exemplification of self-sacrificing femininity, 'the persecuted maiden whose virginity is perpetually refreshed by rape' (*SW* 49), then Juliette, her whorish sister, is 'a little blasphemous guerrilla of demystification in the Chapel' (*SW* 105). While Justine suffers again and again to maintain her virtue, Juliette takes up her place in the world by performing 'all of the crimes of which Justine is falsely accused' and, in turn, 'the pain inflicted on Justine is transformed into Juliette's pleasure, by the force of Juliette's will and desire for self-mastery and heightened extremes of experience' (*SW* 80). Juliette embodies the possibilities of 'sexuality as terrorism' as 'a woman who acts according to the precepts and also the practice of a man's world and so she does not suffer. Instead she causes suffering' (*SW* 79). The importance of Juliette for Carter's analysis lies not in the model of aggressive femininity she represents but in the ways in which her irreverent attitude towards the cult of 'feminine sensibility' embodied by Justine debunks the mystification of virtuous femininity.

However, while Sade's erotic aesthetic exposes the social reality of sexual relations, his challenge to the 'hedges' of patriarchal thought are ultimately limited. To escape the ritualistic violations of the monks at the Saint Mary-in-the-Wood monastery, for example, Justine must make her way through the bars of her chamber and the thorny hedges surrounding the castle (Carter's summary of this episode amplifies the 'Sleeping Beauty' echo). Yet, upon her departure from the monastery, she arrives in another horrifying and dangerous Gothic geography, the vampiric Count de Gernande's castle. She travels, in other words, only to be enclosed once again; her body heals only to bleed once more. Carter's pared down, synoptic reiteration of key episodes of Sade's novel strips it of its excesses to lay bare its schematic treatment of the relationship between the sexes but, in so doing, reveals that Sade's Gothic topography – inside and out – operates under the sign of the phallus. Wherever she is in the Sadeian pornograph, Justine (like Sleeping Beauty) is subject to the 'prick'.

Similarly illusory is Juliette's claim to power. Her assumption of the role of female libertine permits her a degree of social and economic mobility that Justine will never be accorded. Nevertheless, in the end, as Carter's analysis acknowledges, the two sisters exist in a dialectical relationship to one another:

> If Justine is a pawn because she is a woman, Juliette transforms herself from pawn to queen in a single move and henceforward goes wherever she pleases on the chess board. Nevertheless, there remains the question of the presence of the king, who remains the lord of the game. (*SW* 79–80)

The whore to Justine's Madonna, Juliette is, in the end, simply 'Justine-through-the-looking glass' (*SW* 80) – caught up in an endless series of Gothic reflections. She might represent 'an antithetical myth – that of the aggressive phallic woman who is supremely successful and ends her days in wealth and happiness' (Makinen, 1997: 155), but she remains precisely that: another masculinist myth.[18]

Carter's reading of Sade's work in *The Sadeian Woman* resists the kind of opposition between 'reality' and 'representation' that structures Dworkin's and Kappeler's famous indictments. Like Barthes, her analysis places an emphasis on the formal textures of Sadeian representation. However, while Barthes's exposition of Sade's language of erotic freedom looks away from 'the crimes being reported' to focus on 'the performances of discourse' (Barthes, 1976: 36), *The Sadeian Woman* gazes unflinchingly at those crimes against women in their performative aspect. Concerned with the operations of power in Sade's work, Carter's materialist analysis of the ideology of pornography and the conditions of women's oppression keeps in focus the centrality of 'the cock, the phallus, the sceptre of virility, which is not a state-in-itself [...] but a modality', insisting that we 'must not confuse these parlour games with those kinds of real relations that change you' (*SW* 145). Carter more readily challenges what Foucault comes to see as the 'unique and naked sovereignty', the 'unlimited right of all-powerful monstrosity' (Foucault, 1998: 149), that becomes a death sentence for the female subject.

THROUGH A GLASS DARKLY

Sadeian allusions and fragments are scattered through Carter's writing, but they have a peculiarly powerful presence in *The Infernal Desire Machines of Doctor Hoffman*. Written in Japan, and set in an unnamed South American city, this text is nonetheless one of Carter's most resolutely European works. The novel is structured in terms of a conflict between the extremes of rationality and the imagination, embodied by two paternal authorities: the Minister of Determination, who seeks to impose absolute order and control over the city; and Doctor Hoffman, who uses his mysterious 'desire machines' to distort spatial and temporal laws and give material form to hidden desires (the novel was published in the US as *The War of Dreams*). As its title suggests, the novel borrows from and echoes the fantastic and grotesque imaginings of E. T. A. Hoffmann's tales, most notably 'Councillor Krespel' (1818), 'The Sandman' (1816) and 'The Nutcracker and the Mouse King' (1816). Peter Christensen suggests that Carter's text evokes Hoffmann '(minus the second *n* in his surname) in the title as a stand-in for the dangerous, irrational mad-scientist figure in his works' (1994: 64). Nevertheless, he points out the complexity of this intertextual strategy by emphasising Hoffmann's position in a current of German Romanticism bent on extending (rather than rebuking) the Enlightenment pursuit of knowledge. The complex interrelationship between the daylight world of Enlightenment rationality and the shadowy realm of the imagination is suggested from the beginning of *The Infernal Desire Machines of Doctor Hoffman*. Although 'he was the most rational man in the world', the Minister was 'only a witch-doctor in the present state of things' (*IDM* 20–1), dealing with the mirages and spooks created by the Doctor. In this respect, the war between the Minister and the Doctor was 'a battle between an encyclopedist and a poet for Hoffman, scientist as he was, utilized his formidable knowledge only to render the invisible visible, even though it certainly seemed to us that his ultimate plan was to rule the world' (*IDM* 21). In spite of their ostensible polarity, the boundaries demarcating the habitats of reason and unreason occupied by the Minister and the Doctor are already blurred around the edges.

Sleeping Beauty and the Sadeian Gothic

While Hoffmann's tales remain a dynamic presence throughout *The Infernal Desire Machines of Doctor Hoffman*, the text sets in play a profuse, Gothic intertextuality in its allusions to and re-workings of a rich variety of European sources. Its elaborate Gothic style creates, to quote Cornel Bonca, 'some strange and striking verbal effects, much in the line of Sade, Poe, and Baudelaire (and Bataille and Foucault as well), all of whom train the surgical lights and steely instruments of cold reason on the dark chthonic recesses of sexual desire' (1994: 60).[19] Its kaleidoscopic textuality gives new colour to, amongst many other examples, Jonathan Swift's *Gulliver's Travels*, Sadeian pornography, Marcel Proust's *In Search of Lost Time*, Freudian and Lacanian psychoanalysis, Romantic poetry and surrealist art (including Salvador Dalí's melting clocks and Marcel Duchamp's 'bachelor machines').[20] The novel is especially concerned with paternal authority. According to Beate Neumeier, Doctor Hoffman combines 'the father-figures of psychoanalysis (Freud) and of Gothicism (namely E. T. A. Hoffmann, E. A. Poe, and de Sade) respectively, thus reminding the reader in various ways of the inseparability of the fantastic and its Freudian interpretations' (1996: 145). Although this intertextual excess works to disturb the authority of any one text, what holds in place the novel's Gothic intertextuality is a common projection: an idea of femininity imagined through and imaged in the shape of male desire. The novel re-reads what Elisabeth Bronfen refers to as the 'cultural cliché that Woman is man's symptom, the phantom of his desires' (Bronfen, 1992: 420). The signifier 'Woman' circulates persistently and elusively as women in the text appear in transmogrified forms, as puppets, dolls and phantoms. Emerging time and time again in the text's variegated conjuring of phantasmic femininity is Sleeping Beauty, an avatar of the passive woman as an object of male desire and exchange between men (the father-King and the hero-adventurer). Thus, although Desiderio (whose name signifies desire) is sent by the Minister to murder Doctor Hoffman, his journey is shaped and disrupted by his desire for the mysterious Albertina, Hoffman's elusive and metamorphic daughter (whom he eventually murders).

Reading Desiderio as a postmodern Oedipus, Sally Robinson argues that Carter's text 'brings to the surface what often remains underground in male-centred fictions: the trajectories of desire whereby Woman becomes merely a foil or a "prize" in the stories of male subjectivity' (1991: 101). As this 'foil', Albertina is first conjured as an absent space to be filled with Desiderio's narrative. He recounts in his introduction that she is 'the heroine of my story, the daughter of the magician, the inexpressible woman to whose memory I dedicate these pages' (*IDM* 5).[21] Visiting Desiderio in his sleep, Albertina appears 'in a négligé made of a fabric and colour and texture of the petals of poppies which clung about her but did not conceal her quite transparent flesh, so that the exquisite filigree of her skeleton was revealed quite clearly' (*IDM* 22). The dream rather than the dreamer, she is the 'visitor with flesh of glass' who is to be gazed at and looked through. The messages she writes in lipstick on Desiderio's 'dusty windowpane' – 'BE AMOROUS! [...] BE MYSTERIOUS!' – both irritate and haunt him, itching 'away all day inside [his] head like a speck of dust trapped beneath [his] eyelids' (*IDM* 22). The image of dust in the eye sets in play a tension between sight and obscurity, the visible and the invisible, that plays out through the subsequent narrative.[22]

The novel's preoccupation with visuality and the (in)visible is brought into focus when Desiderio visits the peepshow machines at the seaside. Like microcosms of the novel, the exhibits at the peepshow create a phantasmagoria of disarticulated, fragmented and bleeding female bodies. The first set of peepshow images are, as Suleiman argues, 'like Surrealist paintings'; but they are also 'unmistakably male voyeuristic fantasies (as Surrealist paintings often are), representing female orifices and body parts, and scenes of extreme sexual violence' (1994: 137).[23] Exhibit one, playfully entitled 'I HAVE BEEN HERE BEFORE', displays the open legs of a woman and offers an invitation to gaze directly inside the female body:

> The legs of a woman, raised and open as if ready to admit a lover, formed a curvilinear triumphal arch. The feet were decorated with spike-heeled, black leather pumps. [...] The dark red and purple crenellations surrounding the vagina acted as a frame for a perfectly round hole through which the viewer glimpsed the moist, luxuriant landscape of the interior. (*IDM* 44)

The peepshow thus plays with ideas of the female body as a site of the uncanny, one that is already suggested by the eerie presence of the wax body, and especially Freud's notion of the uncanniness of the female genitals as 'the entrance to the former *Heim* of all human beings, to the place where each one of us lived once upon a time and in the beginning' (Freud, 1990: 368). Gazing far into the world opened up by the wax female genitals, Desiderio brings into focus the outline of a castle which becomes increasingly sinister 'as though its granite viscera housed as many torture chambers as the Château of Silling' (*IDM* 45), the 'impregnable' castle in Sade's *The 120 Days of Sodom*. This exhibit parodies, through hyperbole, Gothic associations of the inner space of the Gothic castle and the female body as a womb/tomb – a stark image of the Sadeian conjunction of eroticism and death that runs through European Gothic and is brought into sharp focus through the surrealist imagination.

The images of corpse-like female bodies that haunt the narrative coalesce in the figure of Sleeping Beauty, who is initially referenced by the wax bodies in the peepshow – 'The Sleeping Beauty' is the oldest surviving waxwork in Madame Tussaud's (see Warner, 2006: 47–57). Sleeping Beauty is given her most explicit presence, however, when Desiderio visits the major's daughter, Mary Anne, 'the beautiful somnambulist' who 'sits like Mariana in the moated grange' (*IDM* 49). In order to get to the Major's mansion, Desiderio must first make his way through the 'dense, forbidding hedges' surrounding it: 'roses sprayed out fanged, blossoming whips from cupolas which almost foundered under their weight' (*IDM* 53). Like Sade's Justine, who has to cut her way out of Saint Mary-in-the-Wood, Desiderio is 'lashed', 'scored' and left 'sick, bleeding and dizzy' (*IDM* 54) as he clambers through the 'vegetable maze' enshrouding the castle. Here the *vagina dentata* motif is projected on to the thorny hedge, which reiterates and magnifies the simultaneously erotic and deathly image of the female genitals in the peepshow exhibit. Inside the castle, Mary Anne is not sleeping, but she possesses a 'slippery' quality that aligns her with the waxwork body that only appears to be human:

She did not look as if blood flowed through her veins but instead some other, less emphatic fluid infinitely less red. Her mouth was barely touched with palest pink though it had exactly the proportion of the three cherries the artmaster piles in an inverted triangle to illustrate the classic mouth and there was no tinge of any pink at all on her cheeks. (*IDM* 55)

Envisaged as a compendium of literary and artistic images of suffering femininity (e.g. Ophelia, Mariana, Lady Madeline of Usher), she does not fully inhabit her body but appears as a spectral and strangely disembodied figure.[24]

Mary Anne becomes present when, fully aware of her somnambulant state, Desiderio (like Basile's prince) 'penetrate[s] her sighing flesh' and fills her with (his) meaning. While, at first, it may appear that Desiderio occupies the passive position of Sleeping Beauty (it is he who pricks his finger on the red rose that Mary Anne hands him), this episode brings to the fore the necrophilic undercurrents of the traditional fairy tale. More specifically, the fairy tale scenario is re-cast through a parody of Romanticism's self-conscious staging of nature: the night-time scene that Desiderio describes has the 'precision of a woodcut in the moonlight' and the night itself sighs 'beneath the languorous weight of its own romanticism' (*IDM* 58). Mary Anne's reference, the next morning, to the frightening noise of the nightingales evokes more specifically the dramatic Gothic setting of Samuel Taylor Coleridge's 'The Nightingale: A Conversation Poem, April, 1798'. Mary Anne is, in one respect, aligned with the 'most gentle Maid, / Who dwelleth in her hospitable home / Hard by the castle, and at latest eve' (Coleridge, 1992: 57). But she is also present in the figure of Philomela, another rape victim who is silenced through male violence. This inflection of 'Sleeping Beauty' is positioned in a much wider network of depictions of sexual violence that can be traced through a European Gothic tradition that comes through Sade, Romanticism, surrealism and psychoanalysis.

The second set of peepshow machines that Desiderio visits restages Sleeping Beauty as a series of Gothic set pieces under the title 'SEE A YOUNG GIRL'S MOST SIGNIFICANT EXPERIENCE IN LIFELIKE COLOURS' (*IDM* 62). If the first set of peepshow machines offered a view of dislocated, fragmented femininity as it is conjured in the surrealist imagination, this set of machines generates an image of suffering femininity as it is imagined in Romantic and Victorian visual art and, in particular, the Romantic Idealism of Pre-Raphaelite painting.[25] These machines do not present wax models, but 'actual pictures painted with luscious oils on rectangular plates' (*IDM* 62). In the first plate, 'THE MANSION OF MIDNIGHT', the Gothic mansion offers up precisely the image of 'ivied ruins', complete with a 'lugubrious owl' (*IDM* 62), from which Carter distanced her early writing in the interview with Les Bedford discussed in the Introduction. The second machine (with the warning 'HUSH! SHE IS SLEEPING!') displays a painting of a Sleeping Beauty who resembles Mary Anne, but is lying back 'in the voluptuous abandonment of sleep in a carved armchair where spiders propelled themselves up and down on the high-wires they had spun themselves among the hangings' (*IDM* 63). Dressed in a 'medieval gown of sheer black velvet' and with 'streaming hair' which 'contained several shades of darkness', this Sleeping Beauty evokes the female muses of Pre-Raphaelite painting, most notably Elizabeth Siddal, who was model and muse for John Everett Millais and Dante Gabriel Rossetti (to whom she was married).

In her discussion of *Shadow Dance* and *Love*, Katie Garner argues that an intermingling of surrealist and Pre-Raphaelite commitments works to intensify and double the violence and fragmentation at play in artistic representations of the female body. According to Garner, the texts' engagements with a violent surrealist aesthetic bring to the foreground the subtext of suffering underlying Pre-Raphaelite paintings of tragic femininity (2012: 149).[26] In *The Infernal Desire Machines of Doctor Hoffman*, these two aesthetic movements – both of which celebrate 'the female body as creative sign' (2012: 149) – are similarly intertwined in their obsessive generation of images of deathly femininity (and femininity as death). Thus, the spiders here gesture to the passing of time and layers of dust envisaged by Bataille in his imagining of Sleeping Beauty's discovery (see epigraph), but their mechanical movements also draw attention to the deathly *mise-en-scène* of Romantic femininity. In turn, the golden-locked prince commands the 'ferocious hedge of thorns' to open so that he can enter the mansion and administer the revitalising kiss – a ministration made possible by a 'click of the internal mechanism' (*IDM* 63). However, amidst the 'rampant malignity' displayed in the fifth machine, the prince emerges as a 'grinning skeleton' and figure of 'DEATH', nudging open the thighs of the 'awakened girl'. Foregrounding the deathly eroticism underlying this configuration of Sleeping Beauty, the machine replays Pre-Raphaelite images of somnolent and corpse-like femininity in their Gothic aspect. Stripping back the 'fleshy' beauty of the Pre-Raphaelite subject, this painting unveils the chivalric prince as the grim reaper.

Although varied in their formations, the sadomasochistic frames of the Sleeping Beauty in her surrealist and Romantic configurations can be traced back to the imaginings of Sade. Allusions to Sade are woven into the very fabric of the text. Desiderio discovers in his pocket a scrap of paper with a 'quotation from de Sade written on it in the most exquisite, feminine handwriting': 'My passions, concentrated on a single point, resemble the rays of a sun assembled by a magnifying glass; they immediately set fire to what they find in their way' (*IDM* 111). The presence of this quotation from *Juliette*, which Desiderio believes Albertina placed in his pocket/text, suggests his affinities with the Sadeian libertine. However, looking for (but not finding) a 'personal significance' in the words, Desiderio is unable to recognise these violent passions as his own (see Benedikz, 2002: 89). Nevertheless, this textual fragment anticipates his later encounter with the Sadeian Count, who draws him into an explicitly Sadeian narrative.

A 'blasphemous libertine' and 'blood-thirsty debauchee' with an enormous prick, the Count is a supremely Sadeian figure (*IDM* 146). His oration could be lifted directly from the pages of Sade's work (and bears a particular resemblance to the cannibal giant Minski's narrative in *Juliette*): 'I have devoted my life to the humiliation and exaltation of the flesh. I am artist; my material is flesh; my medium is destruction; and my inspiration is nature' (*IDM* 146). Possessed of the libertine's megalomania, the Count curses 'the womb that bore him' and declares himself to be 'impregnable because I always exist in a state of dreadful tension. My crises render me utterly bestial and in that state I am infinitely superior to man' (*IDM* 146). Cast absolutely in the Sadeian model, he is a parody of Sade's 'sovereign man', as envisaged by Bataille in *Eroticism*. His is the '[m]oral isolation' that 'means that all the brakes are off' because the 'man who admits the value of other people necessarily imposes limits upon himself' (Bataille, 2006: 171). The denial of others' interests that marks the 'ruinous form of eroticism' (Bataille, 2006: 171) in Sade's system is here given a distinct gender inflection as the very notion of a sovereign subjectivity is charted as an exclusively male domain.[27] The self-authoring and authority of the Sadeian libertine manifests as not only a hatred but also an anxiety about reproductive female sexuality (an anxiety that will receive further attention in Chapter 4 of this book).

The power regime of the Sadeian universe is thrown into sharp relief when the Count and Desiderio visit the House of Anonymity, 'a massive, sprawling edifice in the Gothic style of the nineteenth century' (*IDM* 151). With its dark, gloomy corridors and dressing room 'like the interior of a womb', the House of Anonymity echoes the interior of the Saint Mary-in-the-Wood monastery in *Justine*. Dressed in black tights with holes to expose their genitals, the two men are reduced to their pricks: 'The Count began to murmur softly with anticipation and already his prick, which was of monstrous size, stood as resolutely aloft as an illustration of satyriasis in a medical dictionary' (*IDM* 151). These 'unaesthetic, priapic' costumes parody the Sadeian libertine's exercise of phallic power (the flimsy cardboard masks the two men wear suggest the precariousness of this construct). Here human subjects are reduced to linguistic abstractions. In one of the novel's most disturbing Sadeian set pieces, the distorted and disfigured bodies of the prostitutes in the Bestial Room are 'sinister, abominable, inverted mutations, part clockwork, part vegetable and part brute' (*IDM* 154). The Bestial Room is especially reminiscent of the interior architecture of Minksi's formidable Gothic castle in *Juliette*, which, as Carter describes in *The Sadeian Woman*, 'is furnished with girls – chairs, tables, sideboards all formed of the living flesh of captive women. He has reduced women to their final use function, "thingified" them into sofas, tables and candelabras' (*SW* 94). Women become, in other words, part of the paraphernalia of the Gothic *mise-en-scène*.

The Bestial Room, however, is furnished with living animals (for example, grunting bears for armchairs and hyenas for tables), while the barely animate girls in cages are like 'wax mannequins of love' (*IDM* 152). Margret Benedikz suggests that, in this depiction, 'Carter completes Sade's process of dehumanisation of the masculine space by rewriting the women into animals' (2002: 81). But the women are not simply translated into animal form. In an echo of the iconoclastic tableau of women in the Saint Mary-in-the-Wood monastery, their bodies are imprisoned within a more horrifying Gothic iconography:

> There were, perhaps, a dozen girls in the cages in the reception room and, posed inside, the girls towered above us like the goddesses of some forgotten theogeny locked up because they were too holy to be touched. Each was as circumscribed as a figure in rhetoric and you could not imagine they had names, for they had been reduced by the rigorous discipline of their vocation to the undifferentiated essence of the idea of the female. (*IDM* 154)

Assembled to present 'twelve hairy shrines' (*IDM* 155), the women are reduced to their orifices. This sacred synecdoche prefigures Carter's later analysis of pornography's abstraction of human intercourse to 'the probe and the fringed hole' in *The Sadeian Woman* (*SW* 4). But, while the Count positions himself as a 'self-ordained, omnipotent, consecrated man-phallus' (*IDM* 156), the 'unfortunate prostitute' he selects from the brothel is reduced to a 'bleeding moan' (*IDM* 160). Here Carter's text echoes what Annie Le Brun describes as Sade's dramatisation of 'the intolerable deceitfulness of ideas without bodies, the intolerable deceitfulness of any system which denies human and material reality' (1990: 139–40). Unlike Justine, whose subjectivity is located in her suffering, and whose abused body seems to possess supernatural qualities in its ability to constantly heal and regenerate, this disembodied subject is nothing but suffering.

Carter's dialogue with Sade, here and in *The Sadeian Woman*, reveals the expository power of his pornography. However, by stripping back its Gothic machinery, she also unveils its sexual politics. Through its relentless and repetitive intertextuality, *The Infernal Desire Machines* of

Doctor Hoffman projects a kaleidoscope of fragmented, spectral and illusory female bodies that are produced in and through the aesthetic discourses of the Gothic. While Doctor Hoffman's phantasmagoria disrupts the truth claims of the Minister's 'realist' world view it is, in the end, a House of Cards, in which women appear as either a flickering presence or a bleeding nothingness. Thus, when Desiderio arrives at Hoffman's castle, he is disillusioned: 'at last I had reached the power-house of the marvellous, where all its clanking, dull, stage machinery was kept. Even if it is the dream made flesh, the real, once it becomes real, can be no more than real' (*IDM* 239). Dusty and cobwebbed, the interior of Hoffman's workshop of filthy creation echoes the Mayor's office which, with its dusty carpet and 'cobwebs spun from inkwell to pen-rack across blurred surfaces of desks' is itself 'a mausoleum' (*IDM* 51).

Here, however, the 'pen' operates as an actual enclosure. Desiderio discovers that Hoffman's 'reality modifying machines' are powered by copulating couples in 'love pens' (one of which is reserved for Desiderio to share with Albertina):

> here were a hundred of the best-matched lovers in the world, twined in a hundred of the most fervent embraces passion could devise [...]. They formed a pictorial lexicon of all things a man and a woman might do together within the confines of a bed of wire six feet long by three feet wide. (*IDM* 255)

Doctor Hoffman's machinery of desire reiterates Sade's 'ambition to "say everything" about human sexuality [...] to offer his reader an endless variety of postures and combinations' – a desire, argues John Phillips, that is primarily a linguistic matter (Phillips, 2001: 153). The infernal desire machines of Doctor Hoffman reduce women in particular to nameless 'figures in rhetoric'. It is no wonder that, having killed the Doctor and his daughter, Desiderio returns to his own pen: 'Old Desiderio lays down his pen. [...] My head aches with writing. What a thick book my memoirs make! [...] My head aches. I close my eyes. Unbidden, she comes' (*IDM* 265). Albertina is penned in once again by the novel's unremitting textuality; like a waxwork woman, she is enclosed in its dreams forever.

WAKING THE SLEEPING BEAUTY IN THE WOOD

Carter's re-workings of traditional European fairy tales in *The Bloody Chamber* similarly engage with the topologies of the Sadeian pornograph. The publication of *The Sadeian Woman* in the same year as *The Bloody Chamber and Other Stories* has led to the two texts being read alongside one another, with the latter most often considered a fictional re-imagining of the former's analysis of Sade's pornography. Margaret Atwood, for example, interprets *The Bloody Chamber* as 'a "writing against" de Sade, a talking-back to him' (1994: 120), while for Keenan the two works 'are deeply implicated in one another; they are, it could be said, contrasting sides of the same genre' (1997: 136). The stories are, however, more generally steeped in a French literary tradition, echoing the literary and visual representations of women that suffuse *The Infernal Desire Machines of Doctor Hoffman*. The stories' French heritage lies partly in their relation to Perrault's fairy tales, which Carter translated in 1977. For Jacques Barchilon, Carter's translation was the work of someone who 'understood French well enough to translate Perrault with accuracy and imagination' (2001: 26).[28] He finds further proof of Carter's French literary credentials in the 'modern and elegantly French' story, 'The Bloody Chamber', a tale in which quotations from Baudelaire's poetry jostle against descriptions of extravagant gowns by the Parisian couturier Paul Poiret and the very walls of the castle are lined with 'calf-bound volumes' of pornography ('BC' 16).

Perhaps unsurprisingly, some early responses to Carter's re-casting of vulnerable, adolescent heroines within menacing Gothic interiors in *The Bloody Chamber* mirrored those to *The Sadeian Woman*.[29] Two of the most infamous critiques came from Robert Clark and Patricia Duncker. For Clark, Carter's fairy tale re-workings are '[o]ld chauvinism, new clothing' in so far as they reproduce the point of view of the male voyeur (1987: 149). In a similar vein, Duncker contends that the stories reiterate the 'classical pornographic model of sexuality, which has a definite meaning and endorses a particular kind of fantasy, that of male sexual tyranny within a marriage that is grossly unequal' (1984: 10). For Duncker, the fairy tale is inextricably embroiled in patriarchal social and cultural arrangements: her indictment of Carter's re-visionings in *The Bloody Chamber* is, therefore, underpinned by her conviction in the irrevocable fixity of the ideological structures of the genre (see also Lewallen, 1988). Challenging this reading, Lucie Armitt suggests that, by situating the fairy tale as 'so entrenched in patriarchally restrictive kinship systems that no amount of revision can free it up for positive feminist aims', it is critics such as Duncker who remain 'ensnared' by its generic formulae (1997: 89; see also Makinen, 2000: 31–2). Armitt points out that *The Bloody Chamber* invites a re-thinking of the relationship between genres, arguing that 'rather than being fairy-tales which contain a few Gothic elements these are actually Gothic tales that prey upon the restrictive enclosures of fairy-tale formulae' (1997: 89). It is with this notion in mind that my re-reading of *The Bloody Chamber* will turn again to 'Sleeping Beauty' as a paradigmatic narrative of the daughter's exile to interrogate the 'thorny' place of the Sadeian Gothic in Carter's feminist re-visioning of the genre.

Sleeping Beauty lurks half-asleep, half-awake in Carter's drafts and notes for *The Bloody Chamber*. Although motifs from Perrault's 'La Belle au bois dormant' pervade the collection, both 'The Snow Child' and 'The Lady of the House of Love' engage directly with this fairy tale. A number of early handwritten and typescript drafts of 'The Snow Child', which is most often read as a reworking of 'Snow White' (see Chainani, 2003), give the story the title 'The Sleeping Beauty'. One discarded draft is tellingly inscribed with a note that 'there are many ways of beginning this story' (BL Add MS88899/1/34). Certainly, in many respects, 'The Snow Child' follows the patterns of 'Snow White', a paradigmatic narrative of mother–daughter rivalry.[30] However, in its Sadeian emphasis on necrophilic desire and the deathly power of the paternal prick, 'The Snow Child' resonates not only with 'Snow White' but also with 'Sleeping Beauty'. A Count, out riding with a Countess, articulates his wish for a daughter with the familiar red, white and black attributes. And thus she appears, 'the child of his desire'. The Snow Child is the perfect image of virginal girlhood ('SC' 92) and inspires murderous jealousy and rage in the Countess who, from that moment, 'had only one thought: how shall I be rid of her?' ('SC' 92). After two failed attempts at getting rid of the girl – which lead to the Countess's clothes springing off her body and entwining themselves around the body of the Snow Child – the Countess asks her to pick a rose. Pricking her finger on the thorn, the Snow Child, as if following pre-scripted stage directions, 'bleeds; screams; falls' ('SC' 92). The Countess watches on 'narrowly' as the Count proceeds to rape the dead child.

In 'The Snow Child', mother–daughter rivalry is recast across the Madonna/whore binary. Dressed in 'the glittering pelts of black foxes' and 'high, black, shining boots with scarlet heels, and spurs' ('SC' 91), the Countess is cast as a Sadeian Juliette. In one sense, she appears as an exemplary Sadeian woman – that is, a woman who acts 'according to the precepts and also the practice of a man's world and so she does not suffer' (*SW* 79). Aligning herself with the Count, she ensures her own safety within the confines of the pornograph. In the Gothic's 'peep show of terror', Michelle A. Massé suggests, the 'role of spectator seems to promise protection. Minimally, you are safe for the duration of the spectacle: you know at least that it's not you who is burning at the stake this go-round' (1992: 40). An 'invincible, immaculate' virgin, the Snow Child is the Count's antithesis. As 'white as snow,' she is a Sadeian Justine who suffers silently and, in this silence, falls victim to the bloody prick of male desire. Never much more than a figure of speech, she slips from simile to metaphor: 'Soon there was nothing left of her but a feather a bird might have dropped; a bloodstain, like the trace of a fox's kill in the snow; and the rose she had pulled off the bush' ('SC' 92). The snow child – the child made from snow – melts as quickly as she was constructed.

In so far as it strips back the fantasy of female rivalry to reveal it as a projection of male desire, 'The Snow Child' has been read as a critique of competition (for the father/Phallus) within the Oedipal framework of traditional fairy tales (see Bacchilega, 1997: 36–8). However, the strategies of mirroring and reiteration played out in Carter's Gothic re-imagining of fairy tale structures suggest a more complex affinity between the Countess and the Snow Child (or mother/daughter, Madonna/whore). Although there is no magic mirror in 'The Snow Child', the ice-covered lake into which the Countess throws her diamond brooch (the second of her attempts to eradicate the virginal daughter) functions as its symbolic analogue. Located at the centre of the text, the mirror does not simply represent female rivalry; it also reflects back the relationship between the Countess and the Snow Child. In the course of this short narrative, which restages the Justine/Juliette antithesis across the mother–daughter relationship, both the Countess and the Snow Child occupy the same position: the Countess's furs and boots are transferred from one body to the other and back again; what one loses the other gains, but both are cloaked in the costume of the father's desire. When the Count passes the rose to the Countess it 'bites' her too. The repetition of this bloody bite reveals that both women are subject to the exercise of the prick. As Carter writes in *The Sadeian Woman*, Juliette and Justine 'do not cancel one another out; rather, they mutually reflect and complement one another, like a pair of mirrors' (*SW* 78). Reducing the pornographic scenario to its machinery, the stark prose of 'The Snow Child' exposes the chilling mechanisms of power at the heart of this Sadeian Gothic fantasy.

If 'The Snow Child' represents a 'pared down' (Sage, 2001: 74) version of the 'Sleeping Beauty' model, 'The Lady of the House of Love', the next story in *The Bloody Chamber*, exposes its Gothic extravagancies and excesses. Carter's notes for this story appear alongside those for 'The Snow Child', and are similarly shot through with quotations from and allusions to Perrault's 'La Belle au bois dormant'. It too appears to have started its life as a direct reworking of 'Sleeping Beauty', masquerading under several titles in its earlier versions, including 'Thematic Variations: Vampira / La Belle au Bois Dormante' and 'La Somnambula' (BL Add MS88899/1/34). The story that appeared in *The Bloody Chamber* has itself undergone various transformations. Published in *The Iowa Review*, alongside 'Notes on the Gothic Mode' in 1975, the story has its origins in Carter's radio play, *Vampirella*.[31]

First broadcast in 1976, *Vampirella* casts the Sleeping Beauty story through a distinctly Gothic lens. This is the domain of the ghost of Count Dracula, the notorious nineteenth-century Parisian necrophile Henri Blot, the Scottish cannibal Sawney Beane and the bloody devastation of the First World War. Ornately adorned with heavy velvet curtains, Persian carpets and a 'handsome portrait of Gilles de Raie' (*V* 21), the Gothic castle at its centre is inhabited by a vampiric Countess who is caught between two discourses: the Gothic inheritance of the paternal Count ('blood, blood is her patrimony' (p. 12)) and the Enlightenment optimism of the bicycling virgin Hero, the Empire Boy who arrives 'on two wheels in the land of the vampires' (*V* 6) and promises to diagnose her 'medical condition' and restore her humanity (*V* 21). The female vampire is caught up in what Foucault describes as the transition from 'sanguinity' (a society where power spoke through blood) to an 'analytics of sexuality' in the mechanisms of power – a transition with which, he suggests, Sade is contemporary (Foucault, 1978: 148). Suspended between the language of decay (of bad blood) and diagnosis, 'the princess drowses in the castle of her flesh' (*V* 9). She embodies the predicament of the Sleeping Beauty who, as Carter puts it, is imprisoned by 'hereditary appetites that she found both compulsive and loathsome' ('P' 499). What is made explicit, then, is that this bloody inheritance is bequeathed to the decadent daughter by the sovereign father.

Borrowing much of the content, language and structure of *Vampirella*, 'The Lady of the House of Love' similarly depicts the melancholic longing and suffering of a female vampire, though here there are fewer bodies and voices (see Crofts, 2003: 53). The Lady inhabits a textual castle, built from fragments of previous literary and cultural texts. She is caged by a tradition of Gothic femininity. Aligned by turns with Medea, Lady Macbeth, Miss Havisham, 'La Belle Dame Sans Merci' and Lady Madeline of Usher, '[s]he herself is a cave full of echoes, she is a system of repetitions, she is a closed circuit' ('LHL' 93). The reminder that a 'single kiss woke up the Sleeping Beauty in the Wood' echoes in the narrative ('LHL' 97, 103). The House of Love represents a place of perpetual and relentless narrative recycling wherein the 'tenebrous belle' mechanically acts out her auto-narrative by moving towards the inevitable destiny prefigured by the fall of her Tarot cards: 'La Papesse, La Mort, La Tour Abolie, wisdom, death, dissolution' ('LHL' 95). She may be a vampire, but her obscene beauty and spectral demeanour link her to Sade's Countess de Gernande in *Justine*, who is subject to ritualistic acts of phlebotomy by her husband (Sade, 1965: 637). Suspended on the boundaries of the pre-scripted and reiterative syntax of the Gothic, hers is the predicament of the Sadeian Gothic heroine who is both 'death and the maiden' ('LHL' 96).

If the Lady of the House of Love is a Gothic Sleeping Beauty, her situation and location are imagined through the scenario of dust and decay visualised by Georges Bataille. In his entry on 'Dust' for the 'Critical Dictionary', published as part of the journal *Documents* in 1929, Bataille writes:

> The storytellers have not realised that the Sleeping Beauty would have awoken covered in a thick layer of dust; nor have they envisaged the sinister spiders' webs that would have been torn apart at the first movement of her red tresses. Meanwhile dismal sheets of dust constantly invade earthly habitations and uniformly defile them: as if it were a matter of making ready attics and old rooms for the imminent occupation of the obsessions, phantoms, spectres that the decayed odour of old dust nourishes and intoxicates. (1995: 42)

For Bataille, dust is ever-present and invasive; it signifies the lingering presence of the past in the present. But it is also a portentous marker of change and hauntings yet to come (the 'making ready' of attics and old rooms). As Briony Fer puts it, dust 'evokes dirt, spectres and nocturnal terrors of abandoned houses and it renews itself continually. If Sleeping Beauty conventionally stands for a feminine ideal of passive perfection, here she is subject to worm-eaten and rancid decrepitude' (1995: 166). Sleeping Beauty is no longer the image of ideal, untouchable beauty but a Gothic body besmirched by dirt and decomposition – the female body as a site of waste and detritus.

In Carter's story, the bleak castle in which the vampiric Sleeping Beauty endures her solitude is full of the dust and dirt that, as Bataille derisively reveals, has been ignored by previous story-tellers (the diction bears uncanny resemblance to Bataille's description):

> Depredations of rot and fungus everywhere. The unlit chandelier is so heavy with dust the individual prisms no longer show any shapes; industrious spiders have woven canopies in the corners

of this ornate and rotting place, have trapped the porcelain vases on the mantelpiece in soft grey nets. But the mistress of all this disintegration notices nothing. ('LHL' 94)

This mistress of the house may notice nothing but, later, the intrepid young officer (who, like Jonathan Harker in *Dracula*, is an envoy of the law) is surprised to find how 'ruinous the interior of the house was – cobwebs, worm-eaten beams, crumbling plaster' ('LHL' 100). Arriving on his bicycle, 'the product of pure reason applied to motion' ('LHL' 97) – or, as Elaine Jordan puts it, 'the anti-Gothic sign of human rationality' (1992: 126) – he is the Enlightenment adventurer determined to see clearly and gain insight into the mysterious female body at the centre of the castle. In her reading of Bataille's work, Fer argues that dust sets in play a tension between obscurity and insight/enlightenment: 'It is a question of how dust, as a metaphor, can migrate from waste, from matter, to "dust in your eyes" [...] and a blurring of sight and meaning, whose meaning is necessarily and opaque and impervious to light' (1995: 154).[32] In Carter's story too, the metaphor of dust brings into focus an obscurity in the field of vision, delineating the boundary between the visible and the invisible, the seen and the unseen.

Analysing the ambiguous metaphorical meanings attached to dust, Joseph A. Amato proposes that, in the pre-industrial world, dust was like darkness:

> In it images appear and vanish, things are transformed and generated. Dust formed a shadowy realm that harboured secret exchanges and sponsored unexpected transformations. Associated with caves and cellars and other places where neither light nor darkness entirely prevailed, dust was an ambiguous reservoir of important and unimportant, living and dead (2000: 20).

Dust, in other words, marks the place of the threshold. In Carter's story, the ruinous body of the dusty house is analogous with the threshold body of the 'châtelaine of all this decay' ('LHL' 101). Like Stoker's Dracula, who emerges from his dusty vaults and returns to dust again, the Lady of the House of Love represents 'undeath': 'She has the mysterious solitude of ambiguous states; she hovers in a no-man's land between life and death, sleeping and waking, behind the hedge of spiked flowers, Nosferatu's sanguinary rosebud' ('LHL' 103). With its 'closely barred shutters', 'heavy velvet curtains' and kitsch artefacts, this Gothic castle is configured as a carefully staged Sadeian brothel, a 'House of Love' where death is everywhere. The Lady's bedroom is already established as a funereal space in its Gothic restaging of the Sleeping Beauty scenario: the walls of her bedroom are 'hung with black satin, embroidered with tears of pearl' and at the centre is 'an elaborate catafalque, in ebony, surrounded by long candles in enormous candlesticks' ('LHL' 94). Far from an image of pristine and supine femininity, or the renewable flesh of the Sadeian victim, the Lady of the House of Love occupies a shadowy realm of dust and dereliction. This vampiric somnambulist represents the Gothic reality of the Sleeping Beauty's somnolent existence. Suspended in time, she is 'a ghost in a machine' ('LHL' 100).

In her analysis of the imagery of enclosure that dominates *The Bloody Chamber*, Armitt argues that 'it is not the solidity of the three-dimensional chamber or mansion that is important' in 'The Lady of the House of Love' but, rather, 'the seemingly more precarious two-dimensional enclosure of the frame of the ancestral portrait' (1997: 93). For Armitt, Carter's re-working of 'Sleeping Beauty in the wood' ('LHL' 93) is primarily focused on the wooden frame of the portrait as the source of the heroine's enclosure which, 'rather more successfully than the fragile bloody chamber of the coffin, may well "bury the woman alive" by killing her into art' (1997: 94). Although Armitt's argument appositely foregrounds the imprisoning effects of male aesthetic enclosures, the wooden frame of the portrait is only one of the precarious enclosures to which the female body is subject in 'The Lady of the House of Love'. This reading, perhaps, cannot see the trees for the wood. The somnambulant Lady is bounded by a series of Chinese-box enclosures that extend beyond the walls of the Gothic mansion and the derelict bedroom bequeathed by her 'wicked father' ('LHL' 94–5) to the rampant, thorny hedge marking the boundary between the castle and the forest space. For the castle is encircled by 'an exceedingly sombre' garden, which 'bears a strong resemblance to a burial ground and all the roses her dead mother planted have grown up into a huge, spiked wall that incarcerates her in the castle of her inheritance' ('LHL' 95). In this reconfiguration, the hedge of thorns symbolises the threshold of sexual difference. However, its transgression does not represent the 'sexual awakening' of Sleeping Beauty posited in psychoanalytic readings (and exemplified by Bruno Bettelheim's analysis) but, rather, a deathly eroticism.

It is not the dank decrepitude of Nosferatu's Gothic castle that disturbs the young British army officer who must break through these thorns, but this rampant hedge: 'Too many roses bloomed on enormous thickets that lined the path, thickets bristling with thorns, and the flowers themselves were almost too luxuriant, their huge congregations of plush petal somehow obscene in their excess, their whorled tightly budded cores outrageous in their implications' ('LHL' 98). The rose-covered hedge that overpowers the father's house re-contextualises the threshold as an exteriorisation of sexual difference. For the virgin hero is not only unsettled and nauseated by the excess of the rose-covered hedge, but also by its mirror image in the Lady of the House of Love's 'extraordinarily fleshy mouth, a mouth with wide, full, prominent lips of a vibrant purplish-crimson, a morbid mouth' ('LHL' 101). In her 'négligé of blood-stained lace' ('LHL' 96), the Lady of the House of Love embodies the conjunction of death and eroticism envisaged by Bataille. 'Eroticism,' he suggests, 'is assenting to life up to the point of death' (2006: 11). For Bataille, death brings continuity to the discontinuity of human existence: 'We are discontinuous beings, individuals who perish in isolation in the midst of an incomprehensible adventure, but we yearn for our lost continuity' (2006: 15). Erotic nakedness, as a state of communication or continuity with others, contrasts discontinuous existence. It is the orgasm as *la petite mort*.

To assuage his fear of death, the young officer (occupying his disciplinary office) attempts to re-inscribe the Lady into the traditional 'Sleeping Beauty' script, fantasising about treating her for nervous hysteria and turning 'her into the lovely girl she is; I shall cure her of all these nightmares' ('LHL' 107). He dreams of 'himself as donor, liberator, redeemer'. For, as Simone de Beauvoir emphasises, 'in order

Sleeping Beauty and the Sadeian Gothic

to awaken the Sleeping Beauty, she must have been put to sleep' (1988: 216). Nevertheless, the narrative cannot be re-dreamed within the predetermined contexts of the heroine's deathly location – 'There is no room in her drama for improvisation' ('LHL' 106). Within this Sadeian Gothic interior, her narrative is already written. Although the Lady is seduced by the possibilities of the romantic script, when she tries to remove the antique wedding dress (the absent mother's Gothic legacy), she cuts her finger on her broken spectacles and bleeds (her reading is already and always hindered by her defective vision). The officer's kiss marks the beginning of an erotic continuity and her deathly metamorphosis. For the Lady of the House of Love, the 'end of exile is the end of being' ('LHL' 106). The inevitability of the 'prick' is, once again, inescapable as this Sleeping Beauty is not awoken by 'a single kiss' but, rather, sacrificed to it. The Lady of the House of Love is not only a 'cave full of echoes' but Echo herself.

Nevertheless, in Carter's re-visioning, when the heroine bleeds it is not just her body but also the narrative that is 'punctured' by the thorny framework of the Sadeian *mise-en-scène*. Although the Lady of the House of Love cannot be freed from the 'Sleeping Beauty' script, its mechanisation and artificiality are made visible when the light of day pours into her macabre bedroom:

> now you could see how tawdry it all was, how thin and cheap the satin, the catafalque not ebony at all but black-painted paper stretched on struts of wood, as in the theatre. [...]
> But now there was no trace of her to be seen, except, lightly tossed across the crumpled black satin bedcover, a lace négligé lightly soiled with blood, as it might be from a woman's menses, and a rose that must have come from the fierce bushes nodding through the window. ('LHL' 106)

When Sleeping Beauty is finally freed from her somnolence, the stage set is stripped back and the illusion of the Gothic interior is unveiled as contingent on her imprisonment. Carter parodically replays the logic of the Sadeian pornograph, reinstating the traces of menstrual blood effaced from its scripts. However, although her re-imagining (or re-awakening) of 'Sleeping Beauty' disrupts the topographical mechanisms of the Sadeian Gothic, it leaves no place in which to re-imagine female sexual selfhood beyond its enclosures (a limitation that is redressed elsewhere in *The Bloody Chamber* and in Carter's later fiction). What it does permit is the return of history to take its revenge on the 'rational' male hero, whose regiment leaves the next day for France. The Empire boy will find continuity with the vampire once again in the deathly trenches of the First World War.

What Carter exposes in *The Bloody Chamber* and *The Infernal Desire Machines of Doctor Hoffman* is pornography's status as a genre, one with close affinities to the Gothic.[33] Through the conventions of pornography, Sade holds a magnifying glass to the cultural conditions of gender and sexuality to demystify the power structures that underpin them. In 'Notes on the Gothic Mode', Carter writes that Sade was 'the last great figure of the Enlightenment, one of the most rational men who ever lived' ('NGM' 134). The highly mechanistic emphasis of Sade's Gothic composition pushes rationality to its limits to expose the Gothic realities of the exercise of power.[34] However, while Carter finds in Sade's work an analytic method, she does not lose sight of the 'the cock, the phallus, the sceptre of virility' (*SW* 145) as a pre-eminent Sadeian modality. Her texts are not 'threatened by the big dick,' to put it in Hélène Cixous's terms (1993: 347). In *The Infernal Desire Machines of Doctor Hoffman*, she uses a Gothic excess of citation – drawn from the kaleidoscopic projections of the Sadeian Gothic (into Romantic poetry and surrealist art) – to 'impregnate' the enclosures (or pens) of the Sadeian world. The Sadeian fascination with broken and bleeding bodies becomes in Carter's novel a fascination with the flow of textual fragments into new configurations. In 'The Snow Child', the female body is similarly reduced to bits and pieces, while, in 'The Lady of the House of Love', the female vampire is revealed as a part of the dusty, mechanistic stage set. The machinery of the Sadeian pornograph is thus unveiled to expose its fantasies of suffering femininity. Confronting the thorny hedges of the father's house, Carter unmasks the operations of the 'prick' that repeatedly put women to sleep in the Sadeian Gothic.

NOTES

1 The book's relation to the pornography debates is foregrounded by the subtitle used for its publication by Pantheon in the US – *The Ideology of Pornography*. For an in-depth discussion of the book's relationship to the pornography debates see Sheets (1992).

2 For an incisive overview of feminist academic debates about pornography, including a discussion of the limits of Kappeler's argument, see Wicke (1991).

3 According to Dworkin, Barthes 'wallowed in the tiniest details of Sade's crimes, those committed in life as well as on paper' (1981: 70–1).

4 In a short, unpublished biographical essay on Sade, Carter writes '[Sade's] libertarianism, [...] although extreme, is that of a man who enjoyed bondage. He is full of contradictions' (BL Add MS88899/1/70).

5 Carter's strategy in *The Sadeian Woman* comprises an extremely abbreviated, but revelatory, summary of Sade's novel. My readings here engage with both Sade's texts and Carter's interpretation of them.

6 The second part of the tale deals with the murderous jealousy of the King's wife. For more on this tale see Warner (1994: 220–2).

7 In these notes, Carter also links Sleeping Beauty to Brynhildr, the 'magic sleeper' in the Völsunga Saga.

8 This emphasis on the otherworldliness of her beauty is conveyed even more strongly in Perrault's French: 'il vit sur un lit, dont les rideaux étaient ouverts de tous côtés, *le plus beau spectacle* qu'il eût jamais vu: une Princesse qui paraissait avoir quinze ou seize ans, et dont *l'éclat resplendissant avait quelque chose de lumineux et de divin*' (Perrault, 1981: 135–6; emphasis added).

9 Marina Warner discusses the image of the 'tranced' Sleeping Beauty and the bodily passage of the Virgin Mary in *Phantasmagoria* (2006: 50).

10 In Matthew Lewis's *The Monk* (1796), for example, Ambrosio, assisted by Matilda's supernaturally imbued silver myrtle, enters Antonia's chamber in order to drug and rape her. Here he plays the role of the intrepid prince as he penetrates door by door the barriers to her chamber, his design not to wake Antonia (who is associated through the novel with images of the Virgin Mary) but to prolong her sleep: 'He now ventured to cast a glance upon the sleeping Beauty. [...] An air of enchanting innocence and candour pervaded her whole form; and there was a sort of modesty in her very nakedness which added fresh stings to the desires of the lustful Monk.'

That the kiss Ambrosio places on Antonia's 'half-opened mouth' raises his desires to 'that frantic height, by which Brutes are agitated' (1973: 300–1) further emphasises the Gothic eroticism of the image of virtuous femininity embodied by the sleeping woman in Basile's 'Sun, Moon and Talia' and *Perceforest*, the latter of which receives direct reference in the novel (1973: 134).

11 For more on the Sadeian castle see Le Brun (1990: 47).

12 The 1965 Grove Press translation of *Justine, ou les Malheurs de la vertu* appears in the bibliography of *The Sadeian Woman*, but Carter's notebooks on Sade also reveal extensive notes from this volume.

13 Discussing the mutually influential relationship between Sade's *Justine* and Lewis's *The Monk*, Angela Wright shows how the texts fashion pictorial images of their heroines in order to establish them as 'modest, virginal, religiously devout and naive' in 'the eighteenth-century literary tradition which equated feminine beauty and distress'. Wright adds that what marks *Justine* as a specifically French inflection of this tradition is the 'knowing eroticization' provided by the heroine's first-person narration, as opposed to the male focalised narratives that are more typical of the English Gothic novel at this time (2002: 43).

14 La Dubois, the criminal and violent 'surrogate mother' (*SW* 40) who tries to lure Justine into a life of crime, embodies a similar ambivalence. Although she is ostensibly the mirror opposite of the Virgin Mary, as the exemplification of benevolent motherhood, her name (Du*bois*) posits a similitude with the Saint Mary-in-the-Wood monastery that highlights their commonality of location.

15 Helene Meyers describes how '[f]eminist critics such as Susan Brownmiller, Andrea Dworkin, Mary Daly, Susan Griffin, and Dale Spender argue that women are at risk when they roam the streets, when they make love in their bedrooms, when they enter their gynecologists' offices, when they consume or produce culture. Taken together, such accounts of women's lives suggest that the world is a Gothic place for the second sex' (2001: 117; see also Keenan, 1997: 139). Meyers also cites Dworkin's suggestion that sexual intercourse is a 'Gothic crime of transgression' that 'makes all women into Gothic heroines, virgins awaiting, fearing, and, perhaps, desiring their defilement' (Meyers, 2001: 11).

16 Sage points out that, although *Madness and Civilization* appears in the book's bibliography, Carter's argument that '[f]lesh comes to us out of history' moves along the lines of *The History of Sexuality* (1994b: 14).

17 For a discussion of the uneasy dialogue between feminism and Foucault see McNay (1992).

18 I have analysed the relationship between power, victimisation and feminism in *The Sadeian Woman* elsewhere (see Munford, 2007).

19 Foregrounding the novel's surrealist inheritance, Kai Mikkonen also argues that it 'prompts a sense of textual continuum that extends through the surrealists to their precursors like Jarry, Roussel, Sigmund Freud, Lautréamont, de Sade, E. T. A. Hoffmann and literary fairy tales, romanticism, Greek mythology, symbolism, primitivism, and Stéphane Mallarmé [...] in a seemingly endless chain that provides the reader with a history and a critique of modernist avant-garde' (2001: 179).

20 Suleiman argues that the novel is '*of* as well as *about* the Surrealist imagination', with Doctor Hoffman appearing as the surrealist image-maker in the model of, amongst others, Dalí, Magritte, Duchamp and Breton (1994: 128; emphasis in original). See Tonkin (2006a) for a reading of the text as an ironic parody of Proust's *In Search of Lost Time* and Cavallaro (2011: 54) for a discussion of its echoes of Deleuze and Guattari's 'desiring machines'.

21 For more on the figure of Albertina as muse see Bronfen (1992) and Tonkin (2006a).

22 Briony Fer discusses such an image in relation to Bataille's metaphors of dust (1995: 169). I return to this idea later in the chapter.

23 Suleiman suggests that the fourth exhibit of the first sequence, 'EVERYONE KNOWS WHAT THE NIGHT IS FOR', in which a decapitated and mutilated woman lies in a pool of painted blood, evokes Duchamp's peephole installation, *Étant Donnés* (1994: 137).

24 Most particularly, her ethereal representation casts her in the image of a Pre-Raphaelite painting. This connection is foregrounded by the reference to Tennyson's and Millais's imagining of Shakespeare's Mariana in the moated grange – though her staged suicide also links her to Ophelia.

25 In their alignment of Sleeping Beauty and Pre-Raphaelite images of femininity, the pictures in this peepshow machine resonate with, amongst other examples, Edward Burne-Jones's *The Legend of Briar Rose* (1885–90) and Dante Gabriel Rossetti's 'My Sister's Sleep', published in 1850.

26 Garner emphasises the example of Elizabeth Siddall's illness after posing for Rossetti's 'Ophelia' in a bath of water.

27 Arguing that 'Minski is the exception that proves how far Sade's other monsters are from the sovereignty Bataille ascribes to them', Jane Gallop

suggests that Bataille's interpretation of Sadeian 'sovereignty' is something of a misreading (1981: 21). It has, however, maintained a strong critical hold in subsequent treatments of Sade (including, I would argue, that of Carter).

28 For a more in-depth analysis of Carter's translation practices see Heidmann and Adam (2007).

29 For an excellent overview and review of critical responses to *The Bloody Chamber* see Benson (2001).

30 According to Sandra Gilbert and Susan Gubar, 'Snow White' exemplifies the mapping of female sexual identity across the Madonna/whore binary. This fairy tale, they suggest, 'should really be called Snow White and Her Wicked Stepmother, for the central action of the tale – indeed, its only real action – arises from the relationship between these two women: the one fair, young, pale, the other just as fair, but older, fiercer; the one a daughter, the other a mother; the one sweet, ignorant, passive, the other both artful and active; the one a sort of angel, the other an undeniable witch' (1979: 36).

31 Charlotte Crofts notes that critics have mistakenly described *Vampirella*, which was broadcast on BBC Radio 4 in July 1976, as an adaptation of 'The Lady of the House of Love', but its creation in fact predates the short story (2003: 26–7).

32 Fer is referring here to Bataille's discussion of dust in his commentary on Joan Miró's work.

33 Michelle A. Massé argues that the 'Gothic uses woman's whole body as a pawn: she is moved, threatened, discarded, and lost. And as the whole person is abducted, attacked, and so forth, the subtext metaphorically conveys anxiety about her genital risk. Pornography reverses the synecdochal relationship by instead using the part to refer to the whole: a woman is a twat, a cunt, a hole. The depiction of explicitly genital sexual practice which is pornography's metier can be simply a difference in degree, not in kind, from the Gothic's more genteel abuse' (1992: 108) The Gothic's affinities with chess play will be explored in Chapter 3.

34 Carter claims in an interview with Sage that Sade 'sent me back to the Enlightenment, where I am very happy. They mutter the age of reason is over, but I don't see how it ever began so one might as well start again, now. I also revere and emulate Sade's religious atheism' (qtd in Sage, 2001: 69).

2

Poe, Baudelaire and the decomposing muse

When it most closely allies itself to *Beauty*: the death, then, of a beautiful woman is, unquestionably, the most poetical topic in the world – and equally is it beyond doubt that the lips best suited for such topic are those of a bereaved lover.

(Edgar Allan Poe, 'The Philosophy of Composition')

A Muse creates nothing by herself; she is a calm, wise Sibyl, putting herself with docility at the service of a master.

(Simone de Beauvoir, *The Second Sex*)

THE MUSE AS GOTHIC (M)OTHER

The Marquis de Sade's theatre of suffering, with its carefully choreographed cruelty and abominable displays of tormented bodies, casts its profligate shadow over the development of European Gothic forms in the nineteenth century. Emerging foremost from these shadows are Edgar Allan Poe and Charles Baudelaire. Here the transgressive excesses of the Sadeian Gothic find their resemblances in Poe's macabre extravagancies and Baudelaire's dissolute rebellions. The vulnerable, virginal bodies across which the Sadeian libertine acts out his brutal desires are recast in the irresistible but treacherous corporeality of ghastly revenants, femmes fatales, monstrous vampires and lascivious prostitutes; the image of persecuted beauty exemplified by Justine finds its dialectic realisation in the reflection of monstrous and deathly beauty cast by the Medusa. 'This glassy-eyed, severed female head, this horrible, fascinating Medusa' was, Mario Praz describes in *The Romantic Agony*, 'the object of the dark loves of the Romantics and the Decadents' (1970: 27).[1] It is this image of horrible beauty − of beauty in the atrocious, the sad and the painful − that finds form in the work of Shelley and Keats, and of Flaubert and Gide, amongst others; it suffuses too Poe's aesthetic conviction in the beauty in women's death and decay (see Praz, 1970: 27).[2] For Praz, however, Baudelaire is the poet 'in whom the Muse distilled her most subtle poisons,' and whose 'sense of beauty was eminently Medusean' (1970: 40, 43). At once fascinating and appalling, the Medusa represents a tension between female beauty and monstrosity that is vital to the development of the European Gothic imaginary in the nineteenth century.[3] A figure of ominous female sexuality and emblematic of the artistic process itself, the Medusa is the Gothic muse who at once reflects and deflects the male gaze, raising imperative questions about the particular and perverse decompositions of femininity underlying Gothic representation and artistry.

'Woman being the very substance of man's poetic work', de Beauvoir argues, 'it is understandable that she should appear as his inspiration: the Muses are women. A Muse mediates between the creator and the natural springs whence he must draw' (1988: 214). In Greek mythology, the nine muses were the daughters of Zeus and Mnemosyne, and presided over the arts. The classical muse was deemed to bestow the divine gift of poetic creativity upon the poet, giving life to his artistic expression; the poet then reanimated the muse through the creation of a text apostrophising her. In this way, the exchange between the poet and muse implied, in Elisabeth Bronfen's words, 'a moment of loss of self and possession by an Other' (1992: 363). In the Platonic account, the muse's inspiration is figured as a 'possession' or 'divine madness' that requires the poet to lose his senses.[4] Characterised by possession, madness, subjection and loss, the poet−muse relation is, therefore, a peculiarly Gothic one. Although the muse appears to occupy a position of aesthetic authority, she functions as a cipher across and through which the poet inscribes his divinely-appointed vision. Her power, in other words, remains phantasmatic. A present absence, or disembodied presence, the muse is figured as a kind of Gothic mother. Mother of the muses, Mnemosyne is also

> the mother of the source of poetic authority itself and as such the point of origination to be invoked in the poetic act. She is the powerful agent whereby the gap is closed between any poetic endeavour and a timeless source of memory, even though her voice can exist only in absence, as the point of origination, simultaneously put under erasure and articulated in the daughters who repeat and indirectly represent her. (Bronfen, 1992: 363)

As a mother to the poet, the muse represents a forgotten past and an inaccessible knowledge. Amongst this knowledge that is lacking for the poet, and that the muse makes present, Bronfen suggests, is that of death.

The disembodied, deified muse of the classical tradition was, nevertheless, reinscribed as a more corporeal figure over time. Tracing the waning 'vitality' of the muse over the centuries, Bronfen highlights how the move to imagine the muse as a specific human being – to provide her with a 'concrete body' – coincides with the diminishment of her role in the creative process and a reconfiguration of the poet– muse relation.

> As the muse is supplanted by the poet's *usus*, the notion that poetic inspiration implies a fluctuating relation between poet and radical Otherness turns into one where the boundary between self and the other is clearly drawn, with the poet self-sufficient, relying not on alterity but on his own experience to justify the truth of his song. The paradox inherent to this changed poet–muse relation is such that while the poet is portrayed as being possessed, it is he who possesses; while the poet seems dependent on the inspiration by another, he is the lover and begetter with the muse as the beloved, the begotten. (1992: 364)[5]

Bronfen points in particular to Romantic transferrals of the muse on to a 'corporally existent beloved, only now she is dying or already dead' (1992: 365). The poetic invocation of the muse becomes an act of Gothic possession. No longer identified with the divine figure of the Madonna, the muse is transposed into a maternal metaphor for the male poet's creativity as female origination and (pro)creativity are displaced by paternal authority and artistry. It is this dynamic tension between possession and dispossession, and between composition and decomposition, that underlies the transfiguration of the monstrous muse in Poe and Baudelaire's Gothic imaginings – a tension that, in turn, is creatively reignited in Carter's re-imagining of the Gothic muse.

This chapter explores Carter's engagement with and reworking of the figure of the deathly muse in the work of Poe and Baudelaire, two of her most influential and persistent literary models. Both Poe and Baudelaire lurk throughout Carter's writing – in her published texts as well as her notebooks and reading journals – as inheritors of Sade. Carter, as discussed in the Introduction, envisages a 'familial attachment' to Poe, using his imagery as part of the decor of her own fictions. Paraphernalia from Poe's Gothic imagination pops up through her fiction – for example, a waistcoat that was worn in a film adaptation of 'The Fall of the House of Usher' is found in the junk shop in *Shadow Dance* and a large, defaced poster of 'Tristessa wearing the bloody nightdress of Madeline Usher' appears in Zero's room in *The Passion of New Eve* (*PNE* 90). The ornate textures of Baudelaire's poetic are similarly woven into the fabric of Carter's fiction – in the representation of Leilah's bejewelled and perfumed body in the same novel and the Marquis's appropriation of the poet's words in 'The Bloody Chamber'.

Both Poe and Baudelaire are positioned as an intimate – and peculiarly visceral – part of Carter's literary inheritance. Although her oeuvre is peppered throughout with allusions to and citations from their work, in 'The Cabinet of Edgar Allan Poe' and 'Black Venus' the masters of the macabre are disinterred and reanimated as actors in their own Gothic stage sets. Both of these works are published in *Black Venus* (1985), a collection of eight short stories published between 1977 and 1982, which are loosely connected through the theme of the literary and historical past (the collection includes an overture to *A Midsummer Night's Dream*, a re-working of Sergei Prokofiev's *Peter and the Wolf* and a fictional portrait of Lizzie Borden, who was accused of murdering her parents with an axe). In *Black Venus*, proposes Sage, Carter

> is mischievously engaged in supplementing the canon – writing *round the edges* of the known, resurrecting (by means of invention, naturally) materials that didn't quite make it into the record, and voices we didn't get to hear. She inserts apocryphal episodes into various ready-made traditions – into Baudelaire's biography, and Poe's (the *real* role of the black Muse the dead mother's Gothic legacy). (1994a: 44–5; emphasis in original)

In 'The Cabinet of Edgar Allan Poe' and 'Black Venus' Carter is concerned with exploring the artist-muse relation and, especially, the concept of the muse as 'another magic Other [...] another way of keeping women out of the arena', as she puts it in an interview with Kerryn Goldsworthy (Goldsworthy, 1985: 11–12). While the Sadeian Gothic derives erotic enthralment from the representational contortions of the female body in the performative spaces of the Gothic castle, Poe and Baudelaire re-position her Medusan shadow at the centre of their morbid spaces of composition. The threat of sexual violence is thus exchanged for an economy of textual violence in nineteenth-century male Gothic re-imaginings of the monstrous muse.

POE AND THE PHILOSOPHY OF DECOMPOSITION

In 'The Philosophy of Composition' (1846), Poe outlines, with specific reference to 'The Raven', the procedure by which some of his poetic works were put together. In so doing, he offers an aesthetic theory that posits the importance of keeping the '*dénouement* constantly in view' and beginning the process of artistic creation 'with the consideration of an *effect*' (1986b: 480). Poe's theory is positioned as a scientific one, cast in the manner of a 'mathematical problem'. His view thus runs counter to that of those writers, 'poets in especial', who 'prefer having it understood that they compose by a species of fine frenzy – an ecstatic intuition'. These poets, Poe avers, would positively shudder at letting the public take a peep behind the scenes, at the elaborate and vacillating crudities of thought – at the true purposes seized only at the last moment – [...] at the wheels and pinions – the tackles for scene-shifting – the step-ladders and demon-traps – the cock's feathers, the red paint and the black patches, which, in ninety-nine cases out of the hundred, constitute the properties of the literary *histrio*. (1986b: 481)

From the very outset of the essay, the need to keep things 'in view' (for example, the '*dénouement*' and 'originality') is emphasised, foregrounding the importance of looking, and of spectacle, in the philosophy of composition. The enumeration of compositional aspects offered here – articulated in a list-like, mechanical manner – debunks the Romantic view of poetic inspiration and the organic growth of poetry. Poe's essay focuses instead on technical effect and the theatrical. In so doing, suggests Rachel Polonsky, it 'redirects critical attention onto technique, to art as a clever illusion which the artist controls like a mathematical or mechanical problem' (2002: 43). It is a theory of composition that privileges the artificial over the natural and wryly restores creative omnipotence to the male artist.

Having established technical effect as the starting point for the processes of composition, Poe moves on to explore the subsequent steps in his '*modus operandi*'. Taking beauty as his 'province' and melancholy as 'the most legitimate of all the poetical tones' (1986b: 484), Poe arrives at his infamous conclusion that 'the death [...] of a beautiful woman is, unquestionably, the most poetical topic in the world – and equally is it beyond doubt that the lips best suited for such topic are those of a bereaved lover' (1986b: 486). In this formulation, the beautiful 'dead beloved' serves as muse for the male artist; the importance of the female figure lies only in her status as inanimate object to be looked upon by the 'bereaved lover'. Just as he acts, looks and loves, she is acted upon, looked at and beloved as his idealised other. In *Over Her Dead Body*, Bronfen persuasively shows how the conjunction of femininity and death in representation – exemplified by the image of the dead, female body – reveals and assuages a fear about death and mortality. The beautiful, feminine corpse, she argues, becomes the aesthetic site of alterity over which 'culture can repress and articulate its unconscious knowledge of death which it fails to foreclose even as it cannot express it directly' (1992: xi). The cultural connection between femininity and death is so deeply embedded that 'the fear of death translates into a fear of Woman, who, for man, is death' (Bronfen, 1992: 205).

In 'Through a Text Backwards', Carter suggests that Poe 'is suspiciously straightforward about his enthusiasm for dead and dying women'. 'The Philosophy of Composition', she quips with characteristic jocularity, should 'by rights be re-titled: "The Philosophy of Decomposition"' ('TTB' 487).[6] Populated by corpse-like, vampiric and revenant women, Poe's short stories, such as 'Ligeia' (1838), 'The Fall of the House of Usher' (1839) and 'The Oval Portrait' (1842), as well as poems like 'The Raven' (1845), 'Ulalume' (1847) and 'Annabel Lee' (1849), dramatise his infamous expression of necrolatry in 'The Philosophy of Composition'. In many of these texts, however, the death of a beautiful woman is not simply the 'poetical topic' of the work but, rather, its premise and impulsion. The decomposition of the female body, in other words, becomes the precondition for artistic composition.

The intimate relationship that Poe envisages between composition and decomposition is powerfully articulated in 'The Oval Portrait'. Originally titled 'Life in Death', this short story self-consciously situates itself in a European Gothic tradition through its reference, in the opening sentence, to 'one of those piles of commingled gloom and grandeur which have so long frowned among the Apennines, not less in fact than in the fancy of Mrs Radcliffe' (Poe, 1986b: 250). Poe's castles, Carter proposes, are drawn not from 'the castles of European fact but the castles of European fantasy' ('TTB' 484). Although she places Poe's castles and 'gaunt mansions' (the analogy between body and castle is never far away in Poe) in a tradition of Walpole's and Radcliffe's castles ('TTB' 484), she argues that most of all they 'resemble the most forbidden of all the forbidden places of de Sade: the castle in *The Hundred Days at Sodom* [sic] where ritual tableaux of the most extravagant sexual cruelty are acted out daily'. They are 'built of the same imaginative fabric' as the 'mansions, abbeys and castles where Justine is tortured and her sister, Juliette, wreaks her infamies' ('TTB' 485). The interior of the castle in 'The Oval Portrait' thus establishes itself as a highly stylised Gothic stage set in a Sadeian lineage. The remote turret in which the narrator ensconces himself is furnished with dilapidated and antique decorations, candelabra and heavy shutters; his bed is 'enveloped' by fringed, black velvet curtains. The isolation in this story, Carter notes, is 'absolute' ('TTB' 484).

When the fringed curtains are pulled back, the stage is lit by the rays of the candelabrum and the narrator's eye is drawn to 'the portrait of a young girl just ripening into womanhood' (Poe, 1986a: 251). Just as the narrator meticulously describes the Gothic *mise-en-scène* he attends closely to the details of the portrait's frame. The story throughout lays great emphasis on acts of opening and shutting, and of concealment and revelation, as well as the blurred boundary between dream and waking life. Foregrounding an analogy between the architectural and psychological interior that can be found elsewhere in Poe's oeuvre, the heavy shutters of the room are mirrored by the narrator's eyelids, which are described several times as 'closed' or 'shut', and signal an interplay between notions of light and sight in the text – one that echoes in the description of the '*socket* of the lamp' (Poe, 1986a: 253; emphasis added). The turret-chamber can be read, then, in relation to the uncanny as an ambivalent effect of the nebulous boundary between seeing and not seeing – as that which 'ought to have remained secret and hidden but has come to light' (Freud, 1990: 345).[7]

Staring closely at the portrait, the narrator becomes 'satisfied with the true secret of its effect' – that is, 'the spell of the picture in an absolute *life-likeness* of expression' that subdues and appals him – and seeks an explanation for it in the small volume carrying descriptions of the paintings and their histories (Poe, 1986a: 251; emphasis added). The story of the 'oval portrait', he discovers, describes the triadic relationship between the male artist, his beloved and the portrait of which she is the object: 'He, passionate, studious, austere, and having already a bride in his Art; she a maiden of rarest beauty [...] loving and cherishing all things: hating only the Art which was her rival' (1986a: 252). Like the narrator and the portrait, the artist, his canvas and the young bride are enclosed in the 'dark high turret-chamber'. The artist paints the image of his young bride, but he is so concerned with his own creative labour that he does not notice that every stroke of colour he adds to the canvas is drawn from the tints of her face. As the light 'drips' upon the pale canvas, the beautiful maiden becomes pale, withered and weak. The artist, in this instance, is positioned as the vampire, sucking the life-blood from his young wife, who slowly dematerialises under the ghastly light of the 'lone turret'. In 'The Oval Portrait' the death of a beautiful woman becomes a precondition of 'the execution of the work' – the act of artistic 'labour' is a death sentence for the beautiful maiden (1986a: 251). The painter's artistic representation of his bride, his possession of her *ad infinitum*, is inextricable from her bodily dispossession:

> for one moment, the painter stood entranced before the work which he had wrought; but in the next, while he yet gazed, he grew tremulous and very pallid, and aghast, and crying with a loud voice, 'This is indeed Life itself!' turned suddenly to regard his beloved: – *She was dead!* (1986a: 253; emphasis in original)

Here, the artistic process becomes a way to remove the female body from the scene of composition. For this body – 'ripening into womanhood' – is marked as a potentially reproductive body; it is one that, to use Bronfen's words, bears the inscription of 'maternity-materiality-mortality' that the artist must put under erasure through his own creative labour (1992: 364).

THE MATERNAL MUSE

Analysing Poe's Gothic aesthetic in 'Through a Text Backwards', Carter posits that 'the elements' in his 'voluptuous tales of terror' are over-determined ('TTB' 482). Poe's theatricality, she suggests,

> ensures we know all the time that the scenery is card-board, the blade of the axe is silver paint on papier mâché, the men and women in the stories unreal, two-dimensional stock characters, yet still we shiver. [...] We feel we know it so well just because it is so familiar; we feel we have been here before. ('TTB' 482)

Carter links the 'familiarity' of Poe's tales to Freud's suggestion in 'The Uncanny' (1919) that a feeling of familiarity is a memory of the mother's body. However, if 'Poe's mother's body is a haunted house', she adds, it is 'one haunted by allusion' ('TTB' 484). The mother's body is thus positioned from the outset as a textual body – one that, like the castle itself, becomes a creative source of 'weathered stage sets' for Poe's Gothic drama ('TTB' 482). Nevertheless, Carter warns, there has been a tendency to interpret Poe's sexual pathology 'as if everyone loved corpses best' ('TTB' 482). Certainly, biographical and psychoanalytic approaches to Poe's work have been eager to draw a connection between the theoretical emphasis on beautiful, dead women in Poe's writing and his own experiences of bereavement, especially the loss of his mother, Elizabeth Poe, when he was an infant, and his wife, Virginia Clemm (whom he married when she was just thirteen years old).[8] The most famous of these approaches is Marie Bonaparte's study, *The Life and Works of Edgar Allan Poe: A Psychoanalytic Interpretation* (originally published in 1933), which included a preface by Freud. Focusing on Poe's sadistic and necrophilic phantasies, Bonaparte's psychobiographical interpretation posits a reading of his literary themes through the lens of his 'unassuageable longing for a mother left dead, long ago, in a small room' (Bonaparte, 1949: 11). This analysis emphasises Poe's fixation with the mysterious maternal corpse, and the threat of sexual difference, symbolised, for example, by the *vagina dentata* motif in 'Berenice' (see 'TTB' 482).

In one of the few discussions of Carter's critically neglected short story, Maggie Tonkin proposes that 'The Cabinet of Edgar Allan Poe' is a parody of Bonaparte's psychobiographical study, and in particular its focus on Poe's relation to his dead mother. Tonkin's persuasive argument is that, in grounding Poe's representation of femininity in 'his perverse individual psychopathology' (2004: 2), and more specifically his necrophilic desire for his mother, Bonaparte's psychobiographical reading of Poe's work fails to take account of his stylistic strategies and innovations. It also overlooks the historical and cultural specificity of the image of the muse – and specifically the image of the 'deceased beloved as muse' described by Bronfen in *Over Her Dead Body*. Carter's story, Tonkin suggests, 'not only exhumes the classical muse buried in Bonaparte's account, but also mimics the decomposition of the muse trope in Poe's texts by fragmenting the maternal body into tit'n'teeth' (2004: 3). Poe's ambivalent literary treatment of the feminine is not straightforwardly a perverse psychopathological expression but, rather, participates in an existing literary tradition of representing the feminine and, in particular, the maternal (Tonkin, 2004: 3).

While sharing Tonkin's emphasis on the maternal muse, I want to focus instead on the story's treatment of European Gothic conventions and the construction of literary tradition through familial tropes. In 'The Cabinet of Edgar Allan Poe', Carter re-imagines and re-stages the poet's ambivalent relation to the maternal body and his subsequent relationship with Virginia. The 'cabinet' here signifies multifariously as a 'small room' or 'repository', as a 'private space' and as a 'room devoted to the arrangement or display of works of art and objects of vertu; a museum, picture-gallery'.[9] This last meaning in particular gestures towards an (anachronistic) reading of Poe's work in the European tradition of the 'cabinet text' that developed towards the end of the nineteenth century – a reading of the text backwards that locates Poe as progenitor of a decadent Gothic aesthetic. According to Emily Apter in *Feminizing the Fetish: Psychoanalysis and Narrative Obsession in Turn-of-the-Century France*, cabinet fiction emerged as 'the result of the nineteenth-century marriage between the "pathologies of modern life" contrived by Balzac and Baudelaire and the medical literature of psychosexual mania' (1991: 40).[10] In Carter's telling, the cabinet of Edgar Allan Poe, with its representation of pathological interiors, and treatment of women as fetish objects, is at once a repository for repressed maternal longing and a literary lumber room – a perversely domesticated version of the Sadeian torture chamber.

If the maternal body is a site of allusion, it is one that resonates fully and richly in Carter's short story. Carter's fictional biography is constructed from citations from and allusions to Poe's work, alongside biographical material about Poe and his parents, and parodic reiterations of psychobiographical readings of his work. Just as Poe's work is all about the stage set and its paraphernalia, 'The Cabinet of Edgar Allan

Poe' is similarly bursting with theatrical metaphors and analogies. Poe's theatricality is identified as coming from his maternal side: 'There is a past history of histrionics in his family. His mother was, as they say, born in a trunk, grease-paint in her bloodstream, and made her first appearance on any stage in her ninth summer in a hiss-the-villain melodrama entitled *Mysteries of the Castle*' ('CP' 32). The biographical fact of Eliza Poe's appearance in Miles Peter Andrews's *The Mysteries of the Castle: A Dramatic Tale in Three Acts* in 1795, to which Carter also refers in 'Through a Text Backwards', establishes an imaginative framework in which to play out the Gothic drama of Poe's maternal relation. Eliza Poe is, from the beginning of Carter's story, cast as the Gothic mother. Prematurely buried in the script of maternal femininity, her body is marked from the outset as a site of haunting. The boundaries between biographical 'fact' and literary 'fiction' are already blurred. The infant Poe is born into the dressing room, suckling at his mother's bosom 'while she learned her lines' ('CP' 33). Peering out of prop-baskets, he watches his mother slide in and out of different roles, cross-dress, and stage various deaths and resurrections. He grows up, in other words, between the nourishing maternal body and the scripted role his mother plays.

However, if Poe is born of theatrical blood on his mother's side, he is also imagined as the offspring of a Sadeian Gothic ejaculation. As his mother skips out on to the stage 'in the fresh-hatched American republic' to perform in *The Mysteries of the Castle*, the narrative pictures forth a paternal birthing scene on the other side of the Atlantic:

> At this hour, this very hour, far away in Paris, France, in the appalling dungeons of the Bastille, old Sade is jerking off. Grunt, groan, grunt, on to the prison floor … aaaagh! He seeds dragons' teeth. Out of each ejaculation spring up a swarm of fully-armed, mad-eyed homunculi. Everything is about to succumb to delirium. ('CP' 32–3)

David Poe (an alcoholic and mediocre actor who abandoned his family) may have been Edgar's biological father, but Sade is imagined here as offering a surrogate literary paternity. As David Poe grows increasingly insubstantial — 'evaporating until he melted clean away, leaving behind him in the room as proof he had been there only a puddle of puke on the splintered floorboards' ('CP' 34) — Sade bequeaths Poe a male Gothic fantasy of motherless reproduction. The prison floor becomes the stage on to which Sade's daemonic sperm are splattered. Semen is substituted for vomit, marking the paternal body as a site of abjection — even if, as Julia Kristeva suggests, sperm contains 'no polluting value' (1982: 71).

For, in 'The Cabinet of Edgar Allan Poe', it is Poe's relationship with his mother that is at the centre of this abject re-staging of his birth, life and death. According to Kristeva, abjection is fundamental to the constitution of the subject as a separate being. It is the condition of radically excluding that which is other to the self; it is the state of establishing the (precarious) borders of its autonomous being. Kristeva argues that the mother is the first body that must be abjected by the child so that it may ensure its subjective integrity. The abject, she proposes,

> confronts us [...] within our personal archaeology, with our earliest attempts to release the hold of *maternal* entity even before ex-isting outside of her [...]. It is a violent, clumsy breaking away, with the constant risk of falling back under the sway of a power as securing as it is stifling. (1982: 13; emphasis in original)

In order to separate from the mother, the child needs to rid itself of those fluids that threaten the boundaries of the 'clean and proper' body. The impossibility of assuring the delineation of its own body (the 'own and clean self') from that of its (m)other is experienced as a sense of horror (of nausea and disgust) at bodily fluids and particularly those bodily fluids linked to 'the horrors of maternal bowels' (Kristeva, 1982: 53). At once profoundly corporeal (the narrative is punctuated by references to her sore, milky breasts) and mysteriously ephemeral (Edgar watches his mother's 'vague face' swim in the altar-like mirror as she slithers 'through all the nets which desire set out to catch her' ('CP' 36)), Elizabeth Poe figures the abject maternal as an at once enthralling and threatening power.

However, Carter's text punctures the poetic currency of the monstrous mother through a clichéd re-enactment of a Gothic primal scene (the theatrical vocabulary remains important here) as the infant Edgar and his brother observe the bloody birth of their sister through the Medusan lens of a *vagina dentata* motif:

> The midwife had to use a pair of blunt iron tongs to scoop out the reluctant wee thing; the sheet was tented up over Mrs Poe's lower half for modesty so the toddlers saw nothing except the midwife brandishing her dreadful instrument. ('CP' 34)[11]

Underneath her many costumes, and underneath the sheet from which the infant Poe's sister was pulled 'bloody as a fresh-pulled tooth' ('CP' 34), Elizabeth Poe's body is already bound by the cultural inscription of the monstrous feminine. In Carter's Gothic re-staging of Poe's biography, Elizabeth is cast in the hyperbolic role of Freudian mother; when the curtain rises, the mystery of the castle is revealed as the maternal body.

Carter's 'The Cabinet of Edgar Allan Poe' is, then, an exercise in reading backwards through the text. The final part (or 'act') of the story self-consciously dramatises the displacement of Poe's necrophilic desire for his mother on to his virginal and spectral thirteen-year-old cousin Virginia: 'for, not to put too fine a point on it, didn't she always look like a walking corpse? But such a pretty, pretty corpse!' ('CP' 40). With her 'forehead like a tombstone', she already bears the deathly inscription of the poet's predetermined text. In the final scenes of 'The Cabinet of Edgar Allan Poe', the Gothic muse is caught up in an intricate web of literary and biographical allusions: references to Juliet's 'thirteen summers' and 'The Sleeping Beauty' reverberate alongside quotations from and allusions to Poe's poetry and short fiction (including 'The Sleeper', 'The Oval Portrait', 'Annabel Lee' and 'Berenice'). Virginia steps out from the mirror in which Poe's mother had first been reflected at once strangely familiar and 'a perfect stranger' ('CP' 39).

Tonkin points out that Carter's text uses a misquotation from 'Annabel Lee' – 'My darling, my sister, my life and my bride!' ('CP' 39) – to present Virginia as the model for 'Annabel Lee' (2004: 18).[12] 'Annabel Lee' was written in 1849, two years after the death of Virginia, who is taken to be its addressee. According to Bronfen, the poem provides an example of how the 'death of a beloved turns her into the muse for her mourning lover's poetic inspiration.' The speaker of the poem, she suggests, invokes the lost beloved so that he can idealise his love for her and, in so doing, exert his poetic power; this is a power that, in making present the image of the absent lover, is a 'poetic triumph over death' (Bronfen, 1992: 367). However, in Carter's re-reading/re-writing of Poe's necrologic aesthetic, the asynchronous combination of literary citations and biographical history creates a textual disjuncture that confuses the poet–muse relation. Virginia is born of Poe's poetic – like Sleeping Beauty, she is written only to be put into a 'death-like sleep' by 'the magician himself' ('CP' 40). She takes up the pre-scripted role of deathly femininity and starts to 'rehearse the long part of dying' ('CP' 40). The ballad she sings for Poe and his guests at their home ('The Unquiet Grave') makes her a double for the young Elizabeth Poe who skipped on to the stage 'to sing a ballad clad in the pretty rags of a ballet gypsy' ('CP' 32). But Virginia's deathly body also functions as the text on to which Poe projects his *vagina dentata* fantasy:

All sleep. Her eyes go out. She sleeps.

He arranges the macabre candelabra so that the light from her glorious hand will fall between her legs and then he busily turns back her petticoats; the mortal candles shine. Do not think it is not love that moves him; only love moves him.

He feels no fear.

An expression of low cunning crosses his face. Taking from his back pocket a pair of enormous pliers, he now, one by one, one by one by one, extracts the sharp teeth just as the midwife did. ('CP' 41)

As the echoes of 'The Oval Portrait' suggest, the male artist's composition requires the decomposition of the female body. When Virginia ceases to breathe, the dual resonances of her 'consumption' destabilise the fixity of the poet–muse relation: the fragile, corpse-like Virginia does not die the bloody death of tuberculosis; rather, she is consumed and bloodied by Poe's poetic surgery as he births her into death.

Poe's literary cabinet is opened to reveal that the highly coded and heavily inscribed image of the abject maternal body conceals the mother's silence. Polonsky suggests that Poe's female characters often function as a kind of '*tabula rasa* on which the lover inscribes his own needs. His fictional "ideal" is a woman who can be subsumed into another's ego and who has no need to tell her own tale; she is killed off so quickly that her silence is inscribed quite irrevocably' (2002: 150). This silence is redoubled in the case of Poe's mother. As Arthur Hobson Quinn notes, the lack of information about Poe's parents' personal histories means that 'the records of their careers in the theatre [have] become of unusual significance' (1998: 1). Carter's story, however, is concerned with re-inscribing Elizabeth Poe as a historical subject rather than the site of Poe's Freudian drama. At the centre of the text/cabinet is the 'TESTAMENT OF MRS ELIZABETH POE', which lists the various items that Poe's mother passed on to her infant son (including the nourishing breast, skills in performance and transformation, and an awareness of mortality). The presence of Elizabeth Poe's testimony in Carter's text – 'do not think his mother left Edgar empty handed' ('CP' 36) – runs counter to and redresses biographical accounts of her deathly legacy as absence by allowing the Gothic mother to speak.[13] When the theatre burns down shortly after Elizabeth Poe's death, Poe's 'mother' is revealed as a conjuring trick: 'But now the mirror, too, was gone; and all the lovely and untouchable, volatile, unreal mothers went up together in a puff of smoke on a pyre of props and painted scenery' ('CP' 37). The Gothic mother is unveiled as an effect of smoke and mirrors – the effect that precipitates the creative composition. Poe's Gothic artifice may work to counter the mortal threat of the material (and maternal) body but, in Carter's story, it is Poe who decomposes under the blistering stage lights as his 'dust blows away on the wind' ('CP' 42).

BAUDELAIRE'S SICK MUSE

If in Poe's Gothic imaginary it is the corpse-like female subject as muse that enlivens the male artist's Gothic mirror, for Baudelaire it is the strange and contradictory figure of the prostitute that commands his enthralled and appalled gaze. Baudelaire plays a vital, though seldom acknowledged, role in the development of European Gothic forms in the mid-nineteenth century. Bram Dijkstra, for example, foregrounds the ways in which the 'seductively beautiful language' and 'rabidly misogynist point of view' of Baudelaire's writings influenced both 'the image of the godlike male poet' and male-authored representations of unruly and dangerous femininity through the second half of the nineteenth century (1986: 233). Exploiting Sade's aesthetics of evil, Baudelaire is also influenced by Poe's poetics of artificiality. He admires Poe's 'greenish or purplish backgrounds, in which we can glimpse the phosphorescence of decay' (Baudelaire, 1995a: 91) and his work is also fascinated by the female body as a site of decomposition. As he famously writes in his *Intimate Journals*, 'Woman is the opposite of the dandy. Therefore she should inspire horror. [...] Woman is *natural*, that is to say abominable' (1989: 25; emphasis in original). Baudelaire reconfigures female sexuality as the dark abyss – as a dangerous, but compulsive, corporeality representing the destructive drives of Nature.

Such images of dangerous female sexuality converge in Baudelaire's *Les Fleurs du mal*, a collection notable for its macabre treatment of dark desires, decay and supernatural iconography. Quotations and translations from *Les Fleurs du mal* are scattered through Carter's journals. These fragments in turn inform Carter's story 'Black Venus', which takes as its subject the figure of Jeanne Duval, Baudelaire's Creole mistress, prostitute and the putative muse of the so-called 'Black Venus' cycle of *Les Fleurs du mal*.[14] Through playful references to such poems as 'Les Bijoux', 'La Chevelure', 'Le Serpent qui danse', 'Parfum exotique', 'Le Chat', 'Je t'adore à l'égal de la voûte nocturne' and 'Sed non satiata', Carter's story examines Baudelaire's grotesque transformation of the female muse as 'all except herself' (Beauvoir, 1988: 268). Although 'Black Venus' has received relatively little critical attention, a close reading of this text is vital to a reconsideration of the tensions characterising Carter's positioning in relation to a European Gothic heritage and, in particular, her equivocation towards her French, male literary influences and intertexts.

In 'Black Venus', Carter's re-writing of the poet–muse relation is contextualised in relation to the gendered construction of social and literary relations in mid-nineteenth-century French discourse and, in particular, the male artist's fascination with the prostitute as an emblematic figure of the modern, urban landscape. Drawing on Walter Benjamin's concept of the phantasmagoria, Christina Britzolakis describes how '[t]he commodified environment of nineteenth-century Paris becomes a spectral theatre, where commodities disport themselves as fetishes on display. The chief emblem and embodiment of this phantasmagoric landscape, which appears as allegory in the poetry of Baudelaire, is the prostitute' (1995: 463). If the prostitute is its emblem, the alienated hero of this phantasmagoric landscape is the *flâneur*. In 'The Painter of Modern Life', Baudelaire describes the *flâneur* as the 'passionate spectator' for whom

> it is an immense joy to set up house in the heart of the multitude, amid the ebb and flow of movement, in the midst of the fugitive and the infinite [...]. The spectator is the *prince* who everywhere rejoices in his incognito. The lover of life makes the whole world his family, just like the lover of the fair sex who builds up his family from all the beautiful women that he has ever found, or that are – or are not – to be found; or the lover of pictures who lives in a magical society of dreams painted on canvas. (1995c: 9; emphasis in original)

In the mid-nineteenth-century Gothic imaginary, the labyrinthine subterranean passages of the Gothic castle are exchanged for the dark and vertiginous maze of the modern city (the *flâneur* sets up 'house' in the city). Perrault's prince, Sade's libertine and Poe's poet-magician are in turn reincarnated in the figure of the 'perfect *flâneur*', who vampirically feeds off the sights and sounds of the cityscape, giving new vision to this Gothic space where the boundaries between reality and dream worlds dissolve.

Nevertheless, while the transformation of modern space meant new possibilities of experience and desire for the mid-nineteenth-century *flâneur*, it is imagined as a realm to which women were denied subjective and artistic access. Not only is the activity of the *flâneur* in Baudelaire's Paris constructed as the preserve of the sovereign male subject, but it is also a mode of urban mobility from which women are excluded. For women, Griselda Pollock describes, 'the public spaces thus construed were where one risked losing one's virtue, dirtying oneself; going out in public and the idea of disgraces were closely allied' (1988: 69). Out on the streets, the prostitute was the public woman *par excellence* − at once alluring and repulsive for the avidly voyeuristic male *flâneur* and artist, she casts a peculiarly Gothic shadow. In Baudelaire's account, the prostitute's presence is a vital aspect of the kaleidoscopic contours of the modern cityscape at which the male *flâneur* directs his covetous gaze:

> Against a background of hellish light, or if you prefer, an *aurora borealis* [...] there arises the Protean image of wanton beauty. Now she is majestic, now playful; now slender, even to the point of skinniness, now cyclopean; now tiny and sparkling, now heavy and monumental. [...] She is a perfect image of the savagery that lurks in the midst of civilisation. She has her own sort of beauty, which comes to her from Evil always devoid of spirituality, but sometimes tinged with a weariness which imitates true melancholy.
> (Baudelaire, 1995c: 36)

Resplendent in her daemonic majesty, the prostitute takes centre stage in this supernatural spectacle. Just as the virginal heroine is an integral feature of the Sadeian Gothic *mise-en-scène*, and the female revenant is a part of Poe's interior decor, the prostitute and the city assume inextricable Gothic aspects.[15] Woman is, once again, posited as a site or space against the historical subjectivity of the male Gothic agent.

Nevertheless, Charles Bernheimer proposes, male artists' relation to the figure of the prostitute in nineteenth-century France was extremely complex, involving 'both identification and repulsion. As an emblem for their own artistic practice, it represented creative artifice, surface illusion, seductive falsity, even a kind of inspiring void' (1989: 1). Rita Felski similarly describes the social and cultural significance of the prostitute on the mid-nineteenth-century French landscape as generating

> a number of conflicting interpretations; seen by some contemporary writers to exemplify the tyranny of commerce and the universal domination of the cash nexus, it was read by others as representing

the dark abyss of a dangerous female sexuality linked to contamination, disease, and the breakdown of social hierarchies in the modern city. (1995: 19)

Circulating through the city, the female prostitute is a commodified cultural icon, dressed-up in the costume of male desire. Her cosmetics and adornment veil the mortal, rotting and fading realities of her corporeality and, therefore, mitigate her perceived proximity to nature. 'Woman,' suggests Baudelaire, 'is quite within her rights, indeed she is even accomplishing a kind of duty, when she devotes herself to appearing magical and supernatural; she has to astonish and charm us; as an idol, she is obliged to adorn herself in order to be adored' (1995c: 33). Quoting his infamous differentiation between the dandy and woman, Camille Paglia asks why woman inspires such 'horror' for Baudelaire. She proposes that, in the Baudelairean imagination, 'Woman is the dandy's opposite because she lacks spiritual contour and inhabits the procreative realm of fluids where objects dissolve'. Baudelaire's proto-decadent creation of 'a world of glittering art objects' is a response to the 'horror of the female liquid realm' (1990: 430). The decadent vamp, as a Medusan figure, represents the dangerous, all-consuming reproductive body – the female body as leaking vessel.

The prevalence of the prostitute in French literary and artistic representations can also be attributed to phobias about disease and, specifically, the spread of syphilis throughout the century. Significantly, then, the 'dark abyss' is mapped along the axis not only of gender but also of race. The 'foreign-born prostitute' in particular, notes Elaine Showalter, was positioned as 'the alleged source of venereal contagion and the scapegoat for male sexual anxieties' (1992: 189). Sander L. Gilman, for example, highlights the fusion of iconographies of the 'sexualised woman' and the 'black woman' in canonical works of nineteenth-century art, most notably Edouard Manet's *Olympia* (1863), where it is 'the black female as emblem of illness who haunts the background' of the painting (1985: 101). Notions of dark, female sexuality thus became the site for broader fears about contamination, corruption and disease.

An ambivalent fascination with the treacherous female body underlies Baudelaire's iconographic transformation of the muse in the 'Black Venus' cycle of *Les Fleurs du mal*. Baudelaire's 'vamping' of the muse as a figure of corrupt and diseased female corporeality is exemplified by one of the early sonnets of *Spleen et idéal*, 'La Muse malade' ('The Sick Muse'). The invocation to the female muse at the beginning of this poem ostensibly reiterates a classical invocation: 'Ma pauvre muse, hélas! qu'as-tu donc ce matin?' (1996: 44).[16] However, Baudelaire's sick muse is aligned with the figure of the succubus that threatens to sap the poet's creative vitality and virility. With her 'yeux creux', she figures the deadly gaze of the Medusa as the mendacious prostitute who jeopardises his creative project. Although the poet ostensibly questions the muse's sickness, he positions her as the Gothic mirror on to which he projects his anxieties about spiritual degeneration and decomposition: 'Et je vois tour à tour réfléchis sur ton teint / La folie et l'horreur, froides et taciturnes' (1996: 44).[17] Transforming the muse's skin into a textual surface, the poet confronts the Medusa's gaze.

Nevertheless, while the eloquence of Baudelaire's poetic in the opening two quatrains suggests the extent to which the sick muse provides valuable inspiration for the artistic project, it simultaneously functions to contain the grotesque body of the muse within the classical structures of the sonnet. Although the first two quatrains deploy a vocabulary of fluidity and excess associated with the abject body of the muse, the following two tercets work against the threat of the succubus:

> Je voudrais qu'exhalent l'odeur de la santé
> Ton sein de pensers forts fût toujours fréquenté,
> Et que ton sang chrétien coulât à flots rythmiques
>
> Comme les sons nombreux des syllabes antiques,
> Où règnent tour à tour le père des chansons,
> Phoebus, et le grand Pan, le seigneur des moissons.
>
> (1996: 44)[18]

The invocation to Phoebus (god of music and poetry) and Pan (god of nature and fertility) assuages the horror of contaminating and consuming female sexuality by restoring a mythology of male textual and sexual potency. The muse's grotesque and permeable body is thus re-assimilated and enclosed by the highly regulated and closed rhythms of the closing tercets and their reinstatement of patriarchal frameworks. The poet's dis-ease about the processes of decomposition associated with nature and human mortality becomes focused on the muse's disease: Baudelaire's creative project is negotiated over the tensions of this hyphen.

This ambivalent view of the destructive law of nature is, nonetheless, haunted by the memory of, and the hope of returning to, an Edenic paradise. This duality characterises Baudelaire's representation of Duval as 'Black Venus' in *Les Fleurs du mal*. Here, his construction of Duval's sexuality is grounded in an obsession with the wealth, eroticism, excess and primitivism associated with the unknown territories of the Orient in a mid-nineteenth-century Western Imaginary. Exotic and sexually alluring, Duval is aligned with the figure of the veiled woman who embodies mythological inscriptions of the dark continent – concomitant with the equation of the unknown and unknowable *terra* of the female body in Freudian theory at the turn of the century. At once horrifying and enticing, the dark, female body symbolises the possibility of an exotic and idealised elsewhere which, in the 'Black Venus' cycle, may be accessed by way of her sensuous and animalistic corporeal geographies. Baudelaire's fetishistic representation of female hair and natural smell as indicators of primitive animality (and thus key sites for his simultaneous attraction to and horror of the female body) unlocks the gateway for his imaginative wanderings. In 'La Chevelure', for example, the muse's Medusa-like tumbling curls are inhabited by dreams of 'La langoureuse Asie et la brûlante Afrique, / Tout un monde lointain, absent, presque défunt' (1996: 58), while, in 'Parfum exotique', her natural scent conjures visions of 'Une île paresseuse où la nature donne / Des arbres singuliers et des fruits savoureux' (1996: 57).[19] It is through the muse's corporeal immanence that Baudelaire's poet envisages his ecstatic transcendence. Mnemosyne, as silenced Madonna, is refigured as a treacherous Medusa: the muse no longer represents a 'powerful agent whereby the gap is closed between any poetic endeavour and a timeless source of memory' (Bronfen, 1992: 363) but the very opening of the dark abyss. Here, the Gothic muse represents a fetishistic metaphorisation of femininity whereby the horror of decomposition aligned with the material and protean female body is contained in – or 'subdued' by – the male artistic composition.

RE-VAMPING THE MUSE

Foregrounding the figure of the muse as central to Western philosophical and artistic codifications of woman as other and absence, Carter's short story 'Black Venus' disrupts the positioning of Jeanne Duval as the Gothic mirror into which Baudelaire casts his dissolute reflections. In *Speculum of the Other Woman*, Luce Irigaray discusses how woman 'has not yet taken (a) place'. Instead, she is the place from which 'the "subject" continues to draw his reserves, his re-sources, though without being able to recognize them/her' – she holds only the place that she constitutes for the 'male' subject (1985a: 227). In *Les Fleurs du mal*, Duval, as muse, is positioned as the site over which, in Irigaray's terms, the male subject 'struggle[s] to use his specul(ariz)ation to tear apart the representation of the other, thereby preserving the power (of) truth of the spectacle upon which he/ she gazes. Denying the fiction of the mirror that lies beneath' (1985a: 231). For in spite of its break from neoclassical aesthetics, Baudelaire's poetic colludes with the specular logic of dominant representational frameworks by positioning 'woman' as the dark abyss; or, a 'nothing that might cause the ultimate destruction: the splintering, the break in their systems of "presence," of "re-presentation" and "representation"' (1985a: 50). The muse is visible only in so far as she brings into view the male poet's reality. For Baudelaire's aesthetic of exclusion is grounded in a metaphorisation of femininity that exiles the female subject from history and being. Carter, like Irigaray, is interested in interrogating the 'fiction of the mirror' in order to imagine a representational and historical space in which women can take up a place beyond 'the imaginary of the (male) subject' (1985a: 233).

Carter's 'Black Venus' demystifies and humanises Duval not only by 're-presenting' her as a historical subject but by 're-presencing' her as an agent in history. In an interview with Anne Smith, Carter describes the genesis of the story ('something discarded in the final version') as an exploration of 'how awful it is to be a muse':

> I was correlating Jeanne Duval with the Dark Lady of the Sonnets, as the mysterious other, and I read what biographies there were of Baudelaire. Nobody had a good word for *her* … I just can't imagine anything more awful than being Baudelaire's mistress – the *symbolism* put on one's frail shoulders! (Smith, 1985: 28; emphasis in original)

'Black Venus', then, is concerned not only with redressing Duval's representational subjugation in Baudelaire's poetry but also with highlighting the marginalisation she has suffered at the hands of his critics and biographers, who invariably define her against Baudelaire, that is, as his other. Jill Matus, for example, foregrounds the purported erasure of Duval, at Baudelaire's request, from Gustave Courbet's painting of the poet in 'L'Atelier du peintre' (1855), adding that 'a close scrutiny of the painting reveals the ghostly traces of her effacement' (2000: 167). The historical marginalisation of Duval has also been perpetuated by Baudelaire's biographers, whose lengthy accolades most often allude to Duval as an exotic, but deceitful, temptress whose superficial beauty and charm masked petulance and stupidity.[20] In 'Black Venus' Carter seeks to re-animate the 'ghostly traces' of Duval by peeling back the architecture of Baudelaire's poetic and exposing the 'fiction' of his mirror.

In 'Black Venus', Baudelaire's apartment is constructed as an unstable Gothic dream space: 'Soft twists of mist [...] seep in through the cracks in the window frame so that the contours of their high, lonely apartment waver and melt' ('BV' 1). '[F]rosted glass' windows return distorted reflections of its 'inmates': 'The whim of the master of the house has not let the windows alone; he had all the panes except the topmost ones replaced with frosted glass so that the inmates could pursue an uninterrupted view of the sky' ('BV' 2). The uninterrupted view of the sky intimates the possibility of transcendence, represented by the desire for flight that recurs throughout the text. 'Transported' into this dream space, Duval is 'a *tabula rasa*, still. She never experienced her experience *as* experience, life never added to the sum of her knowledge;

rather subtracted from it. If you start with nothing, they'll take even that away from you. The Good Book says so' ('BV' 1). Duval is the blank space – the 'nothingness' – that Baudelaire fills with meaning. For it is not only the frosted glass windows that provide a mirror for Baudelaire's poetic reflections. In 'Black Venus', the interplay of light and dark in the illusory space of the apartment is distributed over the surface of Duval's body, which is illuminated by the fire, another Baudelairean motif:

> She sulked sardonically through Daddy's sexy dance, watching, in a bored, fascinated way, the elaborate reflections of the many strings of glass beads he had given her tracking about above her on the ceiling. She looked like the source of light but this was an illusion; she only shone because the dying fire lit his presents to her. Although his regard made her luminous, his shadow made her blacker than she was, his shadow could eclipse her entirely. ('BV' 4)

Duval's position as muse is articulated through an iconography of the supernatural which figures her as both exotic goddess and demonic vamp. Like that of the sick muse, Duval's skin becomes the site over which the poet–muse dialectic of Gothic dis/possession is enacted. The poet's 'presents' supplant the muse's 'presence'. While the poet is spellbound by the long shadow that his muse casts in the firelight, Duval, with her 'pointed canines still white as vampires' ('BV' 5) and her 'unravelling cape of hair' ('BV' 8), presents an image of the Medusa caught in the reflection of Baudelaire's poetic shield.

Duval is not only possessed by Baudelaire's regard but is also one of the many possessions in his bric-a-brac-cluttered apartment:

> this handsome apartment with its Persian rugs, its walnut table off which the Borgias served poisons, its carved armchairs from whose bulbous legs grin and grimace the cinquecento faces, the crust of fake Tintorettos on the walls (he's an indefatigable connoisseur, if, as yet, too young to have the sixth sense that tells you when you're being conned). ('BV' 2)

The interior of Baudelaire's apartment evokes the object mania and erotic spectacle of the decadent cabinet. According to Apter, 'decadent cabinets, with their murky light, heavy crimson curtains, crevices, cavities, and plethora of "seeing eyes," already seem to theatricalize erotic fantasy, imaging, through decorative accoutrements such as the *oeil-de-boeuf* that facilitate the voyeuristic gaze, the "look" of the bordello client trained on feminine wares' (1991: 45). As a 'perfect stranger' ('BV' 9) Duval becomes another fetishised, exotic 'collectible' – a mesmerising *tableau vivant* in Baudelaire's cabinet of curios. The nineteenth-century decadent cabinet is thus identified as the architectural heir – via Poe – of the eighteenth-century Gothic castle as 'a singularly "possessed" apartment, fostering the folly, caprice and *érotomanie* of its spellbound master' (Apter, 1991: 64).

'Black Venus', however, also foregrounds Duval's status as a dispossessed subject – even if Baudelaire 'cannot believe she is as dispossessed as he' ('BV' 3). The 'mysterious currents of the heavens' may invite Baudelaire's 'well-appointed cabin' to 'loose its moorings in the street below and take off, depart, whisk across the dark vault of the night', but Duval resists the journey back to the 'bloody parrot forest!': 'Don't take me on the slavers' route back to the West Indies, for godsake!' ('BV' 2–3). As Victoria Tillotson proposes, Baudelaire's desire to 'force a home' on Duval, 'whether she's got one or not' ('BV' 3), is that of the 'prototypical nineteenth-century imperial exoticist' (1997: 297). 'Long before Freud's pronouncement,' she points out, 'woman emerged as the predictable "dark continent" in travel and exploration narrative, simultaneously in need of corrective civilizing procedures and offering the promise of unexplored and potentially dangerous territory, replete with the promise of abundance and fulfilment' (Tillotson, 1997: 294).[21] Carter's story atomises Duval's designated status as exotic woman through an interrogation of the cultural and historical stereotypes and iconographies of female sexuality that inform Baudelaire's representation of the 'Black Venus'. In so doing, it foregrounds the symbolic poignancy of Venus as a ubiquitous figure of equivocal female sexuality in decadent art and literature.

At once goddess of love and emblem of female beauty, Venus is a notoriously ambivalent figure. Matus describes how the figure of Venus has 'also been used to suggest whorish seductiveness and voluptuousness, narcissistic female self-absorption, and a variety of other denigrating versions of woman' (2000: 162). Classical portrayals of Venus have conventionally figured voluptuous, white women – for example, Sandro Botticelli's *The Birth of Venus* (c. 1485) and the white, marble Venus de Milo statue. The representation of the 'black Venus', then, is a doubly equivocal figure, exemplifying the contradictions of female sexuality as alluring, mysterious and corrupt. Clare Hanson proposes that:

> If woman is unknown, the unknown is always feared. Venus in this sense is always black: the image of the loved woman in Western patriarchal culture is always a projected image in which the man's thought, to extend an image of Carter's, overtakes the woman's presence. (1988: 79)

Matus similarly foregrounds the broader typological identifications of Venus as epitomising female sexuality with reference to Émile Zola's representation of Nana as 'la Blonde Vénus' (a model for Fevvers in *Nights at the Circus*), where degeneration and blackness are also used to mark the white prostitute: 'Those "snowy thighs" that corrupted Paris mock the association of snow and whiteness with purity, demonstrating that white as they are, hers are no different from the black ones overtly associated with corruption and disease' (2000: 165). In Carter's story, however, Duval is re-birthed as Black Venus, in a colonial recasting of Botticelli's painting: 'A scallop-shell carried her stark naked across the Atlantic; she clutched an enormous handful of dreadlocks to her pubic mound. Albatrosses hitched glides on the gales the wee black cherubs blew for her' ('BV' 9). She is the 'goddess' of the poet's heart; the poet is in turn the albatross – the large-winged bird that, uneasy on the ground, but 'prince of the clouds', illustrates the alienated condition of the poet.[22]

Carter's demythologisation of Duval as Black Venus is concerned with both the poetic and material conditions of her status as Baudelaire's muse – and her ambiguous position as a *femme entretenue*. 'Black Venus' disrupts Duval's situation within (and as) Baudelaire's text by accentuating her position as a Creole woman in the context of French colonial imperialism. The motif of tobacco, as a fashionable European drug, is used to explore the ways in which their poetic relation is inextricable from their economic relation. Images of smoke and smoking recur throughout the short story, from the opening description of the 'smoky-rose, smoky-mauve evenings of late autumn' ('BV' 1), to the representation of Duval twisting 'a flute of discarded manuscript from the wastepaper basket into a spill for her small, foul, black cheroot' ('BV' 2). The image of the 'smoky-rose, smoky-mauve' evening echoes, as Linda Hutcheon notes, Baudelaire's 'Harmonie du soir' and 'Crépuscule du soir' (1989: 142). However, it also evokes the 'bluish clouds' that Baudelaire describes in his famous account of smoking in 'The Poem of Hashish':

> Let's suppose you are sitting down smoking. Your attention will come to rest a little too long on the bluish clouds rising from the pipe. The idea of a certain evaporation, slow, successive, eternal, takes hold of your mind, and you are soon applying this idea to your own thoughts, to your own thinking matter. By a strange equivocation, by a kind of transposition or intellectual misunderstanding, you feel yourself evaporating too, and you attribute to your pipe [...] the strange activity of *smoking you*. (2002: 55–6; emphasis in original)

Baudelaire envisages the effect of smoking as one where the boundaries between subject and object become blurred and individuality is expanded. The creative acts of the imagination involve a kind of evaporation or vanishing of the subject who, as E. S. Burt argues, is 'not after all the stable, seated entity having fixed properties that it first appears. Rather, like tobacco, it is revealed as a natural product, as becoming what it is through shaping and evaporating' (2001: 951).[23] The strange activity of smoking points to a Gothic account of subjectivity as disassembled – or 'de-composed'.

Richard Klein argues that, in Baudelaire's poetry, smoking is endowed 'with the beauty of his women, whose fascination and seduction held poetic charms' (1993: 6). In Baudelaire's 'Black Venus' cycle, it is the intoxicating substance of the body of 'la dame Créole' that is powerfully fetishised as a Gothic other. Carter's 'Black Venus' emphasises this imaginative association through the inclusion of her translation of the first stanza of 'Sed non satiata' in the text:

> Weird goddess, dusky as night,
> reeking of musk smeared on tobacco,
> a shaman conjured you, a Faust of the savannah,
> black-thighed witch, midnight's child …

('BV' 7)

Here, Jeanne – 'the forbidden fruit' ('BV' 7) – figures like tobacco and other intoxicants to open up new imaginative vistas and encounters with otherness.[24] In 'Black Venus', however, it is Duval, as beleaguered muse, rather than the intoxicated poet, who is associated with smoking tobacco:

> Jeanne woke from her trance. Folding another spill out of a dismantled sonnet to ignite a fresh cheroot, her bib of cut glass a-jingle and a-jangle, she turned to the poet to ask, in her inimitable, half-raucous, half-caressing voice, voice of a crow reared on honey, with its dawdling accent of the Antilles, for a little money. ('BV' 7)

Smoking is posited here as a material relation of an economic kind. Jeanne may have 'only the haziest notion of her use value ('BV' 4), but she will 'dance for Daddy' in return for 'pretties' and 'the occasional lump of hashish' ('BV' 3). For Duval, smoking is not an experience of dissolution and evaporation but, rather, a physical pleasure – she possesses a 'slumberous resentment of anything you could not eat, drink, or smoke, i.e. burn' ('BV' 3–4). Folding 'another spill out of a dismantled sonnet to ignite a fresh cheroot' ('BV' 7), Baudelaire's muse irreverently sends his fetishistic poetry up in smoke.[25]

However, the motif of tobacco also foregrounds Duval's position as an 'exotic' commodity in a colonial economy. The narrative shifts from an image of Duval smoking a cheroot to a documentary-style account of her rather scantily chronicled biography: 'Nobody seems to know in what year Jeanne Duval was born, although the year in which she met Charles Baudelaire (1842) is precisely logged [...]. Where she came from is a problem [...] (Her *pays d'origine* of less importance than it would have been had she been a wine)' ('BV' 7). Speculating about her Caribbean heritage in relation to Toussaint L'Ouverture, who 'led a successful slave revolt against French plantation owners at the time of the French Revolution' ('BV' 7), the narrator situates Duval's labour in the context of tobacco production. Drawing a parallel between the historical contexts of French colonial imperialism and the representational colonisation of the female body – Duval 'had been deprived of history, she was the pure child of the colony' ('BV' 8) – the text exposes how Baudelaire's literary metaphorisations of femininity deny Duval agency and voice by positing her as the silent object of a male erotic register:

> It was as though her tongue had been cut out and another one sewn in that did not fit well. Therefore you could say, not so much that Jeanne did not understand the lapidary, troubled serenity of her lover's poetry but, that it was a perpetual affront to her. He recited it to her by the hour and she ached, raged and chafed under it because his eloquence denied her language. ('BV' 9)

As she aches, rages and chafes under the strain of Baudelaire's fetishistic poetic, Duval's sores are not, as Baudelaire would have it, physical, but existential.

The representation of Duval in Carter's fictional biography pivots around a major shift in her self-positioning. Discussing Duval's role as Baudelaire's muse with Kerryn Goldsworthy, Carter highlights the processes of dehumanisation that become a precondition of the muse's status: 'I mean you can't take a muse seriously as a human being, or else they stop being a muse' (1985: 11–12). In a move to 'humanise' Duval, the text intersperses imagined fragments of her speech and thought with evocations of, and direct borrowings from, *Les Fleurs du mal*. A mocking allusion to 'Le Serpent qui danse', for example, allows Duval to reproach Baudelaire for his poetic idealisation:

> He said she danced like a snake and she said, snakes can't dance: they've got no legs, and he said, but kindly, you're an idiot, Jeanne; but she knew he'd never so much as *seen* a snake […] if he'd seen a snake move, he'd never have said a thing like that. ('BV' 6)

Carter's ironic re-contextualisation of fragments of *Les Fleurs du mal* provides a space for Duval's realism and vernacular commentary to deflate Baudelaire's poetic by negating the role of inspiration and charm she is ascribed as muse in his poetry. In this respect, Carter posits a series of metaphorical 'half-rhymes' with her Baudelairean intertexts: the excesses of Baudelaire's poetic register are simultaneously undercut and modified by the interposition of Duval's vernacular commentary on them.

The dynamic tension between representations of and quotations from the opulent and fetishistic register of Baudelaire's poetry and imagined fragments of Duval's speech and inner narrative produces a critical dissonance. As Hutcheon puts it, 'two discourses meet – and clash: the poetic language of male sublimated desire for woman (as both muse and object of erotic fantasy) and the language of the political and contextualizing discourses of female experience' (1989: 141). These conflicting discourses work, she suggests, 'to foreground and contest the history of desire, male desire' (1989: 141). However, from this critical dissonance emerges an alternative space for the articulation of Duval's desire. Baudelaire's muse might ostensibly collude with his poetic projections by performing the dance 'he wanted her to perform so much and had especially devised for her' ('BV' 3), but she exists in a more ambivalent position in his carefully staged choreography. For example, an ironic recasting of 'Les Bijoux' destabilises the poet's view of the muse's collusion in his voyeuristic fantasy by disengaging her from its fetishistic scenario:

> He liked her to put on all her bangles and beads when she did her dance [...]. Meanwhile, she hummed a Creole melody, she liked the ones with ribald words about what the shoemaker's wife did at Mardi Gras or the size of some fisherman's legendary tool but Daddy paid no attention to what song his siren sang, he fixed his quick, bright, dark eyes upon her decorated skin as if, sucker, authentically entranced. ('BV' 3)[26]

Not only do the 'ribald words' of Duval's bawdy song resonate against the eloquent fetishism of 'Les Bijoux', but by calling Baudelaire a

'Sucker!' (also a crude sexual riposte), Duval intimates her awareness that her 'master' has been duped.

The decisive use of 'meanwhile' in this scenario suggests that Duval exists at once inside and outside of Baudelaire's poetic. This double movement that structures Carter's rearticulation of Duval's position in Baudelaire's poetic resonates with Irigaray's theorisation of 'playing with mimesis' as a means of woman 'recover[ing] the place of her exploitation by discourse' by 'making "visible", by an effect of playful repetition, what was supposed to remain invisible: the cover-up of a possible operation of the feminine in language' (1985b: 76). What is significant about this knowing play with mimesis is that it points to an 'elsewhere' space of discourse: 'if women are such good mimics', Irigaray suggests, 'it is because they are not simply resorbed in this function. *They also remain elsewhere*' (1985b: 75; emphasis in original).[27] The female mimic 'still subsists, otherwise and elsewhere than there where she mimes so well what is asked of her. Because her own "self" remains foreign to the whole staging' (Irigaray, 1985b: 152). In this context, the notion of 'foreignness' is assigned new meaning as Duval's performance unveils the artificiality of the exotic idealisation that Baudelaire projects upon her sexuality. Like Irigaray's mimic, Duval is aware of herself as a producer, rather than a simple bearer, of meaning.[28]

Carter's 'Black Venus' destabilises the hierarchical opposition between the male poet and the female muse by placing them in an inter-reflecting relationship that stresses their commonalities rather than their differences. Duval, for example, shares the *ennui* that famously plagues Baudelaire and the *flâneur*: 'the thought of organising a new career made her yawn' ('BV' 4). Their resemblance is also reflected by Carter's playful re-working of Baudelaire's romanticised self-conceptu-alisation as an affronted albatross in *Les Fleurs du mal*. In 'Black Venus', Duval is figured as a 'sooty albatross' who 'hankers for the storm' so that she too may take flight ('BV' 9). Baudelaire, however, in his 'frock coat', is imagined as the 'uxorious penguin' – for 'there isn't room for two albatrosses in *this* house' ('BV' 10). The poet, Hutcheon points out, is imagined as 'that great dandy of birds (from Poe's *Adventures of Arthur Gordon Pym*) the one who always builds its nest near that of the albatross: the penguin – flightless, bourgeois, inescapably comic' (1989: 144). Constrained and grounded by the prohibitive and restrictive dress of 'public nineteenth-century masculine impedimenta' ('BV' 10), the 'poet is demystified, as is the lover' (Hutcheon, 1989: 144).

In Carter's re-presentation of the artist–muse relation, Baudelaire's legacy is not poetic but, rather, 'the veritable, the authentic, the true Baudelairean syphilis' ('BV' 14) that Duval is left to 'continue to dispense, to the most privileged of the colonial administration' ('BV' 13–14). Both Matus and Hutcheon identify this exchange (the attribution of syphilitic contagion to Baudelaire rather than Duval as the contaminating prostitute) as the vital last strike in Carter's ironic re-imagining of their relationship. However, 'Black Venus' goes further than this by imagining the 'unknown end of Jeanne Duval' (Pollock, 1999: 270) and inscribing the empty space left in Baudelaire's biographies. The text retells Félix Nadar's account of Duval's old age: 'Nadar says he saw Jeanne hobbling on crutches along the pavement to the dram-shop; her teeth were gone, she had a mammy-rag tied around her head but you could still see that her wonderful hair had fallen out. Her face would terrify the little children' ('BV' 12). While Nadar portrays Baudelaire's muse, with her terrifying gaze, as a decomposing Medusa whose 'wonderful hair has fallen out', Carter's text envisages Duval buying new teeth and new hair to recompose herself. Baudelaire, in contrast, is left in the later stages of syphilitic degeneration 'so far estranged from himself that, [...] when he was shown his reflection in the mirror, he bowed politely, as to a stranger' ('BV' 12). Freed from the ghostly status of metaphor she is ascribed in Baudelaire's poetic, the sick muse no longer serves as a mirror surface that returns the poet's dissolute reflections. Rather, it is the poet whose sense of self begins to decompose and evaporate in the Gothic mirror.

This Gothic estrangement echoes that experienced by Poe at the end of 'The Cabinet of Edgar Allan Poe'. Unable to recognise himself, Poe 'continued, fascinated, appalled, to stare in the reflective glass at those features that were his own and yet not his own' ('CP' 42). But, while Elizabeth Poe and Virginia go up in smoke in Poe's cabinet-like hall of mirrors, Duval is released from her role as muse in Baudelaire's poetic:

'You could say that Jeanne had found herself; she had come down to earth, and, with the aid of her ivory cane, she walked perfectly well upon it' ('BV' 13). In her 'new dress of black tussore, her somewhat ravaged but carefully repaired face partially covered by a flattering veil' ('BV' 13), Duval subversively appropriates black clothing – 'the cornerstone of Baudelaire's personal dandyism' (Steele, 1998: 91) – and refashions herself. Her black veil no longer signifies her position as an exotic muse and vamp, but her status as a 'respectable widow' ('BV' 13). Through a subversive exchange of costuming and re-veiling Duval reclaims the Gorgon's mask to re-negotiate her position within Baudelaire's poetic landscape. Standing proud with her cane, the symbol of the *flâneur*, she walks the streets not as a prostitute but as an *arriviste* leaving her 'charming house' to take 'last night's takings to the bank' ('BV' 13). 'Chugging away' from Europe on a steamer heading to the Caribbean, it is Duval who mobilises the Baudelairean topos of the boat as a symbol of the poet's transcendental journey to return to her motherland. Carter demystifies and humanises Duval not only by re-presenting her but by re-presencing her as a historical subject – as a re-birthed Black Venus rising from the ashes of Baudelaire's poetic.

In 'The Cabinet of Edgar Allan Poe', the death and dematerialisation of the maternal muse is already scripted – even if this script is, to some extent, disrupted by the presence of Elizabeth Poe's testament at the centre of the text. However, in 'Black Venus', Carter's re-imagining of Duval's historical presence as an embodied subject extricates her more effectively from her designated position as muse. Nonetheless, Carter's stylistic attachment to her intertext – her seemingly spellbound revelry in the voluptuous cadences of Baudelaire's' poetic – raises uncomfortable questions about the sexual politics of her textual practices. Particularly troubled by the vexed question of style in 'Black Venus', Britzolakis argues that the shift between documentary and figurative registers in the text 'enacts an oscillation of identification and desire' (1995: 468). She suggests that, in the end, Carter's 'stylistic investment in Baudelaire's text cannot help but to reinscribe [Duval], at least partially, within the iconic framework of the *Fleurs du Mal*' (1995: 469). There is a danger, then, that Carter's text resubmits Duval to a fetishistic economy of the feminine. It is in this context that Griselda Pollock problematises the feminist irony that, at the end of the text, Duval continues to dispense 'the true Baudelairean syphilis' to the colonial administration. This transformation of 'Madame Duval' into a 'madam', she argues, marks a key 'slip' in Carter's poetic turn that keeps the 'prostitutional image' in circulation so that 'Jeanne is imaginatively reconfigured as the exotic but venal sign of sexuality' (1999: 271).

Carter works a risky edge in her evocation of Baudelaire's fetishistic metaphorisations of femininity. But, in exposing the poet's transformation of Duval into a series of reflective surfaces, Carter's stylistic redeployments and translations of Baudelaire's poetry position the poet himself as the reflective mirror. Carter's language in this story might turn 'Baudelaire into a décor' (Britzolakis, 1997: 468) – just as 'The Cabinet of Edgar Allan Poe' uses Poe 'decoratively'. However, the dissonance between Baudelaire's fetishistic, erotic register and the internal narrative of Duval's musings creates a productive discord that does not just expose the history of desire as the history of male desire. By demystifying the artist–muse relation, it also opens up an imaginative space in which to 're-presence' the muse as a desiring subject. Carter's ironic restaging of the monstrous muse in the 'The Cabinet of Edgar Allan Poe' and 'Black Venus' engenders a process of re-composition – an exhumation of the muse that Poe wants to bury and Baudelaire wants to debase. Carter acts here as a decadent daughter, exchanging the maternal muse for a paternal muse that is at once apostrophised and subordinated in the aesthetic process. Poe and Baudelaire respectively dematerialise into dust and ashes. De-composed, the male artist/muse disappears back into the Gothic mirror.

NOTES

1 Praz opens the first chapter of *The Romantic Agony*, 'The Beauty of the Medusa', with a discussion of Shelley's 'On the Medusa of Leonardo da Vinci' which, in its evocation of the 'livid face of the severed head, the squirming mass of vipers, the rigidity of death, the sinister light, the repulsive animals, the lizard, the bat', gives rise to 'a new sense of beauty, a beauty imperilled and contaminated, a new thrill' (1970: 26).

2 This is a relation already glimpsed in eighteenth-century Gothic representations of appalling femininity. In Lewis's *The Monk*, for example,
confronting Antonia's gaze sends Ambrosio into a state of murderous
panic: 'There was something in her look which penetrated him with
horror' (1973: 387). Leslie Fiedler interprets the figure of the persecuted
'maiden in flight' in Lewis's novel as a kind of muse in so far as she
represents 'the uprooted soul of the artist, the spirit of the man who has
lost his moral home' (1960: 123).

3 One of the three gorgons in Greek mythology, the Medusa was not only
incredibly beautiful but the only one to be mortal. As punishment for
being seduced by Poseidon (some versions state that she was raped) in
Athena's Temple, Medusa is turned, by Athena, into a monster with a snarl
of hissing snakes for hair. With serpents writhing in her head, Medusa's
appearance was so terrible that anyone who looked directly at her was
turned to stone. Charged with the task of slaying her, Perseus used his
shield to avoid looking directly at Medusa and cut off her head. For more
on the Medusa see Garber and Vickers (2003: 2–3).

4 Timothy Clark describes how Plato's notion of inspiration as divine
madness 'simultaneously names and masks a crisis of subjectivity associated
with the process of composition, a crisis difficult to reconcile with models
of the subject as a responsible, self-possessed agency' (2000: 55–6).

5 For an incisive summary of the muse's transformations see Bronfen (1992:
363–5) and Tonkin (2004: 7–10).

6 Carter offers a reading of Poe's famous tale in reverse. She starts, in other
words, from the effect – as advocated by Poe as the starting point for
writing. Alexandra M. Kokoli argues that this is a strategy that Carter
uses in some of the stories in *Black Venus*, for example 'The Fall River Axe
Murders' (2002: 63).

7 The Freudian uncanny will be explored in the following chapter.

8 Karen Weekes highlights how biographical discussions of Poe's work
invariably point out that he 'lost an unusual number of beautiful, relatively
young, nurturing females in his lifetime: his mother, Eliza Poe; his foster
mother, Fanny Allan; the mother of one of his friends, Jane Stanard;
and his own wife, Virginia Clemm'. Poe's foster mother also died of
consumption (2002: 149).

9 See 'Cabinet', *Oxford English Dictionary*, http://dictionaryoed.com. Gina
Wisker highlights the title's Gothic allusion to Robert Wiene's German
Expressionist horror movie *Das Cabinet des Dr Caligari* (Wisker, 2006: 181).

10 Citing Walter Benjamin's commentary on Poe, Apter argues that 'Poe stamped his domestic space with the inimitable stylistic flourishes of his literary haunted houses, but more important for our discussion, he equipped it with the trappings of hidden surveillance' (1991: 44).

11 Tonkin reads this reference to the *vagina dentata* myth as evidence that 'Poe's imagery is drawn from the cultural repertoire rather than from his individual psychopathology' (2004: 17).

12 The line should read 'Oh my darling – my darling – my life and my bride' (Poe, 1986a: 90). Carter's revision foregrounds the subtext of incest.

13 See, for example, Quinn: 'Elizabeth Poe, dying in Richmond in 1811 under distinctly miserable circumstances, could leave her two-year old boy only her high heart, her unremitting industry, and that indefinable charm which made her a favorite from Boston to Charleston among the theatregoers of that day' (1998: 1).

14 The structure of *Les Fleurs du mal* has garnered much critical attention, largely owing to Barbey d'Aurevilly's claim that the collection of poems possessed a 'secret architecture'. Although the overall design of the book continues to be debated, there is a general critical consensus that the volume possesses a number of cycles (see Ward Jouve, 1980: 148).

15 Walter Benjamin foregrounds this connection through the motif of the labyrinth, proposing that '[w]ith the emergence of big cities, prostitution comes to possess new arcana. Among the earliest of these is the labyrinthine character of the city itself. The labyrinth, whose image has become part of the flâneur's flesh and blood, seems to have been given, as it were, a colored border by prostitution' (2006: 166).

16 'Alas, my poor muse! What sickens you at first light?' All translations from 'La Muse malade' are by Helen Vassallo.

17 'And on your skin, reflected each in turn, I behold / A madness and a horror, taciturn and cold.'

18 'Oh! that a fresh breath were exhaled from deep inside / Your breast, where strong thoughts would eternally abide, / And that your Christian blood would flow gently in time / With the antique syllables of a classical rhyme, / As in days when the sceptre in turn would belong / To Pan, lord of the harvest, and Phoebus, lord of song.'

19 'Languorous Asia, scorching Africa, /A whole world distant, vacant, nearly dead' (1993: 51); 'An idle isle, where friendly nature brings / Singular trees, fruit that is savoury' (1993: 49).

20 Matus highlights the misogynistic assumptions underpinning A. E. Carter's

biography of Baudelaire (2000: 166). Amongst other disparagements, Carter describes Duval as 'a mendacious slut [...] a strumpet pure and simple' (Carter, 1977: 64).

21 Freud argues in 'The Question of Lay Analysis' (1926) that '[w]e know less about the sexual life of little girls than of boys. But we need not feel ashamed of this distinction; after all, the sexual life of adult women is a "dark continent" for psychology' (1959b: 212).

22 See the final stanza of Baudelaire's 'L'Albatros': 'La Poëte est semblable au prince des nuées / Qui hante la tempête et se rit de l'archer; / Exilé sur le sol au milieu des huées, / Ses ailes de géant l'empêchent de marcher' (1993: 38); 'The Poet is a kinsman in the clouds / Who scoffs at archers, loves a stormy day; / But on the ground, among the hooting crowds, / He cannot walk, his wings are in the way' (1993: 17).

23 Neil Badmington argues that Baudelaire's descriptions of consuming wine and hashish in *Les Paradis* represent 'the suspension of the knowing subject of humanism' (2004: 100).

24 Tobacco in turn possesses magnificent symbolic value. Writing on Baudelaire's poetics of tobacco and the conditions of gifting and exchange in *Given Time*, Jacques Derrida describes how tobacco 'symbolizes the symbolic: It seems to consist at once in a consumption (ingestion) and a purely sumptuary expenditure of which nothing natural remains' (1992: 112). With reference to Derrida's movement from a discussion of Honoré de Balzac's treatise on prostitution to a consideration of tobacco, Tillotson highlights how Derrida's elision of women – his marginalisation of the material conditions of women in favour of an analysis that privileges the linguistic level of the texts he discusses – brings to the fore 'the explicit linking of women, sexuality, imperialism, and capitalism in nineteenth-century fiction' (1997: 293).

25 Duval is not only situated in a lineage of Carter's heroines who adopt conflagration as an act of protest against imprisoning patriarchal structures (for example, Aunt Margaret who sets fire to the house in *The Magic Toyshop*, and the prostitutes who burn down the brothel following Ma Nelson's death in *Nights at the Circus*) but is also aligned with another silenced Creole woman, Antoinette Cosway in Jean Rhys's *Wide Sargasso Sea* (1966).

26 'La très chère était nue, et, connaissant mon coeur, / Elle n'avait gardé que ses bijoux sonores' (1996: 195); 'Knowing my heart, my dearest one was nude, / Her resonating jewellery all she wore' (1993: 47).

27 Irigaray offers a feminist counter model to Jacques Lacan's conceptualisation of the 'masquerade of femininity' as woman's 'entry into a system
of values that is not hers, and in which she can "appear" and circulate only
when enveloped in the needs/desires/fantasies of others, namely, men'
(Irigaray, 1985b: 131).

28 Irigaray's use of the term 'mimétisme', which links the notion of mimicry
to camouflage, is resonant here. 'Mimétisme', Naomi Schor proposes,
refers to 'a parodic mode of discourse designed to deconstruct the
discourse of misogyny through effects of amplification and rearticulation'
(1994: 66).

3

Dolls, dreams and mad queens

The master of marionettes revitalises inert stuff with the
dynamics of his self.

(Angela Carter, 'The Loves of Lady Purple')

Surrealist beauty is convulsive. That is, you feel it, you
don't see it — it exists as an excitation of the nerves. The
experience of the beautiful is, like the experience of desire,
an abandonment to vertigo, yet the beautiful does not exist as
such. What do exist are images or objects that are enigmatic,
marvellous, erotic — or juxtapositions of objects, or people,
or ideas, that arbitrarily extend our notion of the connections
it is possible to make. In this way, the beautiful is put at the
service of liberty.

(Angela Carter, 'The Alchemy of the Word')

AUTOMATA AND GOTHIC ANIMATION

With its waxworks, clockwork dolls, dark doubles and automata,
uncanny repetitions and phantasmal projections, the Gothic gives form
to what Terry Castle describes as the 'spectralization' of human thought
since the eighteenth century (1995: 141–2). Radically reorganising
ways of thinking about the self, Enlightenment philosophy yielded a
new obsession with technology and the power of the machine. The
mechanistic view of human existence which emerged from Descartes's
dualist description of the human being composed of the material body,
an automaton built by God, and the immaterial soul, was famously

extended by the materialist Enlightenment philosopher Julien Offray de La Mettrie. In *L'Homme Machine* (*Machine Man*) (1747), La Mettrie applied the mechanistic view to both mind and body, concluding 'boldly that man is machine and that there is in the whole universe only one diversely modified substance' (La Mettrie, 1996: 39). La Mettrie's work, which later influenced Sade's fascination with erotic technologies, called into question the very nature of human identity. If the human were a machine, could the opposite be argued?

In the eighteenth century, attempts to explore the complex relation between human beings and machines were under way in the mechanical sciences, especially in the marvellous work of automaton makers. The earliest example, the French scientist Jacques de Vaucanson's life-size mechanical duck, was first exhibited in Paris in 1738, and gave the illusion of digesting and defecating. Between 1768 and 1774, Pierre and Henri-Louis Jaquet-Droz, along with Jean-Frédéric Leschot, constructed three automata – a writer, a musical lady and a draughtsman – which toured Europe from the 1770s. The first of these would later be celebrated by the surrealists as part of a broader fascination with automatism and the marvellous as a counter to rational thought. One of the most controversial of the early automata, and famously a source of fascination for Edgar Allan Poe, was Wolfgang von Kempelen's Chess Player. The Chess Player was constructed of a large desk on one side of which sat a man dressed in Turkish costume who played chess with human adversaries (usually beating them). Exhibited widely in the latter decades of the eighteenth century and into the first half of the nineteenth, the 'Turk' was revealed, in the end, and after much speculation, to be a mechanical illusion, operated by a chess master hiding inside the desk (see Altick, 1978: 68–9). Nevertheless, the 'mystery' of the chess player's 'evolutions', as Poe describes them in 'Maelzel's Chess Player' (1836), foregrounds the complex relationship between the automaton as a figure of inanimate (or 'artificial') intelligence and human agency. For Poe, the Chess Player draws attention to its machine-like status, its countenance 'surpassed, in its resemblance to the human face, by the very commonest of wax-works' (2008: 105). The indeterminate boundary between machine-likeness and life-likeness is further emphasised by chess as a game of rational logic tinged by the madness of the unexpected.

Confusing the boundaries between the animate and the inanimate, the human and the non-human, the automaton serves as an emblem for the Enlightenment's simultaneous championing of human autonomy and freedom and fascination with the mechanical and the automated. Illuminating this paradox, Mladen Dolar proposes that the 'mechanical doll is a metaphor of, and counterpoint to, autonomous subjectivity; autonomous self-determination and the automaton seem to go hand in hand' (Dolar, 2002: 62). It is the contradictions residing in the at once mechanistic and life-like body of the automaton that give rise to its uncanny qualities to the extent that, according to Castle, 'the eighteenth-century invention of the automaton was also (in the most obvious sense) an "invention" of the uncanny' (1995: 11). Castle writes that

> the very psychic and cultural transformations that led to the subsequent glorification of the period as an age of reason or enlightenment – the aggressively rationalist imperatives of the epoch – also produced, like a kind of toxic side effect, a new human experience of strangeness, anxiety, bafflement, and intellectual impasse. (1995: 8)

What had been conceptualised as an image of order and rational thought became an uncanny figure of excess and anxiety, one belonging as much to the sphere of the numinous as to the material world. Andreas Huyssen identifies a shift in the nineteenth century to a more sinister treatment of the automaton in literary works. 'The android', Huyssen writes, 'is no longer seen as testimony to the genius of mechanical invention; it rather becomes a nightmare, a threat to human life' (1988: 70). In its uncanny mode, the android/automaton becomes more closely identified with the idea of a dangerous and duplicitous 'femininity' – a motif that can be traced from E. T. A. Hoffmann's 'The Sandman' (and Freud's reading of it), through Villiers de L'Isle Adam's *L'Ève future* to the automated women that command surrealism's erotic imagination.

Brimming with automata, dolls and mannequins, Carter's writing is inhabited too by a macabre cast of toy-makers, puppet-masters and mad scientists.[1] She told Kim Evans in an interview shortly before her death: 'I'm very interested in the idea of simulacra, of invented people, of imitation human beings because, you know, the big question that we have to ask ourselves is how do we know we're not imitation human beings?' (qtd in Crofts, 2003: 144). Carter's fiction explores in particular the uncanniness of the marionette as another site for the conjunction of female sexuality and death in the European Gothic imagination. But it is enthralled too by surrealist images of automated femininity – in particular, the figure of the mannequin and the chess queen. As Jane Hentges suggests, Carter was especially attracted to the surrealists' attempts to 'reproduce the marvellous, to create a borderline world between dream and reality' (2002: 45). A more general preoccupation with play, inherited from the surrealists, runs through her work in the form of dreams, collage aesthetics and games. Implicated in complex operations of excess and boundedness, chance and convention, the notion of play brings into focus the tension between Carter's textual strategies and her materialist politics. This is a tension that is thrown into sharpest relief in her early novels, where the highly choreographed, violent games of sadistic male artists and toy-makers (for example, Honeybuzzard in *Shadow Dance* and Uncle Philip in *The Magic Toyshop*) are played out across the highly eroticised bodies of doll-like female protagonists.

Following on from the discussions of the virtuous Sleeping Beauty and the monstrous muse, this chapter explores how the female body is dreamed (up) in the Gothic imaginings of psychoanalysis and surrealism. Focusing in particular on Carter's early fiction, it examines these Gothic inventions of automated femininity as another reassertion of male creative authority. With reference to *The Magic Toyshop* and 'The Loves of Lady Purple', texts that evince a particular fascination with the uncanny power of dolls and the precarious power of the toy-maker, I begin by investigating the possibilities of re-imagining the Freudian uncanny from the position of the female subject. Turning to *Shadow Dance* and *Love*, I move on to examine Carter's engagements with surrealist images of woman – in the figures of the mannequin, the hysteric and the chess queen. While the surrealist allegiances of these texts have already been explored by Carter scholars, my analysis foregrounds the hitherto neglected motif of chess, a game that fascinated a number of surrealist artists and appears again and again in Carter's fiction. Reading *Shadow Dance* and *Love* through the image repertoire of chess provides some alternative moves through which to re-visit the vexed questions about attack and submission – and power and victimisation – which frame their problematic gender politics. Foregrounding the chess queen as a figure of enthralling and deathly sexuality, I suggest that the logic of the chessboard offers a vocabulary for rethinking the dark eroticism and intertextual geometries of Carter's texts.

UNCANNY ENCOUNTERS AND LIVING DOLLS

Freud's 'The Uncanny' (1919) provides what Castle describes as 'an obsessional inventory of eerie fantasies, motifs, and effects, an itemized tropology of the weird. Doubles, dancing dolls and automata, waxwork figures, alter egos and "mirror" selves, spectral emanations, detached body parts [...], the ghastly fear of being buried alive, omens, precognition, déjà-vu – all of these, says Freud, are "uncanny themes" par excellence' (Castle, 1995: 4–5). Described by Hélène Cixous as 'a strange theoretical novel' (1976: 525), 'The Uncanny' is a Gothic masterwork in its own right. In it Freud outlines the uncanny as 'undoubtedly related to what is frightening – to what arouses dread and horror' (1990: 339). It is more particularly, he suggests, 'that class of the frightening which leads back to what is known of old and long familiar' (1990: 340). Freud's initial analysis of this strange, indefinable encounter hinges on the slipperiness of the terms *heimlich* (meaning 'familiar' or 'belonging to the home') and *unheimlich* (the unfamiliar). What Freud finds, upon mapping the etymology of these words in different languages, is that the word *heimlich* begins to exhibit a meaning that is identical to that of its opposite, *unheimlich*. In so far as it is associated with the home, with the private, *heimlich* does not only signify 'what is familiar and agreeable'; it can also mean 'what is concealed and kept out of sight' (1990: 345). The relationship between the *heimlich* and the *unheimlich* reveals the uncanny as something 'secretly familiar' that is brought into view – it is something that 'has undergone repression and then returned from it' (1990: 368). Giving rise to troubling sensations and unsettling feelings, the uncanny is the awful recurrence and repetition of material that has been estranged through repression. Having traced this estrangement of the familiar, Freud identifies two types of uncanny experience: the first occurs 'when infantile complexes which have been repressed are once more revived by some impression', the second 'when primitive beliefs which have been surmounted seem once more to be confirmed' (1990: 372). The uncanny is, in part, 'something one does not know one's way about in' (1990: 341). Labyrinthine and dizzying, it is a peculiarly Gothic space marked by uncertainty and ambiguity.

For Freud, the 'unrivalled master of the uncanny in literature' is E. T. A. Hoffmann (1990: 355). Hoffmann's 'characteristic uncanniness', suggests Castle, is 'decisively bound up with the evolution of Enlightenment philosophical and technological innovation' and, specifically, the 'urge toward technological mastery and control' exemplified by the creation and exhibition of working automata in Europe in the eighteenth century (1995: 10, 11). Freud devotes a large chunk of 'The Uncanny' to re-telling Hoffmann's 'The Sandman', the story of Nathaniel, a young man who falls in love with a doll, Olympia, that he assumes to be the 'perfectly proportioned and gorgeously dressed' – though 'sightless' – daughter of Professor Spalanzani (Hoffmann, 1982: 99). Freud's summary of the story, however, places most emphasis on Nathaniel's childhood memories of being terrified by a lawyer called Coppelius, whom he associates with the figure of the 'Sand-Man' who tears out children's eyes, and with the death of his father. He later displaces this figure on to an optician, Coppola, who has supplied – and later removes – Olympia's eyes, the sight of which sends Nathaniel into a state of madness. Nathaniel eventually recovers from his illness, but a trip up the town hall tower with his fiancée Clara – during which he rediscovers and uses Coppola's telescope – leads to another episode of raving madness, as a result of which he hurls himself to his death.

In Hoffmann's tale, Nathaniel describes seeing Olympia as making him 'feel quite uncanny' (Hoffmann, 1982: 99). It is also the sight of Clara, whom he mistakes for a puppet, in front of Coppola's telescope that sends a 'shudder' through him and gives rise to his final nervous episode. Freud, however, is at pains to undo the emphasis placed on the doll as a locus of 'intellectual uncertainty' in Ernst Jentsch's earlier reading of the tale's uncanniness. The 'theme of the doll Olympia', he proposes, 'who is to all appearances a living being,' is not 'by any means the only, or indeed the most important, element [...] of uncanniness evoked by the story'. For Freud, the main theme of the story is, 'on the contrary, something different, something which gives it its name, and which is always re-introduced at critical moments; it is the theme of the "Sand-Man" who tears out children's eyes' (1990: 348). Freud goes on to argue that Jentsch's theory of intellectual uncertainty – which refers to 'the impression made by waxwork figures, ingeniously constructed dolls and automata' (1990: 347) – provides an inadequate reading of the uncanniness in Hoffmann's story. He proposes instead a psychoanalytic reading of the story, one that highlights repressed infantile complexes. For Freud, the uncanny nature of the Sandman is linked to a gruesome anxiety about the loss of sight which, he argues, codifies a fear of castration. Uncertainty about the (in)animacy of the mechanical doll, he avers, is 'quite irrelevant in connection with this other, more striking instance of uncanniness' (1990: 351). Freud confirms in a lengthy note that the 'automatic doll can be nothing else than a materialization of Nathaniel's feminine attitude towards his father in infancy' (1990: 354). Olympia is buried (alive) in the text's footnotes. By shifting the focus from Nathaniel's desire for Olympia to a displaced fear of castration (centred on the figure of Coppelius/Coppola), Freud's reading subjugates the significance of the automaton in the story's uncanny effect. Although later in the essay he acknowledges that he has 'occasionally heard a woman patient' admit that 'even at the age of eight she had still been convinced that her dolls would be certain to come to life' (1990: 355), he asserts that the idea of a 'living doll' does not excite any fear at all in 'The Sandman'.

Freud's marginalisation of the doll marks what Nicholas Royle describes as a 'violent attempt to reduce or eliminate the place and importance of women' in the text (Royle, 2003: 41). Women thus become a haunting presence in Freud's essay, a text that takes as its focus time and time again male subjectivity. For example, to illustrate the uncanny factor of repetition, Freud outlines his own uncanny experience in 'the deserted streets of a provincial town in Italy' of returning again and again to a quarter of dubious character, where '[n]othing but painted women were to be seen at the windows of the small houses' (1990: 359). While the doll motif recurs here in the guise of the prostitutes as 'painted women', a second crucial reference brings into sharp relief the disavowed but strangely familiar place of women in his text. Freud concludes the collection of examples that forms the middle part of his essay with an instance that 'furnishes a beautiful confirmation of our theory of the uncanny': that is, the claim made by neurotic men he has treated that 'there is something uncanny about the female genital organs. This *unheimlich* place [...] is the entrance to the former *Heim* [home] of all human beings, to the place where each one of us lived once upon a time and in the beginning' (1990: 368). The womb is thus figured as the haunted house that is given imaginative form in the threatening and claustrophobic spaces (the womb-like castles, coffins and decaying houses) of the Gothic composition.

In 'Fiction and its Phantoms', Cixous proposes that what unfolds in 'the labyrinthian space' of Freud's text 'is a kind of puppet theatre in which real dolls or fake dolls, real and simulated life, are manipulated by a sovereign but capricious stage-setter' (1976: 525). Here she illuminates the extent to which Freud transforms 'The Sandman' into a 'case history' and redistributes the story to minimise the intellectual uncertainty surrounding Olympia and establish a 'linear, logical account' of Nathaniel (1976: 535). Freud figures in Cixous's text as a Gothic toy-maker – a kind of Spalanzani – who fixes female identity within his representational frame. In terms of the dynamics of the seen/unseen that haunt both 'The Sandman' and 'The Uncanny', Freud refuses to look directly at the female doll who (by embodying the threat of castration) becomes another Medusan figure. But what if, asks Cixous, 'the doll became a woman? What if she *were* alive? What if, in looking at her, we animated her?' (1976: 538). Animating both Olympia and the uncanny lapses in 'The Uncanny', 'Fiction and its Phantoms' reveals how Freud's carefully choreographed puppet theatre works to repress (rather than repudiate) uncertainty (about sexual identity, but also about death) as it is figured by the image and idea of the 'living doll'. It brings to light, in other words, 'what ought to have remain hidden' in Freud's analysis. The 'direct figure of the uncanny' that emerges in Cixous's text is the Ghost as 'the fiction of our relationship to death, concretized by the specter in literature' (1976: 542). What is ultimately repressed in Freud's reading of Hoffmann's text, then, is its fictional status as 'a secretion of death, an anticipation of non-representation, a doll, a hybrid body' (1976: 548). However, for Cixous, as for Carter, the father's doll is not inanimate.

The living doll is a prominent denizen of Carter's fiction. In a seminal discussion of Carter's work, Paulina Palmer argues that her early fictions evince a theoretical interest in 'gender and its construction, the cultural production of femininity, male power under patriarchy, and the myths and institutions which serve to maintain it' (1987: 180). The preeminent image used to explore these theoretical concerns is the puppet. Palmer suggests that, in addition to 'carrying Hoffmann-nesque associations of the fantastic', this motif has connotations of the 'coded mannequin', a term she borrows from Cixous 'to represent the robotic state to which human beings are reduced by a process of psychic repression' (1987: 180).[2] Although the 'coded mannequin' takes form in Carter's first novel, *Shadow Dance*, it provides a powerful focus for her second novel, *The Magic Toyshop*. Replete with images of doubling, violence and mutilation, *The Magic Toyshop* plays directly and strenuously with Freud's notion of the uncanny. The display of 'carved and severed' wooden limbs in Uncle Philip's workshop (*MT* 66) and Melanie's discovery of 'a freshly severed hand, all bloody at the roots' in the kitchen drawer (*MT* 118) echo all too directly Freud's description of the peculiar uncanniness of '[d]ismembered limbs, a severed head, a hand cut off at the wrist' in 'The Uncanny' (Freud, 1990: 366). But, if Freud's text marginalises Olympia, Carter's novel brings the puppet to centre stage, making visible the female subject's uncanny experience.

Taking as its focus the enclosing structures of the home and the family, *The Magic Toyshop* exemplifies what Sage identifies as a 'recurrent plot' in Carter's early novels: 'a middle-class virgin bewitched and appalled by the fictions of femininity falls in love with a working-class boy, a dandified, dressed-up tramp who's meant to make sense of her desires, but doesn't' (1992: 170). While this paradigm might also be identified in the depiction of Marianne in *Heroes and Villains* and Annabel in *Love*, it is Melanie who conforms most closely to the traditional 'female Gothic' heroine.[3] An adolescent girl on the threshold of womanhood, Melanie initially experiences her position as a Gothic daughter through the Sleeping Beauty narrative. Her night-time journey dressed up in her mother's wedding dress takes her beyond the walls of her father's house to encounter the mysterious, and perilous, horrors of the nocturnal garden and its 'huge, still, waiting things with soft, gaping mouths, whose flesh was the same substance as night' (*MT* 19). Although 'under the moon, the country spread out like a foreign and enchanted land' (*MT* 16), this Edenic Garden 'turned against Melanie when she became afraid of it' (*MT* 18). Clambering up the thorny trees surrounding her father's house, this Sleeping Beauty rips her dress on the thorns climbing back into the castle: 'She had bled far more than she realised' (*MT* 22). Once again, the 'prick' is the price that she must pay for crossing the threshold of the father's house. Melanie finds herself confronted by thorns once again when, following her parents' death (a punishment for inhabiting the mother's wedding dress), she is relocated to Uncle Philip's murky and grimy home. Here she wakes up in her bedroom as if 'from a hundred years' night, *la belle au bois dormante* [*sic*], imprisoned in a century's steadily burgeoning garden. But it was only her new wallpaper, which was printed with roses, though she had not before noticed the thorns' (*MT* 53). Once again, the thorny hedge marks the threshold between the inside and the outside, the animate and the inanimate self.

Melanie's questioning of her animacy – and her anxiety about seeing herself clearly – is also negotiated through the figure of the marionette. Aged fifteen, Melanie awakens into adolescence to discover that 'she was made of flesh and blood' (*MT* 1). However, she animates herself through the performance of a series of pre-scripted images of femininity – for example, '[à] la Toulouse Lautrec, she dragged her hair sluttishly across her face and sat down with her legs apart' (*MT* 1) before using a 'net curtain as raw material for a series of nightgowns' in which to gift-wrap 'herself for a phantom bridegroom' (*MT* 2). These acts of auto-objectification portend the involuntary roles and positions she is later forced to adopt when she is removed to Uncle Philip's 'cruel factory of simulacra' (Sage, 1994a: 16). Taking up her domestic role in the family home, she experiences herself as 'a wind-up putting-away doll, clicking through its programmed movements' (*MT* 76). Placing Melanie in the world of the toyshop, the text refocalises the uncanny by bringing to the foreground the disorientating experience of the doll-like woman whose sense of self is thrown into crisis by the rapidly deteriorating boundary between reality and representation. Seeing her double in the five-foot puppet, dressed in tulle with long, black hair, on the toyshop floor, Melanie begins to feel as 'insignificant as dust' (*MT* 162) – her body ceases to matter.

It is Uncle Philip's dramatisation of Leda's rape by the Swan, however, that provides the mimetic centrepiece of the novel. Playing Leda to Philip's mechanical swan, Melanie is at first amused by its artificiality: 'It was almost as tall as she, an egg-shaped sphere of plywood painted white and coated with glued-on feathers. [. . .] It was nothing like the wild, phallic bird of her imaginings. It was dumpy and homely and eccentric' (*MT* 165). Nevertheless, when she is faced with the reality of sexual violence, the mechanical operations of the automaton (which should reaffirm a sense of her own autonomous subjectivity) instead throw Melanie's identity into crisis: 'she felt herself and not herself, wrenched from her own personality, watching this whole fantasy from another place [. . .] the black-haired girl who was Melanie and who was not' (*MT* 166). The double does not figure here as 'an insurance against the destruction of the ego' but, in its reverse aspect, as the 'uncanny harbinger of death' (Freud, 1990: 356, 357). While in 'The Sandman' it is the troubling life-likeness of Olympia that makes Nathaniel feel 'quite uncanny', here it is Melanie's experience of estrangement as a simulated being that brings into view the unsettling gender politics of Freud's 'strange theoretical novel'.[4]

The motif of the living doll similarly structures 'The Loves of Lady Purple', which dramatises the relationship between a male puppet-master

and his beautiful, female marionette – Lady Purple – as a Gothic fantasy
of artistic authority and omnipotence.

> The puppet-master is always dusted with a little darkness. In direct
> relation to his skill, he propagates the most bewildering enigmas for,
> the more life-like his marionettes, the more god-like his manipu-
> lations and the more radical the symbiosis between inarticulate doll
> and articulating fingers. ('LLP' 23)

Lady Purple materialises here as a creation of the male imagination.
Like the eighteenth-century automaton makers, the Asiatic Professor
exhibits his 'marvellous' creation in his travelling, collapsible theatre.
Touching his puppet's strings, he animates her 'curious structure' with
'necromantic vigour' ('LLP' 26). The Professor's puppet show – *The
Notorious Amours of Lady Purple the Shameless Oriental Venus*' – plays and
replays the Gothic predicament of Lady Purple who, as the Professor
assures his audience, is the 'petrification of a universal whore' ('LLP' 28).
A courtesan with a voracious appetite for perversity, pain and murder,
Lady Purple was 'once a woman in whom too much life had negated
life itself' ('LLP' 28). A leather-booted 'mistress of the whip before
her fifteenth birthday' ('LLP' 30–1), she is cast in a Sadeian mould.
Graduating 'in the mysteries of the torture chamber', she 'thoroughly
researched all manner of ingenious mechanical devices. She utilized
a baroque apparatus of funnel, humiliation, syringe, thumbscrew,
contempt and spiritual anguish' ('LLP' 31). Not simply in charge of the
machinery of desire, Lady Purple is the machine itself. Mechanically
wreaking destruction through her syphilitic contagion, Lady Purple's
'dry rapacity' becomes so automated that she eventually metamor-
phoses into a marionette – she becomes 'herself her own replica, the
dead yet moving image of the shameless Oriental Venus' ('LLP' 33).
Transformed into nothing but wood and hair, she materialises the
decay that her automated simulation of the human body is intended to
forestall. Nightly, she rises to act out this ouroboric transformation as
part of the Professor's Gothic theatre.

Positioning the text as a precursor to *The Sadeian Woman*, Sarah Gamble
argues that 'the joyless mechanical contortions of the female libertine

cause her to quite literally *become* a machine' (1997: 105; emphasis in original). But, as the story within the story suggests, this transition is more ambivalent. Lady Purple is identified at various points – before and after her transformation – with the 'mechanical vamp', an image of the machine as, to quote Huyssen, 'a demonic, inexplicable threat and as harbinger of chaos and destruction' (1988: 70). In particular, her depiction echoes nineteenth-century associations between electricity and erotically charged, uncontrollable and alluring femininity: 'Skins melted in the electricity she generated' ('LLP' 31). Both electricity and the vampish woman represented sources of generative energy that needed to be subdued (or appropriated) by the male toy-maker/scientist/author – exemplified by Victor Frankenstein in Mary Shelley's 1818 novel. (The image of the mechanical vamp resonates too with surrealism's imagining of the erotic but dangerous charge of female beauty, to which I will return below.) One night, however, the puppet is recharged by the stirring kiss of the Professor, and brought back to life again:

> The sleeping wood had wakened. Her pearl teeth crashed against his with the sounds of cymbals, and her warm fragrant breath blew around him like an Italian gale. Across her suddenly moving face flashed a whole kaleidoscope of expression, as though she were running instantaneously through the entire repertory of human feeling, practising, in an endless moment of time, all the scales of emotion as if they were music. ('LLP' 36)

Although Lady Purple transforms from a puppet into 'hot, wet, palpitating flesh' ('LLP' 36), this imagery of performance and rehearsal locates her still in the realm of the mechanical.

Lady Purple is aligned especially with the Jaquet-Droz 'Musical Lady', an android that played the harpsichord and whose 'eyes would move coyly from side to side, and [...] bosom would heave lightly' as she played the 'five tunes in her repertoire' (Wood, 2002: xiii). Gaby Wood notes that it is very likely that Mary Shelley, passing through Neuchâtel on a six-week-long tour of Europe, may have seen the Jaquet-Droz automata just two years before writing *Frankenstein* (2002: xiv). Here, though, it is the Asiatic Professor who claims Shelley's subtitle – 'the modern Prometheus' – in his quest for mechanical life. Like Frankenstein's monster, Lady Purple turns on her creator. Draining the Professor of his life's blood and breath, she leaves him 'sprawled on the floorboards', like a discarded puppet, 'empty, useless and bereft of meaning' ('LLP' 36). Gina Wisker argues that, '[b]rought alive, the living doll at last has her revenge' (1997: 130). However, the puppet's retribution is extremely equivocal. A motorised body with an artificial emotional intelligence, Lady Purple is a hybrid of wood, flesh and machine – and remains an uncanny figure of uncertainty. Although she unfurls and unravels her body from its confinements, it remains nebulous whether 'she was renewed or newly born, returning to life or becoming alive, awakening from a dream or coalescing into the form of a fantasy generated in her wooden skull by the mere repetition so many times of the same invariable actions' ('LLP' 37). The distinctions between animacy and inanimacy, and between the automaton and autonomous agency, remain unresolved. Returning again and again – like Freud – to the brothel, the narrative refuses to give up the painted woman and make her human.[5]

SURREALISM'S MANNEQUINS

'Absurd automatons, perfected to the last degree, which would function like nothing else on earth' were also a source of fascination for surrealist artists and writers (Breton, 1978: 26). The surrealist poet Benjamin Péret, for example, located automata in the realm of phantoms and marvellous beings. His article, 'Au paradis des fantômes', which appeared in *Minotaure* in 1933 was illustrated with numerous images of automata and mannequins. Notable for Péret was the uncanny figure of Jaquet-Droz's 'Young Writer', which wrote the word *merveilleux* over and over again and, in so doing, blurred the boundaries between the animate and the inanimate (see Belton, 1995: 109–10). The notion of 'automatic writing', however, was closely associated with the idea of femininity. Katharine Conley argues that the surrealist muse is not an automaton as such but an 'automatic woman', whose beauty is not 'her mechanical nature but the mechanical, short-circuit effect she has on the poet' (1996: 18). As Breton famously puts it in the closing line of *Nadja* (1928), 'Beauty will be CONVULSIVE or will not be at all' (1999: 160). Beauty, he suggests, is like 'a train that ceaselessly roars out of the Gare de Lyon [...]. It consists of jolts and shocks, many of which do not have much importance, but which we know are destined to produce one *Shock*, which does' (1999: 160; emphasis in original). At once mobilised and circumscribed by the language of science and technology, automatic woman is electrifying – dangerous, seductive and beautiful, she is charged with the responsibility to shock.

Closely linked to Breton's imagining of convulsive beauty is the notion of the marvellous which, according to Carter, is the 'most important of all surrealist principles' and, for her, the 'incendiary' slogan that gets 'the old juices' running ('AW' 512). In the first 'Manifesto of Surrealism' (1924), André Breton famously proposes that 'the marvelous is always beautiful, anything marvelous is beautiful, in fact only the marvelous is beautiful' (1972: 14). He goes on to outline its Gothic affinities, linking the marvellous to the 'exalting effect' of Lewis's *The Monk*, a novel that provides a model for '[f]ear, the attraction of the unusual, chance, the taste for things extravagant' (1972: 16). He acknowledges, however, that

> [t]he marvellous is not the same in every period of history: it partakes in some obscure way of a sort of general revelation only the fragments of which come down to us: they are the romantic *ruins*, the modern *mannequin*, or any other symbol capable of affecting the human sensibility for a period of time. (1972: 16)

These two seemingly unconnected examples present a distinctly uncanny confusion of categories. Hal Foster suggests that each 'combines or conflates two opposed terms: in the ruin the natural and the historical, and in the mannequin the human and the nonhuman'. In both images, he argues, 'the animate is confused with the inanimate, a confusion that is uncanny precisely because it evokes the conservatism of the drives, the immanence of death in life' (1993: 21).

This conceptualisation of the romantic ruin and the modern mannequin alongside one another also points to the body of the mannequin – and implicitly the female body – as a conflicted Gothic space. The female fashion mannequin, argues Renée Riese Hubert, 'exemplified some of surrealists' [*sic*] basic paradoxes concerning animate and inanimate, object and subject, the real and the imaginary, for it abolished barriers and made contradictions irrelevant' (1988: 140). This Gothic aspect of the mannequin was exemplified at the International Surrealist Exhibition held at the Galleries Beaux-Arts, Paris, in 1938, which included a 'red-light' surrealist street populated by female mannequins (Mahon, 2005: 43). Each mannequin was (un)dressed by a different surrealist artist (e.g. Marcel Duchamp, Max Ernst, Sonia Mossé, Joan Miró, Salvador Dalí and Man Ray, amongst others). While the prostitute mannequins emphasised the fetishisation of the female body, they also troubled sexual desire by at once evoking and negating female sexuality: 'for it is the nature of the female mannequin', suggests Alyce Mahon, 'that despite the perfect face, breasts, hands and feet she is ultimately sexless, having only a flattened pubic mound' (2005: 44). Representing a lack awaiting inscription, the mannequins blurred the boundaries between the waxen and the fleshy, and the sexual and the sexless.

Such a positioning of the female body as a site of disorder and contradiction informs the work of the German artist Hans Bellmer – whose influence on Carter's work has been illuminated by Jane Hentges (2002) and Anna Watz (2006). Bellmer's series of life-size female dolls, which appeared in the mid-1930s, offers one of surrealism's most intense and troubling experiments with the doll as a figure of uncanny confusion. Inspired in part by Jacques Offenbach's opera *The Tales of Hoffmann*,[6] Bellmer's first doll, which he created in 1933, was approximately four feet tall and constructed of plaster and papier mâché over wood and metal; it became the subject of a series of macabre photographs, which represented the doll in various disassembled and reassembled configurations, at once erotic and deathly. Structured around a central ball joint, his second doll, which appeared in 1935, permitted even more articulation of the doll's body parts and a closer resemblance to skin (see Green, 2005: 17, and Watz, 2006: 24). Diverse in their arrangements, the dolls represented a poetics of the mechanical. In a

1972 interview, Bellmer explained his conceptualisation of the doll as a kind of experimental text:

> I tried to rearrange the sexual elements of a girl's body like a sort of plastic anagram. I remember describing it thus: the body is like a sentence that invites us to rearrange it, so that its real meaning becomes clear through a series of endless anagrams. I wanted to reveal what is usually kept hidden – it was no game – *I tried to open people's eyes to new realities.* (qtd in Mahon, 2005: 30; emphasis in original)

The girl-doll is thus figured as a malleable sentence. The female body is (re)written as a site of violent confusion, disruptive excess and revolutionary possibility; it is also sentenced, like the Sadeian victim and the Baudelairean muse, to a series of sinister and violent assaults by the male artist.

In her essay on petrification and perversion in Carter's early novels, Hentges draws attention to the echoes of Bellmer's surrealist dolls in the depiction of Uncle Philip's workshop in *The Magic Toyshop*, with its 'carved and severed limbs' and 'partially assembled puppets of all sizes [...] blind-eyed puppets, some armless, some legless, same [*sic*] naked, some clothed, all with a strange liveliness as they dangled unfinished from their hooks' (*MT* 66–7; Hentges, 2002: 50). Watz has discussed in detail the influence of Bellmer's work on *Shadow Dance*, a novel that conjures a 'specifically surrealist version of woman' in the characterisation of Ghislaine (2006: 22).[7] Ghislaine, she proposes, appears as 'the novel's *femme-enfant*, doll, devouring mantis and erotic object, locked into the surrealist imagination as a projected image, and never allowed the agency to become a subject' (2006: 32). For Watz, Ghislaine finds an especially striking resemblance in Bellmer's child-woman dolls, which exemplify how surrealism's aesthetics of transgression are played out time and time again over the female body. Disassembled and disarticulated, the female body is 'fragmentized into bits and pieces' (Watz, 2006: 26). It becomes the site of violent, Gothic play.

The dustiest of Carter's novels, *Shadow Dance* belongs to a world of recycling, bric-a-brac and dressing up. It is also the text which plays the most ghastly and deadly games with the female body. The narrative is focalised through the anguished and failing artist Morris, and centres on his violent and intimate relationship with the beautiful and 'indefinably sinister' (*SD* 56) Honeybuzzard, with whom he runs the junk shop, and the spectral, unnerving and scarred Ghislaine, who haunts the shadow world of his imagination. Scavenging in condemned houses and auctions for Victoriana, Morris and Honeybuzzard make a living from, and vampirically live off, rubbish. At an auction held in 'the gutted corpse of what had once been an Edwardian department store', Morris eagerly sucks up 'the smell of dirt, poverty and graveclothes [...]. He loved to nose questioningly among the abandoned detritus of other people's lives for oddments, fragments, bits of this and that' (*SD* 23). It is not, however, just the 'gutted', corpse-like buildings that are plundered by the male protagonists; this image of the auction house mirrors the butchery to which the female body is subjected, actually and imaginatively, throughout the text.

Shadow Dance establishes from the outset a tired and gaudy stage set for its Gothic theatre:

> The bar was a mock-up, a forgery, a fake; an ad-man's crazy dream of a Spanish patio, with crusty white walls [...] on which hung unplayable musical instruments and many bull-fight posters, all blood and bulging bulls' testicles and the arrogant yellow satin buttocks of lithe young men. (*SD* 1)

This self-consciously crafted stage is a kind of surrealist collage, made up of bits and pieces drawn from a variety of literary and artistic spheres. While Morris and Honeybuzzard resemble images from the visual arts – an 'El Greco Christ' (*SD* 9) and an 'illustration from [Christina Rossetti's] "Goblin Market"' (*SD* 130) respectively – other characters appear to be mechanically animated. Morris wonders whether the 'corpulent' Oscar (who drinks in the same bar and who has also slept with Ghislaine) 'kept a laughing machine in his guts, switched on all the time to electronically simulate hilarity' (*SD* 26). His speculation that there would be room for a 'midget technologist' to live inside his gut aligns Oscar with one of Kempelen's automata and seems to locate the novel in the shadowy realms of the uncanny – where the distinctions between dolls and humans are obscure and dead matter might be brought back to life at any moment. But it echoes too Henri Bergson's suggestion that laughter consists in perceiving 'something mechanical encrusted on something living' (Bergson, 2008: 33), and thus also makes risible the text's images of mechanistic human behaviour.

The novel's central thematic of play is embodied most forcibly by the sadistic toy-making, role-playing Honeybuzzard. He is the first in a line of male puppet-masters in Carter's fiction who seek to play erotic games with women. Androgynous, mysterious and violent, Honeybuzzard is, according to Sage, 'an early embodiment of [Carter's] conviction that the fantastical and the actual can exist in the same place. The Gothic need not be locked away in a separate genre' (1994a: 12). Here the Gothic emerges from the materiality of everyday things and places and is often, though not always, a theatrical effect (Honeybuzzard is also a violent murderer). Like Carter's Poe, who is born into the dressing room, Honeybuzzard inhabits a world of disguise and role play; but, if Poe peers out of the prop basket with longing, Honeybuzzard is already fully immersed in its paraphernalia (he dresses in the waistcoat worn in the film adaptation of 'The Fall of the House of Usher'). Making use of false noses, ears and vampire teeth, Honeybuzzard thrives on the prospect of slipping in and out of himself and into other identities: 'I would like to be somebody different each morning. Me and not-me. I would like to have a cupboard bulging with all different bodies and faces and choose a fresh one every morning' (*SD* 78). Hovering on the boundaries of the 'me' and the 'not-me', Honeybuzzard is a peculiarly abject figure, a notion emphasised by his first appearance as 'Honeydripper' in early drafts of the novel (see BL Add MS88899/1/1).

Kristeva describes the abject as that which 'disturbs identity, system, order. What does not respect borders, positions, rules' (1982: 4). It threatens the borders of the subject's 'own and clean' self (1982: 53). The body and its borders are for Honeybuzzard a constant source of enthralment and play. He relishes in his joke-bag full of reproductions of dog excrement, exploding cigarettes and rubber fried eggs, and longs for 'an exploding contraceptive' because 'even sex was a joke, a savage one' (*SD* 76). In terms of the novel's Gothic allegiances, Honeybuzzard's interest in dirt and defilement aligns him more closely with Bataille, whose love of flies (along with dust and filth) led Breton to attack him for wishing only

> to consider in the world that which is vilest, most discouraging, and most corrupted, and he invites man, *so as to avoid making himself useful for anything specific*, 'to run absurdly with *him* – his eyes suddenly become dim and filled with unavowable tears – toward some haunted provincial houses, seamier than flies, more depraved, ranker than barber shops.' (Breton, 1972: 181; emphasis in original)[8]

Honeybuzzard, it would seem, has taken up Bataille's incitement to revolt in the borders of abjection that place the subject 'in perpetual danger' (Kristeva, 1982: 9). His is the condition of the subject sent to its limits, to the 'place where meaning collapses' (Kristeva, 1982: 2).

If, as Sage suggests, Honeybuzzard 'plays tirelessly and cruelly, like a big cat; anything and anyone is fair game', then the masochistic, doll-like Ghislaine is his 'perfectly perverse' plaything (1994a: 11). Hovering on the threshold between dream and reality, Ghislaine is also an abject figure. When she first appears in the bar where Morris is drinking, the touch of her hand sends a 'sudden terror' through him – just as the vampire's 'undead' touch chills Jonathan Harker's blood in *Dracula* (elsewhere in the text, it is Honeybuzzard, with his dark glasses and vampire teeth, who is associated with the vampiric Count). Although Ghislaine 'used to look like a young girl in a picture book, a soft and dewy young girl', her 'almost translucent' skin is now disfigured by a scar that runs the length of her face, leaving it 'horribly lop-sided, skin, features and all dragged away from the bone' (*SD* 2–3). As Morris observes, the scar that runs down her face 'was all red and raw, as if, at the slightest exertion, it might open and bleed; and the flesh was marked with purple imprints from the stitches she had had in it' (*SD* 2). Now resembling the 'bride of Frankenstein', Ghislaine is constructed as a compendium of Gothic fantasies of femininity as at once alluring and fearful. Although it is never made explicit how Ghislaine was scarred, the suggestion is that Honeybuzzard mutilated her face after Morris, following a failed sexual encounter with her, asked him to '[t]ake her and teach her a lesson' (*SD* 34). Exchanged between the two men, she is punished and forced to bear this 'wound' of femininity as a sign of her shame.

Ghislaine is associated at various points in the text with surrealist images of 'automatic' femininity. Remarking on a transformation in her appearance when she returns from hospital, Morris observes that she 'used to speak with the electronic irresistible sing-song of a ravishing automaton; now her voice gave the final unnerving resemblance to a horror-movie woman to her' (*SD* 4). Uncannily blurring the boundaries between the fleshy and the automatic, Ghislaine no longer provides the 'shock' of convulsive beauty, but is an image of mechanical femininity threatening to run out of control. Before her attack, Honeybuzzard and Morris subdue Ghislaine's threatening sexuality by transforming her into a posing doll for their pornographic photographs. Untiringly contorting herself into all kinds of positions, Ghislaine arrays 'herself in a bizarre variety of accessories' as Honeybuzzard rummages through the junk shop for new toys and props – '[m]ilitary boots and a brocaded hat; rhino whips; clanking spurs; a stag's head; a dappled, gilded, flaking fairground Dobbin' (*SD* 17). Full of bric-a-brac and bizarre, out-of-place objects, the inside of the junk shop (like Honeybuzzard's bedroom) echoes the 1938 Surrealist Exhibition where, Simone de Beauvoir describes, there were 'various objects looming up out of the carefully contrived semi-darkness: a fur-lined dish, an occasional table with the legs of a woman' (qtd in Mahon, 2005: 43).

Ghislaine's transformation here echoes in particular the erotically adorned mannequins on the 'surrealist street':

> They would put her in the window arranged on a rug or a sofa, with a label Sellotaped to her navel: 'Hardly used.' With a dome of immortelles beside her. And the dust would snow down, in time, and obscure her face entirely, and mice would nest in her guts. (*SD* 19)

Breton's association of the mannequin with the romantic ruin resonates in this representation. As well as anticipating her actual death, the imagined picture of mice nestling in Ghislaine's guts echoes the earlier description of the gutted and plundered department store – a connection that reaffirms the figure of the mannequin as 'the very image of capitalist reification' (Foster, 1993: 21). But the representation of the mannequin here is less an instance of Breton's beautiful marvellous than it is an example of Bataille's language of intoxicating dust. Dust here marks the precarious line between past and present, between life and death. It both obscures and acts as a reminder of the materiality of things, demarcating the border between imagination and reality, the dream and the flesh.

CHESS AS GOTHIC PLAY

Staying within this ambivalent field of surrealist play, I wish to trace another strand in the Gothic composition of Carter's fiction: the symbolic currency of chess play and, especially, the troubling allure of the chess queen. Since the Middle Ages, chess has functioned as a crucible for diplomatic tensions of various kinds – political, social and erotic. Representing multifarious modes of engagement (from military warfare and moral guidance to courtship and seduction), the game has proved to be a capacious metaphor for human activity and has influenced both artistic production and conceptions of art and artistry. Chess motifs and metaphors have a powerful presence in modernist aesthetic practices (in, for example, the writing of Samuel Beckett, T. S. Eliot and Vladimir Nabokov); chess analogies similarly inform theoretical understandings of language in the work of Ferdinand de Saussure and Ludwig Wittgenstein, amongst others. For Freud, 'the noble game of chess' was a parallel for the analytic situation: in *Studies on Hysteria* (1895), he likens the turns of the human mind to 'the zig-zag that results when one solves a chess problem by moving a Knight across the squares of the board' (Freud and Breuer, 2004: 291). In 'On Beginning the Treatment' (1913), he later suggests that psychoanalysis, like chess, involves negotiating a series of 'openings and end-games' (Freud, 1959c: 123).

Chess was also of particular significance to a number of surrealist artists, for whom the game (with its vocabulary of 'gambits', 'exchange', 'traps' and 'sacrifice') set in play a dynamic tension between passion and rational thought, and free play and deathly design, as well as dramatising sexual and gender personifications and conflicts. Surrealist interest in chess and its paraphernalia was exemplified by the 1944–45 exhibition on The Imagery of Chess, held at the Julien Levy Gallery in New York City. Besides Max Ernst and Marcel Duchamp, both of whom were involved with the organisation of the exhibition, participants included Man Ray, André Breton, Dorothea Tanning and Yves Tanguy, and exhibits ranged across chess sets, photographs, musical scores, paintings and sculptures. For Man Ray, the geometric form of the chessboard represented the creative process itself as 'the origin and goal of a graphic art, field for clear thinking, impromptu imagination, surprise, planning for the abstract, solid ground to walk on' (qtd in Grossman, 2005: 34). His chess-influenced work *Endgame* (1942) used wooden mannequins as chess pieces, confusing the boundary between piece and player. Such a preoccupation also informs Max Ernst's *The King Playing with the Queen* (1944 and 1954), which deals even more directly with the gender politics of play. In Ernst's sculpture, the queen is positioned as a piece rather than a player; her agency is delimited by the king. Nevertheless, this is a somewhat ambivalent image: the horned king is both a predatory minotaur figure, who threatens to devour the queen, and the image of a cuckolded ruler (see List, 2005: 81). The tension between violence and seduction in this image brings into focus the problematic gender politics of chess and, more broadly, surrealist play.

Chess play's dynamic of power and submission centres on the most alluring and threatening of the chess pieces: the queen. For André Breton, whose ambivalence about chess is famously expressed in 'Profanation' (1944), the queen is a 'suspicious character. The ease with which she moves over the battlefield would have you think that she is a *general* in drag' (qtd in List, 2005: 74). The gender/general ambiguity surrounding the queen's position alludes to the complex history of her position on the chess board. For the queen did not always wield such power; neither did she enjoy such mobility. Over the centuries, chess has undergone several transformations. Although the origins of chess are still disputed, its beginnings are most often located in India by the sixth century. The game initially represented a military formation with the queen's position occupied by a general or counsellor.[9] In *Birth of the Chess Queen*, Marilyn Yalom describes how it was not until 1000, two hundred years after chess arrived in southern Europe, that the queen took up her place on the chessboard. By 1200, Yalom argues, the queen could be found all over Western Europe. Nevertheless, at this time, her mobility was limited: she was allowed to move only one square, diagonally, at a time. By the end of the fifteenth century, however, the queen had acquired new levels of power – incorporating the free diagonal move of the bishop and the horizontal/vertical moves of the rook. Luis Ramírez de Lucena's *Discourse on Love and the Art of Chess with 150 Problems*, published in 1497, outlined the new rules of chess and the chess queen's heightened power, referring to the new game as 'lady's chess' or 'queen's chess' (see Yalom, 2004: 195).

For Alexander Cockburn, whose *Idle Passion: Chess and the Dance of Death* offers a predominantly Freudian take on the game, the ascendance of the queen marks something of a sinister moment in the history of chess: 'The new game caught on in an astoundingly short time. Within a decade the old game had been almost completely abandoned. *Why* the Queen should suddenly have been endowed with such extended powers is a darker, though absorbing problem' (1974: 121; emphasis in original). Less troubled by the dark problem of the queen's unprecedented power, David Shenk notes how the rise of the chess queen registered the emergence of a new female power across Europe: 'In the fifteenth and sixteenth centuries, a cluster of charismatic and powerful queens emerged in Europe: Catherine of Aragon, Isabella of Castile, Mary Tudor, Elizabeth I, Catherine de Médicis [*sic*] of France, Queen Jeanne d'Albret of Navarre, and Mary, Queen of Scots' (2006: 65). Yalom similarly highlights how 'the reality of female rule was [...] undoubtedly entwined with the emergence and evolution of the chess queen' rendering her, in time, 'the quintessential metaphor for female power in the Western world' (2004: xxiii). Still, the queen might have been the most powerful piece on the chessboard, but the king remained the most important, dominating its narrative centre. A lost queen, after all, is not the same as a lost game. That the new modality of chess was also referred to as '*eschés de la dame enragée*' ('mad queen's chess') reflects the cultural anxiety surrounding the queen's newfound power on and off the chessboard (see Yalom, 2004: 214; Weissberger, 2004: xxv).

It is not surprising that Carter, who specialised in Medieval Studies as a student, was interested in chess and, especially, its troublesome queen (she cites chess as one of her favourite games in a 1991 interview with *Marxism Today*). The imaginative landscape of Carter's fiction is imprinted throughout with thematic and metaphorical representations of chess – its board, its pieces and its players. The image of the 'hieratic knight', for example, is used in both *The Infernal Desire Machines of Doctor Hoffman* and 'The Loves of Lady Purple' to gesture to the closed symbolic world of the fair ground: 'hieratic as knights in chess, the painted horses described perpetual circles as immune as those of the planets to the drab world of the here and now inhabited by those who came to gape at us' (*IDM* 112). The almost direct repetition of this image in 'The Loves of Lady Purple' signals the ways in which Carter reuses particular 'moves' across her oeuvre, as if her text too is caught in 'perpetual circles as immutable as those of the planets' ('LLP' 25).[10] The movement of the knight thus provides an image language for a limitless representation of limited play.

Elsewhere, Carter's texts play their own games with Freud's chess analogy. Desiderio, in the introduction to *The Infernal Desire Machines of Doctor Hoffman*, describes killing Albertina in terms of a 'metaphysical chess game' in which he takes away 'her father's queen and mated us both' (*IDM* 6). The narrative geography of *Several Perceptions* is similarly established as a kind of chessboard on which the symbolism of chess play gives form to sexual relationships: 'When it was sunny, Joseph and Charlotte used to sit on the little parapet among the eaves like king and queen of a counterpane country, for all the city was laid out before them, a very expensive toy indeed' (*SP* 14). Here Joseph surveys the space before him, just as Alice does in *Alice's Adventures in Wonderland* (1865), a text that is referenced repeatedly throughout the novel.[11] But the novel also mobilises the resonances of chess play as part of its exploration of the dramatic life of the mind, a thematic preoccupation exemplified by its epigraph from David Hume: 'The mind is a kind of theatre, where several perceptions successively make their appearance, pass, re-pass, glide away and mingle in an infinite variety of postures and situations.' If this conceptualisation of the human mind echoes Freud's account of the zig-zagging moves of the knight, then the description of Joseph and his psychoanalyst Ransome exchanging 'the long, hooded glance of chess masters in a grand tournament' (*SP* 62) reinforces the text's mobilisation of chess as an analogy for the psychoanalytic situation.

Although chess images and metaphors pervade Carter's fiction, both *Shadow Dance* and *Love* have actual chess games embedded in their narratives. In both instances, chess is implicated in a broader rearticu-lation and disruption of surrealist play. From the beginning of *Shadow Dance*, Ghislaine is linked to the enthralling and ambiguous power of the chess queen. When Morris sees her in the bar after she has returned from the hospital, he remarks upon her fragile frame and translucent skin, recalling 'how the red wine had seemed visible, running down the white throat of Mary, Queen of Scots, as she drank' (*SD* 2) – this reference to the famous 'white queen' sets in play the first of the text's obsessive references to decapitation.[12] Amidst the text's multiple images of the white queen emerges another example of the queen as a figure of despoilment and decay. During a night-time scavenge for Victoriana in a deserted house, Morris and Honeybuzzard uncover a 'cake-tin produced as a souvenir of the coronation of Edward VII and his queen, whose faces, wreathed in roses, thistles and leeks stared with the modest imperiousness of constitutional monarchs through a web of *lèse-majesté* dust' (*SD* 88). Here the queen (alongside the philandering king) appears, like the mannequin, as an image of death and decay, the *lèse-majesté* dust a portent of her imminent defilement.

Like several male surrealists, Morris envisages his relationship with women in terms of chess positions – for example, he refers to himself as 'checkmated again' during an argument with his suffering wife, Edna (*SD* 75). For Honeybuzzard, however, the game more fully represents a desire to control and manipulate others (a wish presaged by the Jumping Jack he has crafted in the image of Morris): '"I should like," said Honey dreamily, "to have a floor set out in chequers and to play chess with men and women. I would stand on a chair and call out my moves from a megaphone and they would click their heels and march forward"' (*SD* 117–18). The extent to which Ghislaine functions as a symbolic object of exchange, swapped and assaulted by the two male artists/players, is illustrated by the game of chess played by Morris and Honeybuzzard after they are attacked outside the junk shop by a gang of men and women staggering haphazardly in the 'ghost light' in the street. There is from the beginning of this chapter a menacing violence as Morris and Honeybuzzard stand in the shop 'among a raped pile of broken crockery' (*SD* 114). While Morris abstractedly imagines 'the crimson garlands of his guts spaced and gleaming across the yielding floorboards' Honeybuzzard tells him that he rather enjoys being 'under siege' (*SD* 116) from the group, most of whom go to the aptly named pub, The Cornet of Horse. As this name suggests, chess is already set up as a game of attack and defence that suffuses the narrative geography of the novel. Traumatised by the attack, Morris wishes to stay in the junk shop, but does not want to be alone. He does not want 'to play patience' as Honeybuzzard suggests. Upon Morris's plea, however, Honeybuzzard agrees to stay and play a game of chess, conjuring a chess set from a box and stroking the wooden men emerging from it 'as if greeting old friends' (*SD* 117).

It is against this violent and erotically charged backdrop that Morris and Honeybuzzard take their places across the table like two chess masters and set the board ready to embark upon 'the ancient and hieratic game' (*SD* 117). Honey describes the staging:

> 'First the castles, one at each corner, like the legs of a cow. Then the knights – I love the knights; such proud horseheads, such flaring nostrils and, besides, they move obliquely. Now the reverend gentlemen, next to the caballeros. And the Queen, the travelling lady; she's my favourite piece, she can go anywhere on the board – zip, zip. And a femme fatale, she is, whose kiss is death. Uneasy lies the head that wears the crown, here is the King. Vulnerable, your King – in the last resort he has to hop off one by one, stage by stage, like Louis XIV escaping from Versailles. Morris shall be black and

I white. There are our infantry, our pawns, all ready to go over the top. Let's begin.' (*SD* 117)

This game is rich in allusion as chess initiates a network of intertextual echoes – an exchange of fragmented bodies and literary fragments pointing to the precariousness of kingly power. Most notable is the reference to Shakespeare's *Henry IV Part II*, to the transformation of the reprobate, practical joker into a worthy future king and, more immediately, to the ailing king's own anxieties about the responsibilities of kingship. The 'vulnerability' of the king's power to rule is more pressingly mobilised by the (erroneous) reference to the French king, which points not to the steadfast, absolutist dominion of Louis XIV but to the indecisive rule of Louis XV, who was King of France during the French Revolution – and who took flight from Versailles with his wife, the extravagant Marie Antoinette (a figure much reviled by the similarly profligate but Republican Sade). This reference raises once again the spectre of decapitation, signalling that the stakes of this combat are high (it is no coincidence that Honeybuzzard wants to work on his toy guillotine when the game of chess is put away).

The game increases in pace and excitement and the two men chase one another around the board until they fall into a 'deadly chess impasse'. As the scene culminates in a reference to Carroll – 'Pawn to the back line! Pawn to Queen, like in *Through the Looking-Glass!*' – Morris wins and Honey overturns the table, setting the chess pieces flying across the floor (just as Morris had imagined his guts flying everywhere earlier in the chapter). He sobs: 'You're cheating, you're tricking! I won't have it, you can't have another Queen, you can't!' (*SD* 118). Erotic, bloody and visceral, this vampiric game (Morris taking a pawn is described as drawing 'first blood') lays bare an anxiety about masculine potency and power, especially in the face of the seductive and mobile Queen, the 'femme fatale' whose 'kiss is death'. The *femme fatale*, suggests Mary Ann Doane, blurs the boundaries between passivity and activity. She 'is an ambivalent figure because she is not the subject of power but its *carrier* (the connotations of disease are appropriate here)' (1991: 2). The queen's power here is, at least partly, her ability to displace homoerotic desire (her gender ambiguity is already signalled by Breton's fantasy of the queen as a general in drag).

Throughout *Shadow Dance*, Ghislaine exemplifies the *femme fatale* as an appalling, Gothic fascination. In Morris's imagination, she is 'a vampire woman, walking the streets on the continual qui vive, her enormous brown eyes alert and ever-watchful, and the moment she saw him she would snatch him up and absorb him, threshing, into the chasm in her face' (*SD* 39). The sight of Ghislaine's bloody wound may inspire horror in Morris, but he is also tormented by dreams that he is cutting open her face himself: 'He dreamed he was cutting Ghislaine's face with a kitchen knife. The knife was blunt and kept slipping. Her head came off in his hands, after a while, and he cut her into a turnip lantern, put a candle inside and lit it through her freshly carved mouth' (*SD* 39–40). As this image of decapitation suggests, Morris aligns Ghislaine with the Medusa as an exemplification of the *femme fatale*.[13] Haunted by his memory of spending the night with her, Morris, who at one point finds a plastic doll's head in his pocket, recalls possessing Ghislaine's 'white body and all this long, yellow hair writhing over the pillow like crazy snakes' (*SD* 7). It is this uncontrolled and uncontainable excess of Medusan femininity that must be disciplined (Ghislaine must be 'taught a lesson'). As Doane argues, the 'textual eradication' of the *femme fatale* 'involves a desperate reassertion of control on the part of the threatened male subject' (1991: 2). Mobile, dangerous, and fascinating, the *femme fatale*, like the chess queen, is a deadly woman; she must be punished or effaced to allay fears about her sexual agency.

The queen threatens Honeybuzzard's omnipotence – both as a 'travelling lady' and as one who can be captured, or taken, by another. His desire to master Ghislaine – to play with his queen, to put it in the terms of Ernst's sculpture – culminates in his painstaking choreography of her punishment. Towards the end of the novel, Honeybuzzard returns to the destitute house full of abandoned prayer-books and religious paraphernalia, where he had previously imagined 'chaining' Ghislaine, a clergyman's daughter, to a crumbling crucifix and raping her (*SD* 132). This time, he constructs a makeshift altar in the image of a chessboard: 'On the table lay a mound, covered with a chequered tablecloth. At each of the four corners of the table burned a candle' (*SD* 176). Ghislaine, the white queen, is then sacrificed in a spectacle of violence and defilement that marks one of the most troubling moments of Carter's oeuvre.

> Naked, Ghislaine lay on her back with her hands crossed on her breasts, so that her nipples poked between her fingers like the muzzles of inquisitive white mice. Her eyes were shut down with pennies, two on each eyelid, and her mouth gaped open a little. There were deep black fingermarks in her throat. (*SD* 177)

In her final transformation, Ghislaine is reduced to an object or thing, a mere pawn in Honeybuzzard's game to be assailed, assaulted and despoiled.

Read in terms of the novel's aesthetic allegiances, the denouement gestures towards surrealism's use of blasphemy to shock established values and categories. Honeybuzzard is associated throughout the novel with profanation: amongst the eclectic clutter of bits and pieces in his room there is 'a bust of Queen Victoria wearing one of Honey's ubiquitous false noses', as well as 'a drawing over the fireplace of a woman, a child and a dog in an obscene parody of the Nativity' (*SD* 98). His erotic blasphemy is perhaps most strikingly indebted to the sacrilegious aesthetic of Bataille, whose presence on the Gothic landscape of *Shadow Dance* is hinted at from the fleeting reference to 'bulging bulls' testicles' (*SD* 1), with its direct echo of *Story of the Eye* (1928), at the very beginning of the novel. In an essay on Bataille, Carter points to the 'fine European tradition of anti-clericalism' that is central to Bataille's surrealist preoccupations. She argues that, in *Story of the Eye*, Bataille 'puts pornography squarely in the service of blasphemy. Transgression, outrage, sacrilege, liberation of the senses through erotic frenzy, and the symbolic murder of God' ('GB' 68). The erotic frenzy exhibited by the narrator and Simone in Bataille's pornographic novella is mirrored here by Honeybuzzard's frantic acts of sexual violence.

According to Aidan Day, Honeybuzzard's malevolent fantasy of raping Ghislaine on a crucifix aligns him with a 'culture oppressive to women which is shot through with the attitudes of religious patriarchy' (1998: 16). While acknowledging the misogyny at work in Honeybuzzard's victimisation of the female body, Watz complicates Day's analysis by reading Honeybuzzard's subversive violence in the opposite direction. She suggests that 'the killing of the clergyman's daughter and the desecration of the crucifix simultaneously become the final revolt against the Western patriarchal tradition the surrealists so fervently attacked in their art and writing' (2006: 36). This interpretative divergence reflects the complexity of Carter's surrealist engagements in the novel, especially the fault line delineating aesthetic violence and material violence. However, the tension between a reading of Honeybuzzard's incorporation of the crucifix as either an expression of misogynistic collusion or a blasphemous attack on the law of the father is further muddied by Morris's final glimpse of Honeybuzzard 'cradling' the plaster Christ in his right arm (*SD* 179). This image, which is swiftly juxtaposed with that of the pregnant Emily vomiting, prompts a further iconoclastic resonance with pictorial representations of the Madonna and Child. Honeybuzzard's transgression might in one respect be read as a sacrilegious attack – in the tradition of Sade and Bataille – on (paternalistic) religious authority. However, his ritualistic defilement of Ghislaine's body might also be understood as a conjuring up and abjection of the maternal. Read in this way, Honeybuzzard's assault betrays an anxiety about the 'generative power' of the female body (Kristeva, 1982: 77) – an anxiety suggested earlier in the narrative when it is revealed that he keeps a foetus in a jar. By the end of the novel Honeybuzzard is lost to the shadows. An image of living death, his hair trailing like 'mad Ophelia's' (*SD* 179), he descends into a violent and irretrievable state of '[a]bjection, or the journey to the end of the night' (Kristeva, 1982: 58).

What is most troubling about Carter's first novel, however, is Ghislaine's complicity with Honeybuzzard's violent games. Lying before him on the floor, she awaits her violation and, like Sade's Justine, makes of herself a martyr to his desire: 'I've learned my lesson, I can't live without you, you are my master, do what you like with me' (*SD* 166). Disavowing her subjectivity, she remains a 'projected image' – an automaton rather than 'an autonomous being', to return to Carter's phrasing in 'The Alchemy of the Word' ('AW' 512). Still, if Ghislaine represents an image of assailed and sacrificed femininity, of the queen brutalised and defeated, the text offers another – albeit ambivalent – vision of the queen in the more self-assured figure of Emily: Morris 'was awed by her stolidity, her resolution. He glanced at her and saw that her mouth had never been so firmly closed, locked and padlocked. He was oddly reminded of the bust of Queen Victoria' (*SD* 175). Unlike the fragile and insubstantial Ghislaine, who drifts in and out of Morris's imagination, Emily 'walked in a disciplined, almost martial stride and her arms swung to the rhythm of her walk. [...] She walked as if she had a destination ahead of her of which she was quite sure' (*SD* 174). Moving easily across the battlefield, Emily echoes Breton's notion of the queen as a 'general in drag'. But, while Ghislaine becomes a mannequin-object across whose translucent skin Morris and Honeybuzzard hang their Gothic fantasies, Emily has 'a firm sense of occupancy inside her clothes and her strong, well-made body and the firm features of her quiet face. She was always at home in herself' (*SD* 98). Emily inhabits her own body and the material world of which it is a part. She cannot be co-opted into Honeybuzzard's pornographic imaginary and instead, in the first of a series of conflagratory acts in Carter's opus, burns the junk in Honeybuzzard's bedroom and flushes his foetus down the lavatory. Still, just as the chess queen started out with only one move, the queen motif in Carter's first novel is similarly limited. The question of the chess queen's agency and artistry is 'developed' in Carter's later novel, *Love*.

THE GOTHIC HEROINE AS MAD QUEEN

Similarly set in 1960s bohemian Bristol, *Love* is also concerned with a violent, erotic triangle – this time between the orphaned half-brothers Lee and Buzz and Annabel, an art student. The 'sentimental' Lee and 'malign' Buzz stay together only because 'they were alone in a world with which both felt themselves subtly at variance' (*L* 11). Their violently desirous relationship is set against the backdrop of their mother's 'spectacular psychosis in the grand, traditional style of the old-fashioned Bedlamite' (*L* 10). It is into the role of the 'madwoman' that Annabel, the middle-class virgin, steps and subsequently becomes drawn into the brothers' deadly game of violence, loss and sacrifice. One of Carter's most compelling works, *Love* traverses the territories of the Gothic, surrealism and psychoanalysis in its exploration of the torturous pain of love, sex and desire. Dostoyevsky reverberates through the text: not only does Buzz refer to Lee as Alyosha but the novel throughout bears echoes of *The Brothers Karamazov*. Poe too exerts a characteristic influence: dressed in a black suit, Buzz looks 'fresh from a visit to the tomb of Edgar Allan Poe' (*L* 36) at Annabel and Lee's wedding. In her interview with Bedford, Carter recounts how 'the girl in *Love* was called Madeleine for a long time, after Madeleine Usher', but she changed it to avoid 'giving the game away'. Annabel though, she admits, has 'even more literary connotations. I was completely ... I hadn't realised until this moment! It's Annabel Lee' (Bedford, 1977).[14] Although this disingenuous comment situates Annabel in a lineage of Poe's deathly women, her position as a Gothic subject is far more complex.

From the beginning of the novel, Annabel is located within a self-consciously crafted Gothic stage set, but here the eighteenth-century Gothic landscape is restaged as a fragmented and artificial surrealist theatre. Now overgrown, the park was originally planned by an 'eighteenth-century landscape gardener' as an 'artificial wilderness'. The Gothic mansion itself is reduced to just 'a few architectural accessories' (*L* 1), but the ivy-covered tower in its Gothic North continues to perform 'its original role, transforming the park into a premeditated theatre' (*L* 2). It is against this deliberately composed backdrop that the opening of the novel stages a disturbing psychological encounter with the Gothic landscape:

> One day, Annabel saw the sun and the moon in the sky at the same time. The sight filled her with a terror which entirely consumed her and did not leave her until the night closed in catastrophe for she had no instinct for self-preservation if she was confronted by ambiguities. (*L* 1)

This opening passage echoes Edmund Burke's conceptualisation of the sublime as a force that 'excite[s] the ideas of pain and danger' and

Dolls, dreams and mad queens

'operates in a manner analogous to terror' (Burke, 1990: 36). Like the Burkean subject, whose mind is 'so entirely filled with its object, that it cannot entertain any other, nor by consequence reason on that object which employs it' (Burke, 1990: 53), Annabel experiences the power of the sublime.

However, unlike the eighteenth-century Gothic heroine (for example, Emily St Aubert in Radcliffe's *The Mysteries of Udolpho*, who finds an imaginative and subject freedom in her experience of the natural landscape), Annabel is '[w]holly at the mercy of the elements' (*L* 3). Although the sublime confuses and restores the boundaries separating the subject from the object, the inside and the outside, Annabel's lack of an instinct for 'self-preservation' (a Burkean category of the sublime) takes her to the brink of catastrophe. Her sublime experience more closely approximates Radcliffe's conceptualisation of horror in 'On the Supernatural in Poetry' (1826). While for Burke the sublime is linked to a mode of terror, Radcliffe makes a further distinction between terror and horror in the Gothic mode, arguing that they 'are so far opposite, that the first expands the soul and awakens the faculties to a high degree of life; the other contracts, freezes, and nearly annihilates them' (Radcliffe, 2000: 168). A 'mad girl plastered in fear and trembling against a thorn bush' (*L* 3), Annabel experiences the sublime as an overpowering force that threatens to obliterate her subjectivity.

'[W]ispy and tenuous, like a phantom rag-picker' (*L* 27), Annabel hovers on the border of being and non-being. Standing in the hospital grounds after his appointment with her psychiatrist, Lee observes that Annabel 'spoke in sweet, fallacious music like the song of a mechanical nightingale and now she seemed to him a ghostly woman, white as a winding-sheet and shrouded in hair' (*L* 62). This reference to Hans Christian Andersen's 1843 fairy tale 'The Nightingale' (and Stepan Mitussov's libretto) hints at Lee's preference for the mechanical woman. Yet, Annabel, with her 'almost dissolving edges and transparent' skin remains spectral and ghoulish (*L* 62). Ethereal, fragile and operating outside of the limits of the rational and the fully present, Annabel's somatic expressions link her to the abject figure of the vampire as hysteric — a position that is constructed in and through multiple representations of female madness (most notably allusions to Ophelia).[15]

According to Christina Britzolakis, the 'Gothic staging of the mad girl as spectacle' in *Love* is an effect of the 'psychiatric stance of the clinical "case-study", beloved of late nineteenth-century French novelists' (1995: 464). However, the novel also engages with late-nineteenth-century discourses of hysteria as they are understood in and mediated by surrealist aesthetics. For Louis Aragon and André Breton, hysteria was 'the greatest poetic discovery of the late nineteenth century' and 'a supreme expressive medium' (1928: 20; qtd in Beizer, 1993: 2). Rather than treating it as a pathological category, Aragon and Breton located in hysteria a mode of aesthetic expression unhindered by rational thought. They celebrated, for example, the supremely visual work of the French neurologist Jean-Martin Charcot at La Salpêtrière hospital in Paris and, in particular, the photographs of the hysteric Augustine that appeared in the second volume of the *Iconographie photographique de la Salpêtrière* (1878). Transforming the hospital space into his 'museum of living pathology', Charcot, during his infamous *leçons du mardi*, staged the hysterical convulsions of his female patients for the medical gaze and analysis of his male colleagues.[16] As Janet Beizer summarises, Aragon and Breton identified in the hysteric's 'inarticulate cries a delivery from syntax, a subversion of social and cultural codes, a transgressive poetics, as they discovered in the well-photographed postures and convulsions of the generally female hysterical body an alternative theater, a living erotic art' (1993: 2).

Love, perhaps more so than any other text in Carter's oeuvre, makes its allegiances to surrealism quite explicit, playing throughout with references to various surrealist aesthetic techniques and games – in her conversation with Lee, for example, the psychiatrist diagnoses Annabel and Lee with a 'mutually stimulated psychotic disorder known as "*folie à deux*"' (*L* 60). Describing *Love* as Carter's 'Surrealist poem for the forlorn daughter', Sue Roe argues that the text 'cannot take Annabel as its subject, except as *peinture-poésie*, photomontage, *cadavre exquis*, collage' (1994: 62). Annabel, she proposes, 'exists outside even the traditions of the female Gothic which, like other literary solutions in this novel, have, it is hinted, broken down along with much else' (Roe, 1994: 63). Caught up in surrealist expression, she is inarticulate and disarticulated; spoken rather than speaking, she is unable to inhabit her subjectivity.

Nevertheless, while Ghislaine's body, like that of the mannequin, is unequivocally played with, written on and spoken for, Annabel reimagines, from the position of the female subject, the hysteric as a 'paragon of the artist' (Foster, 1993: 53). She makes sense (or non-sense) of herself and others through image and artistry, painting the walls of her bedroom and drawing visual images of both Lee and Buzz in her mind's eye. Annabel's fragile sense of being in the world emerges, at least partially, from her negotiation of her position as an (animate) artist and (inanimate/animated) *objet d'art*. Following their first sexual encounter, during which she bleeds profusely, Lee looks at Annabel 'nervously, as if she might not be fully human'. However, unlike Ghislaine, she returns his gaze, wondering 'if he might be magic'. Rolling over the pastel crayons that are scattering the bed sheets, their bodies become marked with 'brilliant dusts' and 'spotted with blood' as each becomes 'a canvas involuntarily patterned by those workings of random chance so much prized by the surrealists' (*L* 34).

Annabel's 'favourite painter' is Max Ernst (*L* 31), who was profoundly interested in mental illness (and the artistry of the mentally ill), and who experimented with chance as a creative process. Ernst's presence in Carter's novel is explored in some detail by Roe in relation to the significance of collage aesthetics in the novel.[17] However, I would like to take my reading of the novel's surrealist allegiances along a slightly different, though similarly haphazard, path in order to explore Annabel's simultaneous position as artist/*objet d'art* in relation to the images and vocabularies of chess as a game of 'disorder'. The story of chess has, as Cockburn illuminates in *Idle Passion*, been closely knitted with accounts of mental illness and neurosis (1974: 12). In *Studies of Hysteria* Freud identified pleasure and ability in the game in certain female patients, most famously his insomniac patient Frau Cäcilie M, who reportedly had a chess player ready to play outside her bedroom (Freud and Breuer, 2004: 232). For Annabel (whose name echoes the 'real' identity of Cäcilie, Anna von Lieben) chess similarly represents a place of pleasure and refuge. Although, like Ghislaine, she is identified with the queen, Annabel is positioned as not only a piece but also a player in the text's ludic economy.

Annabel sometimes plays chess with Lee because 'she liked to handle the pieces of a red and white Chinese ivory set that Buzz had somehow acquired for her' (*L* 40).[18] As the ambiguous and probably dubious provenance of the chess set suggests, the game works a risky edge. Annabel's mesmerised and peculiarly tactile attitude to chess echoes that of Honeybuzzard in *Shadow Dance*: 'she would fall into a reverie, her eyes fixed vacantly on the board caressing the knight or castle in her hand while Lee gnawed his fingernails and waited for some startling, irrational move which would throw his mathematical attack into disarray' (*L* 40). Like Honeybuzzard, she too plays a passionate and imaginative game, the disorder of which unsettles the cool and calculating method of Lee, who describes his experience of one particular game to his lover, Carolyn:

> 'She plays chess from the passions and I play it from logic and she usually wins. Once, I took her queen and she hit me.'
> Though, he recalled, not sufficiently brutally to require that he tie her wrists together with his belt, force her to kneel and beat her until she toppled over sideways. She raised a strangely joyous face to him; the pallor of her skin and the almost miraculous lustre of her eyes startled and even awed him. He was breathless with weeping, a despicable object.
> 'That will teach you to take my queen,' she said smugly. There were bruises on her shoulders and breast when she took off her sweater to go to bed. She stroked herself thoughtfully and suggested: 'I should like a ring with a moonstone in it.' (*L* 40)

This reference to chess play appears just after Lee recounts to Carolyn an instance of 'Annabel being beaten' (*L* 40). Notions of power, play and strategy coalesce around the idea of 'being beaten' – as a state of defeat and assault. That Lee ignores Annabel's request for a moonstone ring and buys her instead a 'print of Millais' "Ophelia"' from a second-hand shop (*L* 41) represents his move to read her, as Garner argues, through 'the established and commercialised discourse of the image of the hysteric'. Here Lee occupies the role of the 'Pre-Raphaelite artist, for whom the sensual beauty of his muse is enhanced by (or perhaps even a product of) her restrictive, unhealthy female body' (Garner, 2012: 153). Annabel's passion and artistry are contained and controlled as she is placed back in the position of hysteric as victim.

In *Love*, chess comes to figure a mime of the violent erotic relations between its players, who are engaged in a deathly game of confrontation, manoeuvre and, as the game progresses, sacrifice. Its symbolic schema works to foreground the material world by drawing attention to the physical situation of the bruised and assaulted female body that underlies the violence of representation. Play here has consequences. In the act of stroking herself, as she had caressed the chess pieces, Annabel foregrounds the ambiguity of her position; at once a player and a piece, the dangers of the game in which she is engaged are redoubled. Roe, in her analysis of the novel, aptly highlights the text's resonances with the work of the surrealist writer Leonora Carrington (who had an intimate relationship with Ernst for several years), most notably 'My Mother Is a Cow', which explores how '[t]o be one human creature is to be a legion of mannequins' (qtd in Roe, 1994: 67). But the chess game described in *Love*, which renders raw and vulnerable the bodies of its players, also echoes the chess playing and artistry between Ernst and Dorothea Tanning, an avid chess player and artist (who was later married to Ernst).

A famous photograph of Max Ernst and Dorothea Tanning playing chess (1948) shows the partially clothed couple through a picture frame. Replaying medieval associations of chess and courtship, it highlights the vulnerability of the chess-playing body engaged in erotic and desirous exchange. This position of vulnerability is one that Annabel 'develops' as part of her aesthetic game. For, if Ghislaine appears to be a passive victim of Honeybuzzard's mastery, then Annabel wills her victimhood. The image of Annabel toppling over sideways in the passage above reworks the idea of 'resignation' – when a player recognises the inevitability of losing a game and topples over his/her king. Her suicidal despair and desire (the manifestation *par excellence* of her masochism) are given symbolic representation in the Gothic vocabulary of chess play. After watching Lee and Carolyn together at the party, an episode which she experiences as if 'an infatuated spectre' (*L* 44), Annabel reasserts her corporeal presence by proceeding 'immediately to the bathroom to kill herself in private'. This calculated 'move' leaves her waiting to bleed to death 'as content as if she had won another game of chess by unorthodox means' (*L* 45).

The nihilistic focus of Annabel's (chess) play as self-destruction, especially in its final stages, has especial affinities with the Dadaist artist and chess player Marcel Duchamp, whose elaboration of esoteric endgames in *Opposition and Sister Squares Are Reconciled* (1932) brought into focus the 'chess' problem as an aesthetic endeavour.[19] For Annabel too, chess play is inextricably connected to her artistry. Whereas, in *Shadow Dance*, Ghislaine is transformed into an aesthetic object and sacrificed on Honeybuzzard's improvised chessboard, Annabel prepares for her suicide by dressing herself in the costume of the white queen, 'a long, plain, white dress of cotton with a square-cut neck and long, tight sleeves' (*L* 102). With a final, Gothic flourish, she converts herself into a 'marvellous' and carefully crafted chess piece:

> With her glittering hair and unfathomable face, streaked with synthetic red, white and black, she [...] had become a marvellous crystallization retaining nothing of the remembered woman but her form [...]. No longer vulnerable flesh and blood, she was altered to inflexible material [...] for now she was her own, omnipotent white queen and could move to any position on the board. (*L* 104)

Annabel's 'endgame' – the 'distinct and stark final stage of chess' (Shenk, 2006: 190) – sees her collapsing the boundaries between artist and *objet d'art* by transforming herself from chess player to chess piece to become the 'omnipotent white queen'.

Cockburn concludes *Idle Passion* by describing chess, in its 'eternal unresolvable struggle', as not necessarily 'an image of discovery or a portent of the new' but 'a process of suicide; a mime of despair' (1974: 216). In this light, Annabel is *la dame enragée* who brings madness and fury to the game. As Cockburn notes, although Duchamp did not make the 'final commitment to becoming "a madman of certain quality"', some of his fellow Dadaists 'ended their lives with suicide, the only solution they could find to the juxtaposition of the absurdity of art and the absurdity of the world' (1974: 196). For Annabel too, the drama of the board represents the disintegration of the distinction between life and art. She concludes her masochistic auto-narrative by committing suicide in her 'darkened bedroom' (*L* 102):

> now she lay in her ultimate, shocking transformation; now she was a painted doll, bluish at the extremities, nobody's responsibility. Lee returned to the house only to retrieve a little money and a few clothes. He found her in the bedroom. Buzz crouched at the end of the bed, at the feet of the bedizened corpse.
>
> 'I think you should stand with your foot on her neck,' said Buzz. 'Then I would take your picture with your arms crossed and, you understand, your foot on her neck. Like, in a victorious pose.' (*L* 112)

Annabel's strategic sacrifice is, in the end, something of a pyrrhic victory. Although, in turning herself into a painted doll, she authors/ authorises herself as a work of (surrealist) art, she has nonetheless sacrificed herself to the brothers' deadly play. The white queen is removed from the game.

In a 1987 'Afterword' to *Love*, Carter reflects on the 'text that is Annabel's coffin' (*L* 114) as an 'almost sinister feat of male impersonation' with its 'icy treatment of the mad girl and its penetrating aroma of unhappiness' (*L* 113). Linked throughout with images of victimisation, both Annabel and Ghislaine belong in the tradition of 'self-regarding masochism' (*SW* 57) that Carter associates with Sade's Justine, who remains 'a pawn because she is a woman' (*SW* 79). Annabel occupies the position of a surrealist artist who enlivens contradictions and opens up new imaginative vistas through an aesthetic of disorder but, in the end, she sacrifices herself to the violence of a surrealist 'pawnography' that returns her to the position of an inanimate doll.

Carter's textual practices echo surrealism's accommodation of contradictions, its openness to the possibilities of unconscious life and its commitment to social and cultural change (the desire to 'open people's eyes to new realities', to use Bellmer's words). As Carter puts it in 'Notes on the Gothic Mode', with reference to Sade, 'I do not aspire to the boring-sublime; the "perpetual immoral subversion of the established order" is more like it' ('NGM' 134). However, while Carter's fiction revels in surrealist strategies of play and profanation as part of its challenge to the structures of the bourgeois social order, it simulta-neously subjects those strategies to a feminist critique that uncovers the female body as a site of anxiety and desire. In 'The Alchemy of the Word', Carter concludes that the 'surrealists were not good with women. That is why, although I thought they were wonderful, I had to give them up in the end. [...] I knew I wanted my fair share of the imagination, too. Not an excessive amount, mind; I wasn't greedy. Just an equal share in the right to vision' ('AW' 512). *Shadow Dance* and *Love* reveal how surrealism, as part of a broader European Gothic aesthetic, often envisages femininity in spectral and mystical formations but, at the same time, requires a body to brutalise and sacrifice. 'Surrealism's undercurrent of joy, of delight', suggests Carter, 'springs from its faith in humankind's ability to recreate itself; the conviction that struggle *can* bring about something better' ('AW' 507). What Carter emphasises, then, is the need for a feminist surrealist aesthetic that insists upon recreation (play) as a mode of re-creation and re-making. After all, she points out, '[s]omething that women know all about is how very difficult it is to enter an old game. What you have to do is to change the rules and make a new game' (Katsavos, 1994: 13).

NOTES

1 In an interview with John Haffenden, Carter claims that the figure of the 'mad scientist/shaman/toy-maker/male-authority figure' has 'remained remarkably consistent [...] in the particular schema of [her] novels' (1985: 88).

2 Palmer goes on to propose that the puppet is supplanted in Carter's later work by a more utopian model of femininity, exemplified by the image of Fevvers's 'miraculous wings' in *Nights at the Circus* (1987: 180) – a suggestion to which I will return in the next chapter.

3 As Carter clarifies in an interview with Olga Kenyon, 'I usually put my adolescent heroines through the mangle. [Melanie is] a bourgeois virgin, a good screamer, like the Hammer films I enjoyed as a child' (Kenyon, 1992: 27).

4 Where Olympia remains 'sightless' – rendered, paradoxically, invisible by the scopic economy of Freud's analysis – Melanie disrupts the voyeuristic structures of the text's Gothic theatre by resisting the gaze. She looks back, for example, through Finn's peephole (which echoes again Duchamp's *Étant Donnés*), and can never fully be captured by his equivocal squint. Further, at the end of the novel, the paternal prohibition is broken when Margaret and Francie's incest is made visible as the secret concealed at the heart of the family home.

5 In so far as Lady Purple's body comes to matter in the context of a regulatory heterosexual regime (and the fantasy of the brothel), the use of the puppet motif in 'The Loves of Lady Purple' presages Judith Butler's theorisation of the 'matter' of sex as *'a process of materialization that stabilizes over time to produce the effect of boundary, fixity, and surface we call matter'* (1993: 9; emphasis in original). Gender construction, Butler argues, 'not only takes place in time, but is itself a temporal process which operates through the reiteration of norms [...]. As a sedimented effect of a reiterative or ritual practice, sex acquires its naturalized effect, and, yet, it is also by virtue of this reiteration that gaps and fissures are opened up as the constitutive instabilities in such constructions, as that which escapes or exceeds the norm' (1993: 10).

6 See Malcom Green, who suggests that Bellmer also 'knew his Freud and would have been familiar with the latter's study *The Uncanny*, which directly addresses his own nascent Pygmalionism' (2005: 15).

7 The surrealist resonances in this novel are also heightened by the echoes of Léona-Camile-Ghislaine D, on whom Breton's Nadja is purportedly based (see Polizzotti, 1999: x). The name Ghîslaine is used in early manuscripts for *Shadow Dance*, but the circumflex is removed in the published version (see BL Add MS88899/1/1).

8 For more on Breton's criticism of Bataille's 'vulgar materialism' see Fer (1995: 162–3).

9 Called 'chaturanga', meaning 'four members' in Sanskrit, it is comprised of four parts – chariots, elephants, cavalry and infantry – plus a King and his general (see Yalom, 2004: 3).

10 This passage is reiterated and re-worked to describe the travelling fair

in 'The Loves of Lady Purple': 'Hieratic as knights in chess, the painted horses on the roundabouts describe perpetual circles as immutable as those of the planets and as immune to the drab world of here and now whose inmates come to gape at such extraordinariness, such freedom from actuality.' ('LLP' 25)

11 Lewis Carroll's *Through the Looking-Glass, and What Alice Found There* (1871) and the 'A Game of Chess' episode from T. S. Eliot's *The Waste Land* (1922) frame Finn and Melanie's trip to the disused pleasure ground to see 'the Queen of the Waste Land' in *The Magic Toyshop*. This is also the site of what Finn names as the National Exposition of 1852, meaning the Great Exhibition of 1851: 'They built this vast Gothic castle: a sort of Highland fortress, only gargantuan, and filled it with everything they could think of, to show off,' he explains (*MT* 99). The year 1851 was also that of the first international chess tournament, organised by the *Illustrated London News* chess columnist Howard Staunton, to coincide with and mirror the imperial splendour and spectacle of the Great Exhibition.

12 In the neo-Victorian context of the novel, the white queen is also a figure of madness, exemplified by the White Queen as mad woman in Carroll's *Through the Looking-Glass*. In *The Female Malady*, Elaine Showalter discusses the phenomenon of queen delusions amongst women diagnosed as female lunatics during Victoria's reign (1985: 87–90).

13 In 'The Medusa's Head', Freud famously draws a link between the fear of castration-as-decapitation and the fear of a horrific sight, namely the female genitals: 'To decapitate = to castrate. The terror of the Medusa is thus a terror of castration that is linked to the sight of something. [...] The sight of Medusa's head makes the spectator stiff with terror, turns him into stone' (1959a: 273). For more on the Medusa and surrealism see Conley (1996: 16–17).

14 For a reading of *Love*'s intertextual references to Poe's 'Annabel Lee' see Peach (2009: 55–8).

15 In this respect, Annabel hovers uneasily between the eighteenth-century Gothic and early-twentieth-century surrealism (illuminating the connections between these two discourses). She also echoes Anne Blossom in *Several Perceptions*, whose limp is interpreted as a 'hysterical paralysis' (*SP* 145).

16 In *Ventriloquized Bodies*, her study of the hysteric's semiotic body, Janet Beizer highlights how the dermographic patient in particular becomes an inscribed body that is not only spoken about but spoken for: 'In fact the

body does not speak; it is spoken, ventriloquized by the master text that makes it signify' (1993: 26).

17 Roe argues that the novel uses the collage and photomontage techniques developed by Ernst where 'words interact with images and function *as* images' as part of an aesthetic of 'disorder' that 'outlaws' the female subject so that 'she effectively disappears from view' (1994: 65–6).

18 *Love* was published in 1971, one year before the Match of the Century, the Fischer-Spassky chess match that was battled out against the backdrop of Cold War politics.

19 Roe nods to Duchamp's artwork *The Bride Stripped Bare by Her Bachelors, Even (The Large Glass)* (1915–23), when she notes that '[t]here's no bride stripped bare at Annabel's wedding' (1994: 78). For Duchamp, the aesthetics and practice of chess were intimately entwined. In an address to the New York State Chess Association in 1952 he outlined: 'I believe that every chess player experiences a mixture of two aesthetic pleasures: first, the abstract imagery akin to the poetic idea of writing; secondly, the sensuous pleasure of that ideographic execution on the chessboard. From my close contact with artists and chess players I have come to the conclusion that while all artists are not chess players, all chess players are artists' (qtd in Cockburn, 1974: 190).

4

Daddy's girls and the Gothic fiction of maternity

In the beginning was ... what?

Perhaps, in the beginning, there was a curious room, a room like this one, crammed with wonders; and now the room and all it contains are forbidden you, although it was made just for you, had been prepared for you since time began, and you will spend all your life trying to remember it.

(Angela Carter, 'Alice in Prague
or The Curious Room')

Transgressive feminism might be said to have foregrounded the concerns of daughters over mothers.

(Ashley Tauchert, *Against Transgression*)

LOOKING FOR MOTHER

Gothic writing returns again and again to the image of the dead mother's body. If the maternal body is a primal scene of transgression in a French Gothic tradition that can be mapped from Sade to Bataille, a maternal spectral presence has haunted Gothic writing by women from Radcliffe to Margaret Atwood. This displacement of the mother resonates with Luce Irigaray's conspicuously Gothic suggestion that culture is founded on symbolic matricide. Challenging Freud's thesis that Western cultural and social formations lie in an act of an ancient parricide, Irigaray locates their foundations in 'a more archaic murder, that of the mother, necessitated by the establishment of a certain order of the polis' (1991: 36). The maternal relation becomes 'a mad desire, because it is the "dark continent" *par excellence*. It remains in the shadows of our culture; it is its night and its hell' (1991: 35).[1] Patriarchal social configurations are thus founded on the silencing of the maternal body so that desire for (and of) the mother is 'forbidden by the law of the father, of all fathers: fathers of families, fathers of nations, religious fathers, professor-fathers, doctor-fathers, lover-fathers, etc' (Irigaray, 1991: 36).[2] Symbolic matricide in turn becomes the precondition of meaning. The mother, writes Ashley Tauchert in her reading of Irigaray, 'has to be killed off to allow the dream of language' (2008: 98). The death of the mother begets writing.

So, Gothic writing returns again and again (and again) to the image of the dead mother's body. Leslie Fiedler, for example, envisages (male) Gothic artistry as marked by an antagonistic relation to the maternal body:

> Beneath the haunted castle lies the dungeon keep: the womb from whose darkness the ego first emerged, the tomb to which it knows it must return at last. Beneath the crumbling shell of paternal authority, lies the maternal blackness, imagined by the gothic writer as a prison, a torture chamber. (1960: 112)

This threat of maternal blackness in the face of a precarious paternal authority is given form from the earliest Gothic fictions. In Walpole's *The Castle of Otranto*, the Gothic mother, Hippolyta, is exiled by Manfred in an attempt to secure his unlawful inheritance. He turns his incestuous attentions instead to Isabella, his pursuit of whom leads to him stabbing his daughter, Matilda. In its representation of murderous and incestuous desires, illegitimate inheritance and aristo-cratic primogeniture, Walpole's novel depicts patriarchy as a Gothic structure that requires 'the suppression – and sometimes outright sacrifice – of women' (Heiland, 2004: 11). Lewis's *The Monk* evinces a yet more sinister matriphobia, punishing Agnes for her pregnancy by burying her alive in the grim recesses beneath the convent. If the reproductive body is the object of vehement and relentless violence in the Sadeian Gothic, the maternal corpse becomes a constant fascination and site of poetic play for Poe. Muse, Madonna or whore, the mother is always Gothic.

The mother's body is also an uncanny presence in Gothic writing by women. Claire Kahane, for examples, famously identifies the Gothic heroine's confrontation with the 'spectral presence of a dead-undead mother, archaic and all-encompassing' as a key trope of the female Gothic (1985: 336).[3] Such maternal 'haunting' is exemplified by Radcliffe's *A Sicilian Romance*, and Julia's rediscovery of her mother, Louisa Bernini, in an ancient subterranean vault in the Gothic castle. Shifting the focus from Fiedler's conceptualisation of the male Gothicist's confrontation with the maternal blackness, Alison Milbank argues that the image of the Gothic heroine fleeing a tyrant through the passages of an ancient castle can be seen to represent 'both female anxieties about male penetration, and the need to flee the recesses of the castle as maternal body, with its blurrings of inside and outside, self and not-self, into individuation' (1993: xxi). However, while psychoanalytic feminist criticism has opened up a space in which to re-think the mother–daughter relationship within the Gothic context, does it provide a way out of alienation for the Gothic mother? There is a danger that foregrounding the Gothic daughter means that the Gothic mother is left 'buried alive' within the labyrinthine spaces of the Gothic castle – as a manifestation of either the Freudian uncanny or the horror of female sexual identity.

Carter's claim that in her 'imaginative topography houses stood in for mothers' (Sage, 1994a: 6), echoes the synonymy of Gothic structures and the maternal body. Houses and buildings in Carter's fiction are marked by their dusty and cobwebbed interiors, eclectic furnishings and theatrical paraphernalia; they also represent, as Sage describes, a 'sense of the past as a store-room of properties and costumes to try on – including, more narrowly, literature's past, the house of fiction's heritage. The houses in [the] early books are fascinating, threatening places [...]. For houses may symbolise mothers, but they belong none the less to patriarchal proprietors' (1994b: 6). Very often, these houses are inhabited by young women in the thrall of illusory father figures. Melanie's father is a lecturer (or a 'lecher' in Victoria's parapraxis), whose death turns her over to Uncle Philip, who presides over the sinister toyshop, a Gothic parody of the family home. Marianne's father in *Heroes and Villains* is also a professor who teaches his daughter 'reading, writing and history [...] in the white tower' (*HV* 7) and she in turn 'loved him so much she only wished she could be more sure he was really there' (*HV* 10). Albertina too is an obedient daughter who turns her father's dreams into flesh while her mother's embalmed body lies still in his castle like a wax Sleeping Beauty; although a Gothic Sleeping Beauty herself, the Lady of the House of Love is similarly caught up in a relentless script of death and destruction as a daughter of Dracula.

Carter's fiction may be populated by daddy's girls but mother, Sage suggests, is 'almost a missing person' in her writing (1994a: 6). However, while biological mothers may be frequently absent from the pages of Carter's fiction, images of motherhood and the maternal proliferate in her writing. A closer inspection of the dusty houses reveals that they are occupied too by an animated cast of maternal figures. In *Shadow Dance*, for example, Morris projects a maternal affection on to the singing Struldbrug (*SD* 34) who, echoing Swift's immortal Struldbruggs, squats in one of the abandoned and decrepit houses that he plunders with Honeybuzzard. When Honey – in the guise of a 'spectre, a madman, a vampire' (*SD* 136) – tries to scare her (to death), Morris cries out in his sleep that he has killed his own mother (*SD* 145). Carter's fiction is filled too with surrogate mothers – from Aunt Margaret and Mrs Rundle in *The Magic Toyshop* and Mrs Green in *Heroes and Villains* to Lizzie in *Nights at the Circus* and the Chance sisters in *Wise Children*.

Nonetheless, Carter has been accused of both taking up and privileging the daughter's perspective in her writing – and more specifically of adopting the position of the daddy's girl (Ward Jouve, 1994: 150) – in terms of both her thematic preoccupations and her own enthralled relation to her paternal literary inheritance. Returning once again to Sade as a founding father of transgressive writing this chapter begins by exploring the matricidal impulse that underlies the education of the Sadeian Gothic heroine. Carter is clear from the beginning of

The Sadeian Woman that the 'particular significance' of Sade's work is its 'refusal to see female sexuality in relation to its reproductive function, a refusal as unusual in the late eighteenth century as it is now, even if today the function of women as primarily reproductive beings is under question' (*SW* 1). In what follows, I analyse Carter's explorations of the freedoms afforded to the Gothic daughter by the Sadeian Gothic as well as the re-education of the Sadeian heroine – by the mother – in 'The Bloody Chamber'. Related to this is the focus in the second half of this chapter on iconographic re-inscriptions of maternal mythologies in both decadent Gothic imaginings of female sexuality and certain strands of Anglo-American feminist discourse in *The Passion of New Eve*. The last part of the chapter returns both daughter and mother to the Gothic text to examine *Nights at the Circus* as a fiction of maternity.

SADEIAN DEATH SENTENCES

Sade's work is shot through with matricidal and matriphobic impulses. While the mother is treated as a figure of revulsion, the reproductive body becomes a frequent site of violence and humiliation. Arguing that '*the active negation of the mother*' is the primal fantasy underpinning the Sadeian imaginary, Susan Rubin Suleiman notes that the womb and the breasts are 'favourite loci of torture, but not of pleasure' in the Sadeian text (1990: 68; emphasis in original). Such a hatred of both mothers and the maternal is powerfully present in *Justine*, which offers up gruesome violations of the reproductive body – with particular expressions of disgust directed at the vagina and uterus. For example, one of Dom Séverino's many acts of torture involves using a 'perfidious machine' to blast a powerful stream of nearly boiling hot water 'into the last depths of [Justine's] womb' while he showers 'an uninterrupted stream of invectives upon the parts he is molesting' (Sade, 1965: 620). Elsewhere the (male and female) buttocks are brought into view as a constant source of erotic delight, while the female genitals most often rouse derision and brutality (the effeminate boys who service the Count de Gernande break into 'gales of laughter' upon seeing Justine's female body (1965: 631)). Later in the narrative, the counterfeiter Roland assaults Suzanne, one of the prisoners in his isolated castle, by opening her legs to reveal her 'workshop of generation', diving his fingernails inside her 'and rummaging about for a few minutes' until his fingers are covered in blood (1965: 684–5). Surgically opened and marked, the reproductive female body is subject to various scientific operations that serve not to relieve pain and injury but, rather, to inflict them. Scientific and technological enquiry work time and time again to assuage an anxiety about the 'generative power' of the female body.

It is not, however, just the male libertine who finds in the mother's body a target for matriphobic violence. A ferocious disavowal of the mother is also vital for those women who seek to escape a life of illimitable servitude in a patriarchal social structure that offers only the positions of wife or whore. As Kathy Acker remarks:

> No wonder that the women who want more than [subservience to men], who want their freedom, hate their mothers. In de Sade's texts, mothers are prudes, haters of their own bodies, and religious fanatics, for they are obedient to the tenets of a patriarchal society. The daughter who does not reject her mother interiorizes prison. (1997: 69)

Freedom from the strictures of social and familial subservience, however, does not simply require a rejection of the mother as a cultural role but also a violent repudiation of the maternal body. In order to be free (as contingent as that freedom might be), the Sadeian daughter must interiorise another prison and become the father's daughter.

In Sade's 'Eugénie de Franval' (1788), a father and daughter plot to murder Madame de Franval, the wife and mother who prohibits their incestuous desire. Removed from her mother at birth and educated under her father's supervision, Eugénie is tutored in the arts and sciences, and instructed in fencing, dancing, riding and music; she is also seduced by his amorous and sexual advances and 'educated' into her role as his lover – an education that involves having her head filled 'with far more hatred and jealousy than with the kind of deference and respect she should have felt for such a mother' (Sade, 2005: 246). Her fourteenth birthday marks the 'consummation' of the father's crime.

Dressing his daughter, like a doll, 'in the style of those virgins who in olden times were dedicated to the service of the Temple of Venus' (2005: 247) the father restages the bedding of 'Sleeping Beauty'. But here the Sadeian ingénue is a willing victim of her father's desire. This 'crime of love' is founded more explicitly on the sacrifice of the mother on whose 'pitiful corpse' the father and daughter will 'consummate' their crimes (2005: 263). The prospect of the mother's dead body is thus positioned as the site for the conspiracy between father and daughter.[4]

Although Carter's drafts for *The Sadeian Woman* include notes from this Gothic story, they are not developed beyond a brief reference in the final version.[5] However, Carter's positioning of 'Eugénie de Franval' as 'a "straightforward moral tale" rather than something that is "explicitly pornographic"' (BL Add MS88899/1/72) establishes a framework for her analysis of Sade's longer and much crueller work, *La Philosophie dans le boudoir* (1795), translated as *Philosophy in the Bedroom*. Primarily 'a detailed account of the erotic education of a Sadeian heroine' (*SW* 117), *Philosophy in the Bedroom* provides the focus for the fourth chapter of *The Sadeian Woman*, 'The School of Love: the Education of a Female Oedipus'. This is a text that positions itself firmly, if ambivalently, in the female space of the boudoir (mistranslated as 'bedroom' in the English edition) and, as Jane Gallop suggests, makes a specific address to women about liberation.[6] Although *Philosophy in the Bedroom* does not share the same narrative structure as *Justine* and *Juliette*, its themes of sex, death and cruelty remain quintessentially Gothic. Comprised of seven dramatic dialogues, the text has at its core a violent hatred of the mother that culminates in the spectacle of a deathly, sexual attack on her body. The matricidal daughter whose education structures the text's action is Eugénie de Mistival, a fifteen-year-old virgin 'more beautiful than Love itself' (1965: 190). Positioned quite explicitly as a daddy's girl from the first dialogue, she is introduced as the daughter of a father who is 'as libertine as his wife is pious' (1965: 192). Eugénie's education takes place at the hands of the wicked Dolmancé, the lubricious Madame de Saint-Ange and her brother, the Chevalier de Mirval (they are joined at a later point by the gardener Augustin and Dolmancé's valet).

Daddy's girls

In this pedagogy of sexual debauchery, the three libertines initiate Eugénie into the arts of sodomy, masturbation and various contraceptive methods, through a mixture of orgy, tutoring and philosophical sermon. The boudoir thus becomes a Gothic inversion of the Garden of Eden, where no sexual knowledge is forbidden and where destruction, like creation, 'is one of Nature's mandates' (1965: 275). It is a place where female sexuality is antonymous, rather than synonymous, with reproduction. Running throughout the text is a violent repudiation of not only the mother but also her reproductive agency. For Dolmancé, procreation is exclusively the domain of the father because 'uniquely formed of our sires' blood, we owe absolutely nothing to our mothers' (Sade, 1965: 207). Saint-Ange gives voice to another expression of non-reproductive sexuality. At the heart of her educational treatise on sexual freedom is a denigration of the reproductive body and refusal of pregnancy. Thus, she urges Eugénie to 'be the implacable enemy of this wearisome child-getting' (1965: 248) and advocates freedom from the reproductive body as the only path to women's sexual and social emancipation. In her recommendation of sodomy, abortion and lesbian desire, Madame de Saint-Ange serves as a Gothic double to Madame de Mistival, Eugénie's mother. No angel, though, her name mocks the maternal ideal that the other embodies.

It is not an infanticidal urge that drives Eugénie. Rather, the 'most certain impulse' of her heart is a matricidal one (1965: 244). When asked by Dolmancé if she has ever wished the death of anyone, she replies: 'Yes! there is every day before my eyes an abominable creature I have long wished to see in her grave. [...] I abhor her, I detest her, a thousand causes justify my hate; I've got to have her life at no matter what the cost!' (1965: 239, 245). The denunciations of the mother which intersperse the group's orgiastic activities culminate in the horrific assault against Eugénie's mother, the ferocious victimisation of whom provides the focus for the seventh and final act of *Philosophy in the Bedroom*. Towards the end of the sixth act, the libertines receive a letter from Eugénie's father, warning of his wife's imminent arrival to rescue her daughter and urging them to *'punish her impertinence with exceeding rigour'* (1965: 350; emphasis in original). This paternal instruction, an effective death sentence, is welcomed by the daughter who participates joyfully in the vicious brutalisation of her mother. Where Eugénie de Franval plotted with her father to remove Madame de Franval as a sexual rival, Eugénie acts here as the father's emissary, engaging in an incestuous assault against her mother. Eugénie ecstatically exclaims:

> EUGENIE – Come, dear lovely Mamma, come, let me serve you as a husband. [...] Here I am: at one stroke incestuous, adulteress, sodomite, and all that in a girl who only lost her maidenhead today! ... What progress my friends! ... with what rapidity I advance along the thorny road of vice! (1965: 359)

A vengeful Sleeping Beauty (the exemplary father's daughter), she perpetrates and perpetuates the father's crimes on the mother's body, which is already heavily scarred by her husband's violence. The daughter's matricidal desire converges with the libertines' matriphobic anxieties as Madame de Mistival is beaten, raped and whipped with thorns.

While each of the libertines has ideas about a suitable 'sentence' for the mother, as an embodiment of virtue and prohibition, Dolmancé commands his syphilitic valet, Lapierre, to rape her and 'inject his poison into each of the two natural conduits that ornament this dear and amiable lady' (1965: 363). His vicious pronouncement, then, transforms the pious mother into a syphilitic whore. In representing the degradation and torture of the mother, Mary Jacobus suggests, 'Sade makes it clear that the mother is the object of abomination in exact proportion to her conventional sacredness' (1995: 98). This problem of the mother is finally 'sewn up' by Eugénie herself who, having already penetrated her mother in the vagina and anus with a dildo, demands a needle and thread to stitch up her genitals:

> EUGENIE, *from time to time pricking the lips of the cunt, occasionally stabbing its interior and sometimes using her needle on her mother's belly and* mons veneris. Pay no attention to it, Mamma. I am simply testing the point.
>
> LE CHEVALIER – The little whore wants to bleed her to death! (1965: 364)

The red stitch marks and 'pricks' of the needlepoint re-enact the bloody cuts inflicted by Eugénie's father that have left Madame de Mistival's skin looking like 'moire taffeta' (1965: 356). The vampiric daughter thus re-inscribes the sins of the father on the mother's body and aligns herself with the paternal sentence. As a substitute for the absent father, Dolmancé requests a 'panorama of asses' on which to gaze as he metes out Madame de Mistival's final punishment (sewing up her anus) in a spectacular display of non-reproductive sexuality. Just as his sperm flows across the mother's buttocks at the finale of this brutal, Gothic theatre, Dolmancé issues the closing words of the text. The mother's body becomes a pornographic palimpsest, written over in the father's bloody and spermatic ink.

In *The Sadeian Woman*, Carter interprets Sade's treatment of the mother—daughter relationship in *Philosophy in the Bedroom* as 'an extreme and melodramatised, indeed, pornographised description of the antipathy between mothers and daughters', one that 'retain[s] elements of the early erotic relation with the mother that has been more fully explored and documented in men' (*SW* 123). Carter's distinctly Freudian reading of Sade's work rearticulates Eugénie's attitude towards her mother as an Oedipal conflict: Eugénie punishes her mother for attempting to curtail her sexual experience and freedom, but also 'to remove the possibility of rivalry, the only reason her mother might possibly have to wish to repress her daughter's sexuality' (*SW* 117). The Sadeian daughter, she proposes, 'fucks her mother out of vengeance and so finds herself in the position of a female Oedipus but she is not blinded, she is enlightened; then, in spite and rage, she seals up the organs of generation that bore her and so ensures that her mother will not fuck again with anyone' (*SW* 117). In her assault on the mother, Eugénie (like Eugénie de Franval) becomes the father's accomplice and commits her crime knowingly. The boudoir becomes in turn 'an inverted Eden beyond the knowledge of good and evil' (*SW* 122). Closing up the maternal body, Eugénie is able to establish her own position as a 'liberated' sexual subject: a new Eve re-born of the father.

The daughter's liberation does not only require freedom from reproductive sexuality; it also requires the sacrifice of the mother.

Although Eugénie frees herself from maternal control, she remains under the authority of the father, whose letter authorises the matricidal assault. Carter highlights, then, that the destruction of the mother creates Eugénie's autonomy at the very same moment that it marks the limits of that autonomy – an autonomy that 'is well policed by the faceless authority beyond the nursery, outside the mirror, the father who knows all, sees all and permits almost everything, except absolute freedom' (*SW* 131). Like Juliette, Eugénie is a Sadeian woman who 'subverts only her own socially conditioned role in the world of god, the king and the law. She does not subvert her society' (*SW* 133). Sade's text ostensibly makes claims for a sexual space for women – in terms of both its location in the female domain of the boudoir and the promise of sexual freedom articulated in its accompanying political pamphlet ('Yet Another Effort, Frenchmen, if You Would Become Republicans').[7] But, in the end, the philosophy brought into the female space of the boudoir is a resolutely masculine one. Its script belongs, once again, to the male libertine.

The messy philosophy – written in blood and sperm – evinced in *Philosophy in the Bedroom* may free up the Sadeian daughter, but only at the expense of the mother. In her analysis of matriphobic sexual politics in Sade's work, Jacobus calls attention to the ways in which Sadeian pleasure involves a 'discursive elaboration of pain' that takes the female (and often the maternal) body as its 'text' (1995: 85): 'In the Sadeian imaginary, sexuality is a sign-system inscribed on a feminine surface with pen, whip and even needle. The phobic object of Sade's libertine imaginary is the interior of the reproductive body that forever threatens to elude his legible system' (Jacobus, 1995: 86). Thus, while *Philosophy in the Bedroom* would seem to grant the libertine daughter a degree of sexual autonomy and freedom, Eugénie's violation of the maternal body not only closes down reproductive sexuality but also effaces sexual difference and makes female sexuality invisible. Here, as elsewhere in the Sadeian opus, 'cacher le con', as Roland Barthes highlights, becomes synonymous with the broader Sadeian impulse, 'cacher la femme' (Barthes, 1971: 127–8).[8] In spite of its promise of sexual freedom for the Sadeian daughter, *Philosophy in the Bedroom* offers an extremely ambivalent view of female sexuality in which the female body becomes a hole in representation – or, in Irigaray's terms, a 'nothing-to-see' that has to be 'excluded, rejected, from such a scene of representation. Woman's genitals are simply absent, masked, sewn back up inside their "crack"' (Irigaray, 1985b: 26).

Although Carter proposes that Madame de Mistival is only an object of attack in so far as she represents the synonymy of female sexuality and reproduction (*SW* 123), her analysis of Eugénie's assault has been seen as evidence that she privileges the daughter's point of view at the expense of the mother (see Ward Jouve, 1994: 140). This position is one, then, that exemplifies Tauchert's suggestion that '[t]ransgressive feminism might be said to have foregrounded the concerns of daughters over mothers' (2008: 11). However, Carter's reading of *Philosophy in the Bedroom* does not rest only on a repudiation of reproductive definitions of female sexuality. It brings to the surface too, albeit more subtly, the subject of the mother's desire. For Carter argues that the taboo that cannot be transgressed in Sade's text is the mother's sexual pleasure. While violating her mother, Eugénie declares that Madame de Mistival looks as if she is about to orgasm – 'I believe, dear mother, you are discharging' (Sade, 1965: 359) – at which point Madame de Mistival loses consciousness. Carter's interpretation of this crucial silence in the text is significant in so far as it recontextualises Madame de Mistival's sexuality:

> Mother must never be allowed to come, and so to come alive. She cannot be corrupted into the experience of sexual pleasure and so set free. She is locked forever in the fortress of her flesh, a sleeping beauty whose lapse of being is absolute and eternal. If she were allowed to taste one single moment's pleasure in the abuses that are heaped upon her, abuses that would glut Saint-Ange or her own daughter with joy, that would overthrow the whole scheme. (*SW* 128)

It is the mother's orgasm, Carter proposes, that cannot be contemplated within the confines of Sade's sexual economy. What Sade's text might intimate is the potential of a desirous encounter between mother and daughter from which the father is absent. Perhaps, Carter suggests, 'Father is always absent from this scenario because, in fact, he does not exist' (*SW* 133). What is most radical about *The Sadeian Woman*, then, is not just its debunking of the illusory power of the father, or even the daughter's freedom to fuck, but its returning of the mother–daughter relationship – and the mother as a desiring subject – to the Sadeian text.

RETURN OF THE MOTHER

The mother's return to save the daughter from the Sadeian libertine is dramatically restaged in 'The Bloody Chamber', an extravagantly literary re-writing of Perrault's seventeenth-century fairy tale 'La Barbe Bleue' ('Bluebeard') (1697) that is firmly entrenched in the structures of the Sadeian pornograph. Traditionally interpreted as a cautionary tale about female curiosity and the punishment that befalls the Eve-like young woman who seeks too much knowledge, Perrault's version of 'Bluebeard' emphasises the figure of the victim heroine at the hands of a violent and murderous patriarch. In 'The Bloody Chamber', Bluebeard is re-imagined as a profligate Marquis (an identification that places him in a specifically Sadeian tradition) with a taste for Wagner, Baudelaire, literary and visual pornography and the opulent fashion designs of the Orientalist couturier Paul Poiret (see Kaiser, 1994; and Roemer, 2001). The depiction of the Marquis references in particular the 'real' Bluebeard, Gilles de Rais, the fifteenth-century Breton nobleman and companion of Jeanne d'Arc who tortured, sexually abused and murdered children. Representing the limits of evil, Gilles de Rais was a source of fascination in decadent art and literature (see Birkett, 1986: 86–8) and famously provides the focus of J.-K. Huysmans's *Là-bas* (*The Damned*), published in 1891, a copy of which from 'some over-exquisite private press' is displayed in the Marquis's library ('BC' 16).[9] 'The Bloody Chamber' is thoroughly saturated with literary and artistic allusions to the pornographic scenario at the heart of the Bluebeard narrative. As its specifically French setting (in both geographical and literary terms) intimates, it is also concerned with interrogating a tradition of fetishistic representations of victimised and dehumanised femininity that comes up through Sade's Gothic pornography and takes reinvigorated form in decadent Gothic imaginings of female sexuality.

Seduced by the Marquis's lavish gifts – which include a white muslin Poiret dress and a 'choker of rubies, two inches wide, like an extraordinarily precious slit throat' – and the 'sheer carnal avarice' of his lustful gaze, the nameless narrator senses in herself 'a potentiality for corruption' that takes her breath away ('BC' 11). It is with this masochistic willingness that the daughter makes her journey from adolescence to womanhood – a journey that requires her to leave behind the 'white, enclosed quietude of [her] mother's apartment' ('BC' 7) for the sumptuous, decadent interior of the Marquis's Gothic castle. The castle, with its spiked gate (a version of the thorny hedge) and embedded torture chambers, is explicitly identified as operating under the sign of the 'prick'. At 'home neither on the land nor on the water, a mysterious, amphibious place, contravening the materiality of both earth and waves' ('BC' 13), it bears a particular resemblance to the cannibal Minski's castle in Sade's *Juliette* which, Carter describes in *The Sadeian Woman*, is 'a place of privilege with a strong symbolic resonance to the great original of all places of privilege, the womb' (*SW* 94). It is this womb-like space that becomes the site of the daughter's education in Sadeian femininity at the hands of a violent patriarch. Nevertheless, the ambivalent borders of the Gothic castle are signalled from the outset. As soon as the nameless narrator steps off the train she smells the 'amniotic salinity of the ocean' ('BC' 12) that at once parodies and presages the mother's return.

Like Eugénie de Franval and Eugénie de Mistival, the nameless narrator embarks upon a sexual education under the Marquis's supervision. The 'formal disrobing of the bride' that takes place in the bedroom echoes 'a ritual from the brothel' ('BC' 15). This most 'pornographic of all confrontations', the narrator notes, imitates the scenario of a 'living image of an etching by Rops' in which a 'child with her sticklike limbs, naked but for button boots, her gloves, shielding her face with her hand' is examined by an 'old monocled lecher' ('BC' 15). Relentlessly caught up in the reflections of male desire, the narrator remarks upon the preponderance of mirrors surrounding the marital bed: 'so many mirrors! Mirrors on all the walls, in stately frames of contorted gold [...] a dozen husbands [...] in a dozen mirrors' ('BC' 14–15). Here she is aligned with Eugénie de Mistival who, in the early stages of her education, remarks upon the many mirrors in the boudoir. The purpose of 'all these mirrors', Madame de Saint-Ange assures her, is to ensure that the whole body is visible so that 'no part of the body can remain hidden: everything must be seen [...] so many delicious tableaux' (Sade, 1965: 203). Although the narrator does not praise this 'marvelous invention' with the same excitement as Eugénie, she is nonetheless 'aghast to feel [herself] stirring' ('BC' 15) in response to this pornographic exchange. And thus the Marquis closes 'her legs like a book' and the first lesson is over ('BC' 15). Absorbed in this 'brief scene from a voluptuary's life' ('BC' 15), the Sadeian Gothic heroine in process is 'disgruntled' ('BC' 16) when it is abruptly drawn to a close by the Marquis's business trip.

The next stage of the narrator's Sadeian education takes place in the library which, with its dark, gleaming panelling and pulsing red rugs, is a simulacrum of the womb space. It echoes in particular the 'womblike haven' of Huysmans's *À rebours* which, '[r]eplete with an embalmed alcove, sacred ornaments, and an altar dedicated to poetry, [...] provides a consummate illustration of the bourgeois idolatry of art' (Apter, 1991: 44). As she browses the '[r]ow upon row of calf-bound volumes, brown and olive, with gilt lettering on their spines, the octavo in brilliant scarlet morocco' ('BC' 16), the tingling in the narrator's fingertips brings her to an image she had not 'bargained' for:

> the girl with her tears hanging on her cheeks like stuck pearls, her cunt a split fig below the great globes of her buttocks on which the knotted tails of the cat were about to descend, while a man in a black mask fingered with his free hand his prick, that curved upwards like the scimitar he held. The picture had a caption 'Reproof of curiosity'. ('BC' 16–17)

The narrative focalisation emphasises that, although she is startled by the image, the pornographic language here belongs to the narrator. For, as Robin Ann Sheets points out, she is also in possession of knowledge passed on from her mother who, 'with all the precision of her eccentricity, had told me what it was that lovers did; I was innocent but not naive' ('BC' 17; see Sheets, 1992: 352–3). Catching sight of another steel engraving entitled 'Immolation of the wives of the Sultan', the narrator's recall of her mother's teaching gives her enough awareness this time to 'gasp' ('BC' 17). 'The Bloody Chamber' does not only re-inscribe the maternal relation that is often effaced in fairy tale and Gothic narratives. It also provides the 'eagle-featured indomitable mother' with her own history and agency – 'what other student at the Conservatoire could boast that her mother had outfaced a junkful of Chinese pirates, nursed a village through a visitation of the plague, shot a man-eating tiger with her own hand and all before she was as old as I?' ('BC' 7). The mother is thus re-positioned as vital to both the daughter's sexual education and her emancipation from the pornographic structures of the Gothic discipline of suffering.

The Marquis has identified in the nameless narrator a 'promise of debauchery only a connoisseur could detect' ('BC' 20). He is not, however, the only authority in this text. It is following a phone call with her mother and the newly found 'exhilaration of the explorer' that the nameless narrator decides to search the castle looking for evidence of her husband's 'true nature' ('BC' 24). She faces the bloody chamber at the heart of the Marquis's castle with the 'nerves and will' she has inherited from her mother: 'My mother's spirit drove me on, into that dreadful place, in a cold ecstasy to know the very worst' ('BC' 28). Set against the mother's spirit is a peculiarly corporeal representation of the torture chamber located in 'the viscera of the castle' ('BC' 27), its walls gleaming 'as if they were sweating with fright' ('BC' 28). Here, in an emblematic Gothic transformation, the womb is exchanged for the tomb.

The spectacle of the multiple bleeding and mutilated dead bodies of the Marquis's previous wives in the forbidden chamber echoes both the mirror images of the multiple 'impaled' brides in the bedroom ('BC' 17) and the images of the dismembered bodies in the library: this is the final tableaux in the Marquis's Sadeian pedagogy. Embalmed and bearing the 'blue imprints' of the strangler's fingers, the body of the opera singer, one of the Marquis's previous wives, is displayed like a Gothic Sleeping Beauty, while the skull of another young woman is 'utterly denuded' and 'strung up by a system of unseen cords, so that it appeared to hang, disembodied, in the still heavy air'. Crowned with a veil of lace and a wreath of white roses, it is the 'final image of his bride' ('BC' 29). The Gothic centrepiece of this macabre theatre is the body of the Romanian Countess, which lies bleeding in an Iron Maiden, 'pierced, not by one but by a hundred spikes, this child of the land of the vampires who seemed so newly dead, so full of blood' ('BC' 29). Straight from the recesses of the Sadeian Gothic imagination, these female bodies have been used to play out the pornographic scripts of femininity that are embedded in the deathly spaces of this Gothic castle. They are reduced to just another set of collectibles in the Marquis's 'museum of perversity' ('BC' 28).

Whereas Madame de Mistival arrives under the shadow of a paternal instruction that is tantamount to a death sentence, the mother in 'The Bloody Chamber' arrives to lift the death sentence that has been inflicted upon the daughter in response to a kind of maternal telepathy. A 'crazy, magnificent horsewoman in widow's weeds' ('BC' 38), the mother returns to the text to liberate her daughter. Storming the Gothic castle (the daughter's prison) just at the moment the Marquis raises his heavy sword over the narrator's head, she ruptures the pornographic fantasy: 'The puppet master, open-mouthed, wide-eyed, impotent at the last, saw his dolls break free of their strings, abandon the rituals he had ordained for them since time began and start to live for themselves; the king, aghast, witnesses the revolt of his pawns' ('BC' 39). It is the mother, then, who animates the daughter by liberating her from a position as the father's doll/pawn. The mother's appearance, armed and on horseback, echoes Jeanne d'Arc (who haunts the text through her associations with Gilles de Rais). But, she is also reminiscent of the pistol-carrying revolutionary, Théroigne de Méricourt:

> You never saw such a wild thing as my mother, her hat seized by the winds and blown out to sea so that her hair was her white mane, her black lisle legs exposed to the thigh, her skirts tucked round her

waist, one hand on the reins of the rearing horse while the other clasped my father's service revolver. ('BC' 39–40)

Celebrated as an 'amazon of the [French] Revolution, both sexually and politically liberated' (Beckstrand, 2009: 18), the famously fiery Méricourt played an active role in the French Revolution and the pursuit of liberty – for men and women. She represents, then, an image of the political possibilities of the Sadeian woman who seizes the father's power, placing the question of paternal authority in a broader political and historical context. The Marquis, in turn, 'stood stock-still, as if she had been Medusa, the sword still raised over his head as in those clockwork tableaux of Bluebeard that you see in glass cases at fairs' ('BC' 40). Turned to stone by the Medusa's gaze, he falls victim to his own iconography and the mother's death sentence. 'The point is,' Carter writes in a letter to Elaine Jordan, that 'Bluebeard, it turns out at the end, is only cardboard – a construction – an invention – nothing. Like the authority of the father' (BL Add MS88899/1/84).[10] The authority of the father is revealed to be as fragile as it is atrocious.

'MOTHER IS A FIGURE OF SPEECH'

If *The Sadeian Woman* exposes the illusory freedom granted to the daddy's girl who operates within the patriarchal structures of the pornograph, it is equally engaged with challenging mythologised notions of motherhood and the maternal emerging from Anglo-American second wave feminist celebrations of the 'mother goddess'. From the beginning of the book, Carter insists on the dangers of installing 'hypothetical great goddesses' as consolation for women's 'culturally determined lack of access to the modes of intellectual debate' (*SW* 5):

> All the mythic versions of women, from the myth of the redeeming purity of the virgin to that of the healing, reconciling mother, are consolatory nonsenses; and consolatory nonsenses seems to me a fair definition of myth, anyway. Mother goddesses are just as silly a notion as father gods. (*SW* 5)

The Sadeian Woman proposes the demythologisation not only of the structures of paternal power, but also of the maternal archetype and its iconographies. Reviving the myth of the mother goddess might, Carter suggests, give 'women emotional satisfaction', but 'it does so at the price of obscuring the real conditions of life. This is why they were invented in the first place' (*SW* 5). The mystification of the maternal-feminine and the reproductive function, she argues later in the book, puts 'those women who wholeheartedly subscribe to it in voluntary exile from the historic world, this world, in its historic time that is counted out minute by minute' (*SW* 106). Carter links the rejection of the institution of motherhood to the political emancipation of women from imprisoning mythological frameworks. What she identifies in Sade's work are the revolutionary possibilities of its desacralisation of the mother as a site of mystification.

The demystification of the mother goddess and the eternal feminine provides a focus for *The Passion of New Eve*. A peculiarly 'raw and savage book' (Sage, 1994a: 36), this text anticipates some of the theoretical preoccupations elucidated in *The Sadeian Woman*. A novel framed by two pregnancies and structured around the surgical procedure that transforms Evelyn into Eve, the novel was 'conceived' (Carter's choice of word here is knowing) as 'a feminist tract about the social creation of femininity' ('NFL' 71). The text is narrated retrospectively by Evelyn, a 'Baudelairean dandy' (*PNE* 132) who is obsessed with Tristessa de St Ange, a Hollywood movie star who embodies the victimised Gothic femininity that is exemplified by Sade's Justine and Poe's Madeline Usher: 'Suffering was her vocation. She suffered exquisitely until suffering became demoded' (*PNE* 8). Susan Sellers suggests that Tristessa's full name 'effectively heralds her appeal of angelic suffering' (2001: 110), but it also links her to Madame de Saint-Ange from Sade's *Philosophy in the Bedroom* (for Tristessa, who is revealed to be a man, also upholds a male fantasy of femininity).

When she is eventually discovered, Tristessa inhabits a moonlit Gothic house made of glass. This 'mausoleum', like Sleeping Beauty's castle, is a space touched by time – '[s]piders had woven their vague trapezes between the friable heads of dead peonies in enormous glass jars' and 'clouds of dust' fill the air (*PNE* 113). But, in its mystification of suffering femininity, it is a glass house located outside of history, revolving on 'a mysterious axle deep in the earth' (*PNE* 114). When Eve/lyn finally finds his 'dream woman', she is lying on her bier in the midst of a waxwork collection called 'the hall of immortals': 'She had cheated the clock in her castle of purity, her ice palace, her glass shrine. She was a sleeping beauty who could never die since she had never lived' (*PNE* 119). Embodying femininity as a mystification, the celluloid 'Tristessa' exists only in the mirror images and reflections of male desire. Evelyn retrospectively acknowledges that 'he only loved her because she was not of this world' (*PNE* 8).

It is with a similar Hollywood dream in mind that Evelyn leaves London and arrives in the 'lurid, Gothic darkness' of a stinking, shimmering New York where civil war is about to break out (*PNE* 10). With its skies full of 'strange, bright, artificial colours [...] reeking of decay' (*PNE* 12), the cityscape echoes the 'greenish or purplish backgrounds, in which we can glimpse the phosphorescence of decay' that Baudelaire admired in Poe and recreated in his construction of the city in 'The Painter of Modern Life' (Baudelaire, 1995a: 91). From the wanton savagery of the city emerges the prostitute 'Leilah, a girl all softly black in colour' (*PNE* 14), who leads Evelyn 'deep into the geometric labyrinth of the city, into an arid world of ruins and abandoned construction sites, the megapolitan heart that did not beat any more' (*PNE* 21). Not so much Ariadne as 'a little fox pretending to be a siren' (*PNE* 20), Leilah is interpreted by Evelyn as 'the city's gift' to him (*PNE* 25).[11] Dancing her 'naked dance' for Evelyn and as 'black as [his] shadow', Leilah, like Duval, is a creation of the Baudelairean imagination; she is also the whore to Tristessa's suffering femininity. Evelyn's desire for Leilah 'vanishes', however, when she becomes pregnant and nearly bleeds to death after an illegal abortion – when her reproductive body emerges from the performance of sexualised femininity she is supposed to uphold. 'Infected' by the 'slow delirious sickness of femininity' (*PNE* 37), Evelyn leaves New York and heads West where he is kidnapped and imprisoned by a group of guerrilla warrior women. Evelyn's re-education – his transformation into Eve – begins at the hands of Mother.

Decadent daughters and monstrous mothers

The Passion of New Eve, as Suleiman notes, defies summary — which is 'one of its charms and one of the ways in which Carter succeeds in producing a new kind of writing even while apparently remaining within the bounds of a certain "traditional" narrative logic' (1990: 137). The idea of envisaging the 'new' — a new kind of writing and 'a new kind of being', as Carter puts it ('NFL' 74) — is central to the text. Like *The Infernal Desire Machines of Doctor Hoffman*, the text presents a kaleidoscopic intertextuality. According to Britzolakis, '*The Passion of New Eve* is [...] locked into a regressive circulation of literary metaphors of fatal, apparitional and mechanical femininity, from Poe and Baudelaire to the Symbolists' (1995: 467). The novel undoubtedly engages in (and even indulges) an excessive intertextuality, drawing on a tradition of fetishistic representations of femininity. It is constructed as a kind of Frankenstein's monster, built out of literary fragments and allusions. This echo of Mary Shelley's 'hideous progeny' is also important in terms of the novel's Gothic inheritance, both in its interpretation as a 'birth myth' that encodes 'the drama of guilt, dread, and flight surrounding birth and its consequences' (Moers, 1978: 93) and also in its laying bare of the male scientist's fantasy of procreative power.

Most directly, as Suleiman points out, the title of the novel references Villiers de L'Isle Adam's *L'Ève future*. A key work of French decadence, *L'Ève future* bears the Gothic influence of Poe's and Hoffmann's fetishised visions of mechanical femininity, as well as *Frankenstein*'s reworking of the creation myth. The text centres on the creation of a female android by Thomas Edison, a fictionalised version of the American scientist and inventor of, amongst other devices, the phonograph.[12] Built in his subterranean, womb-like laboratory from a combination of dark magic and electricity, Elison's android, Hadaly, is a magical mechanical being in the image of perfect femininity. She is not simply one of his many inventions but, as Raymond Bellour describes, located 'at the very source of his capacity to invent' (1993: 122). In *The Passion of New Eve*, Edison, the 'father' inventor', is reborn as Mother, the leader of a radical feminist sect who presides over the underground town, Beulah. An antidote to the male scientists and puppet-masters elsewhere in Carter's fiction, Mother is born of an unlikely dialogue between second-wave feminist notions of goddess feminism and male-authored decadent representations of femininity. The 'ironic negation of Tristessa's punishing definition of femininity' (Makinen, 1997: 160), Mother is 'the great, black, self-anointed, self-appointed prophetess, the self-created god-head that had assumed the flesh of its own prophecy' (*PNE* 58). With two tiers of nipples, giant limbs and a 'false beard of crisp, black curls like the false beard Queen Hatshepsut of the Two Kingdoms had worn', she incarnates the 'spectacle of the goddess' (*PNE* 59). Nevertheless, at once Frankenstein and her creation, she is a woman self-made by the surgeon's knife:

> She was her own mythological artefact; she had reconstructed her flesh painfully, with knives and with needles, into a transcendental form as an emblem, as an example, and flung a patchwork quilt stitched from her daughter's breasts over the cathedral of her interior, the cave within a cave. (*PNE* 60)

She may embody the figure of the mother goddess, envisaged by Mary Daly in *Beyond God the Father*, but she also gives form to decadent imaginings of the castratory *femme fatale*. This woman 'who calls herself the Great Parricide, also glories in the title of Grand Emasculator' (*PNE* 49): a knife-wielding surgeon, she behaves, to quote Nicole Ward Jouve, as 'the Freudian little boy's worst nightmare' (1994: 156).

Although, like Edison, Mother is a 'great scientist', her 'extraordinary experiments' involve not the making of woman but the re-making of man. Having made herself in the image of the Mother Goddess, Mother plans to re-make Evelyn as her daughter Eve by surgically removing his genitals, excavating a 'fructifying female space' inside him and turning him into 'a perfect specimen of womanhood'. Finally, she plans to 'reactivate the parthenogenesis archetype' by impregnating him with his own sperm (*PNE* 68). The spectacle of Evelyn's transformation re-imagines the self-consciously theatrical assault and infection of Madame de Mistival in *Philosophy in the Bedroom* in a reimagined Garden of Eden. Here, however, it is the mother who wreaks vengeance upon Evelyn, punishing him for his misogynistic treatment of her daughter Leilah by turning him into her identical. Evelyn will be reborn a new Eve and 'the Virgin Mary, too' (*PNE* 70). She will become, in other words, both mother and daughter – the virgin mother of her new self. The second part of this daughter's education is later taught by the Sadeian Zero who, through rape and violence, trains her in the discipline of victimised femininity. The 'passion' of New Eve is primarily an education in suffering.

Mother's separatist, feminist counter-culture, Beulah, is a place 'where contrarieties exist together' (*PNE* 48). With its reference to William Blake's Beulah (see Day, 1998: 113–14), this is a matriarchal space where 'Myth is more instructive than history' (*PNE* 68). Beulah, then, is a comic satire of feminist idealisations of the maternal that valorise the mythic and the spatial over the historical and the temporal: 'Down, down, down into the dark, down into a soft, still, warm, inter-uterine, symmetrical place hung with curtains of crimson plush, into a curtained cabinet where there was a white bed' (*PNE* 69). Underground and cavernous, it is in some respects an exemplary image of the female 'grotesque' which, as Mary Russo highlights, is inextricably tied to the space of the cave:

> As bodily metaphor, the grotesque cave tends to look like (and in the most gross metaphorical sense be identified with) the cavernous anatomical female body. [...] Blood, tears, vomit, excrement – all the detritus of the body that is separated out and placed with terror and revulsion (predominantly, though not exclusively) on the side of the feminine – are down there in that cave of abjection. (1994: 1–2)

But this underground interior is equally reminiscent of the 'womblike haven' of the decadent imaginary (Apter, 1991: 44). Echoing Mother's artificially ornamented anatomy, it is a heavily stylised space adorned in the style of the decadent cabinet which, as discussed in Chapter 2, 'theatricalize[s] erotic fantasy' (Apter, 1991: 45). Although, in Beulah, the gaze is inverted, and turned back upon the misogynist and voyeuristic Evelyn, *The Passion of New Eve* unveils the proximity of feminist and decadent iconographies of the maternal, suggesting that both are derived from the same mystification – a mystification that exiles women from history.

Carter's dystopic depiction of the technologically enhanced world of Beulah critiques the ahistorical underpinnings of its foundational philosophy – that 'time is man, space is a woman' (*PNE* 53). The text suggests that Mother's attempts to eradicate time from space by way of a 'complicated mix of mythology and technology' (*PNE* 48) cannot be sustained. In this respect, Beulah prefigures what Carter later describes in *The Sadeian Woman* as 'the timeless, placeless, fantasy land of archetypes where all the embodiments of biological supremacy live' (*SW* 106). Carter deconstructs the cult of the mother goddess to insist upon an engagement with history – the need for a female speaking subjectivity within a world that is 'counted out minute by minute' (*SW* 106). Thus, when Mother finds that she cannot make time stand still she has a nervous breakdown: 'History overtook myth', Leilah tells Eve, and 'rendered it obsolete' (*PNE* 172–3). It is precisely because she places herself outside of time, outside of the historical world, that Mother must eventually 'abdicate from her mythology' (*PNE* 179). Her retreat back into a cave, the archetypal space of the grotto-esque at the end of the narrative, is not a re-instatement of the maternal principle but a reflection that her 'arcane theology [...] has gone underground' (*PNE* 181). Eve realises in the end that 'Mother is a figure of speech and has retired to a cave beyond consciousness' (*PNE* 184). The woman whom she meets on the beach, who seems to be Mother, is now a 'mad old lady' whose distinctly ageing body appears both physically and metaphorically deflated by its faded glamour: 'She was wearing a two-piece bathing costume in a red and white spotted fabric and, round her shoulders, a stole of glossy and extravagant blonde fur but her flesh was wrinkled and ravaged and sagged from her bones' (*PNE* 177). Her mythology demystified, Mother is freed from the constraints of symbolism and reinstated as a flesh and blood subject. 'Mother' is exchanged for mother.

Carter's construction and deconstruction of the maternal in *The Passion of New Eve*, especially when read in dialogue with *The Sadeian Woman*, demystifies the maternal metaphor and pares down 'the fraudulent magic from the idea of women, to reveal us as we are, simple creatures of flesh and blood' (*SW* 109–10). Ward Jouve argues that:

> if Simone de Beauvoir and countless others are right, and it is
> woman's biology, her being the 'sex that gives life,' which 'destines'
> her for second place, then Carter's systematic and endlessly inventive
> attacks on images of motherhood, her divorcing 'biology' from
> mothering, are so many blows for women's freedom. (1994: 156–7)

Carter is concerned not only with lambasting the figure of the mother
in its patriarchal configuration but with challenging the essentialist
definitions of femininity and motherhood implicit in some aspects of
feminist theory. Both *The Passion of New Eve* and *The Sadeian Woman*
reveal the proximity (and allure) of radical feminist mystifications of
the mother goddess and decadent fantasies of the at once enthralling
and terrifying castratory *femme fatale*.[13] At the close of *The Passion of
New Eve*, Eve is pregnant with the child she conceived with Tristessa
and is sent off by mother to give birth to the 'new kind of being' that
Carter envisages in 'Notes from the Front Line' ('NFL' 74). It is, in the
end, the maternal archetype – rather than the maternal subject – that
is 'buried' underground.

THE FLIGHT OF THE DECADENT DAUGHTER; OR, THE MOTHER'S STORY

The 'new kind of being' heralded in *The Passion of New Eve* might, at
first glance at least, appear to be given form in the figure of Fevvers,
the winged bird-woman of *Nights at the Circus*. Located at 'the fag-end,
the smouldering cigar-butt, of a nineteenth century which is just
about to be ground out in the ashtray of history' (*NC* 11), *Nights at
the Circus* is profoundly concerned with historical change and the
new.[14] For Paulina Palmer, Fevvers, with her 'miraculous wings',
represents a key shift away from the image of the 'coded mannequin'
that marked Carter's earlier fiction to the celebratory '"bird-woman",
courageously exploring new realms, both personal and political' (1987:
201). In contrast to the modes of suffering and automated femininity
represented by, for example, Ghislaine and Annabel, Fevvers saturates
herself with fetishistic myths about female sexuality and adapts them to
assert her own sexual agency. Rejecting a birth by 'the *normal channels*',

she constructs her genesis from a dust-covered Titian depicting the myth of Leda and the Swan: 'I always saw, as through a glass, darkly, what might have been my own primal scene, my own conception, the heavenly bird in a white majesty of feathers descending with imperious desire upon the half-stunned and yet herself impassioned girl' (*NC* 28).[15] In re-imagining her coming into being through this image (one that directly recasts the depiction of Melanie's rape by the mechanical swan in *The Magic Toyshop*) Fevvers takes on the bird-like qualities of her father to become both Leda and the Swan. Her body subsequently becomes the site on to which multiple, and often conflicting, images of the woman with wings become inscribed. She is by turns (and often at once) the Winged Victory, *l'Ange Anglaise* (a reference that links her to Sade's Madame de Saint-Ange), W. B. Yeats's golden bird and Guillaume Apollinaire's winged woman.[16]

While the novel is replete with illusions and references drawn from diverse literary and cultural spheres, its French literary inheritance is especially striking. In her notes for *Nights at the Circus*, for example, Carter identifies Eugène Sue's *Les Mystères de Paris* and Louis Aragon's *Le Paysan de Paris* as literary contexts for the novel (BL Add MS88899/1/97). From the beginning of the narrative, Fevvers's position as a performer is one inflected by Parisian theatre culture: 'Fevvers, the most famous *aerialiste* of her day; her slogan, "Is she fact or is she fiction?" And she didn't let you forget it for a minute; this query, in the French language, in foot-high letters, blazed forth from a wall-size poster, souvenir of her Parisian triumphs, dominating her London dressing-room' (*NC* 7). Attributed with 'deform[ing] the dreams of that entire generation who would immediately commit themselves wholeheartedly to psychoanalysis' while in Vienna, Fevvers causes something of a stir in Paris: 'not just Lautrec but *all* the post-impressionists vied to paint her; Willy gave her supper and she gave Colette some good advice. Alfred Jarry proposed marriage.' (*NC* 11) Constructing herself as 'figure of ultimate spectacularity, a compendium of cultural clichés, worn and soiled from circulation' (Russo, 1994: 166), Fevvers births herself as a decadent daughter made up from bits of pieces drawn from the 'lumber room' of the European Gothic imagination.

Decadent daughters and monstrous mothers

Within the *fin-de-siècle* context of the novel's setting, Fevvers crafts herself more specifically as a pastiche of nineteenth-century decadent Gothic inscriptions of femininity, playfully embodying iconographic representations of the decadent vamp and the figure of the female performer as 'a staple of male-authored *fin-de-siècle* literature, where it is often aligned with the figure of the prostitute and that of the mechanical woman' (Britzolakis, 1995: 466). For example, her blonde hair and physical bulk link her to Miss Urania, the acrobat in Huysmans's *À rebours* and, most strikingly, Émile Zola's Nana, 'La Blonde Vénus', whose sexual and financial vampirism is linked to the political and moral destructiveness of the Second Empire. She also bears echoes of Djuna Barnes's more playful representation of the female performer in the figure of Frau Mann, the androgynous acrobat in *Nightwood* (1936). Sexually aware and economically independent, Fevvers is associated with the New Woman as 'an anarchic figure who threatened to turn the world upside down and to be on top in a wild carnival of social and sexual rule' (Showalter, 1992: 38). Her position as a 'new woman' also emerges powerfully from the Sadeian Gothic and, specifically, from Apollinaire's famous celebration of Sade's Juliette as an image of renewal, a 'being of whom nothing is yet known, detached from humanity, who will grow wings and renovate the universe' (qtd in Le Brun, 1990: 195). Carter explains to Anna Katsavos that

> [o]ne of the original ideas behind the creation of [Fevvers] was a piece of writing by Guilliaume [*sic*] Apollinaire, in which he talks about Sade's Juliette. He's talking about a woman in the early twentieth century, in a very French and rhetorical manner. He's talking about the new woman, and the very phrase he uses is, 'who will have wings and will renew the world'. (Katsavos, 1994: 13)

Carter had already discussed Apollinaire's celebration of Juliette in *The Sadeian Woman* (*SW* 79), but in *Nights at the Circus* the image of the winged woman is brought to life – with all of its promise and its limitations – in the characterisation of Fevvers, who sees in her body 'the abode of limitless freedom' (*NC* 41).

In endowing Fevvers with wings, the text redeploys the image of flight (from persecution) that has been a critical feature of Gothic writing by women since the eighteenth century. However, this is not a straightforwardly transformative endeavour because, as Sage points out, the 'image of the woman with wings has served throughout the centuries as a carrier of men's meanings' (1994a: 47) – a reservation that Carter also expresses about the deployment of the image of the winged woman by 'male intellectuals' (Watts, 1985: 169). Annie Le Brun sounds another note of ambivalence about Apollinaire's definition of Juliette which, she suggests, 'has too many wings and halos [*sic*]' (1990: 195). There is a sense in which this celebratory vision of the winged woman is also caught up in representation; it becomes too emblematic. While Sage argues that Fevvers 'makes meanings on her own account, and evades the symbol-hunters who try to murder, vitrify, petrify, and pin her down' (1994a: 48), Fevvers's inhabiting of the iconography of the winged woman is more ambivalent. She appears to re-embody (and give wings to) the image of automated femininity by playing with the borderline between the mechanical and the fleshy body. For example, Walser, the journalist intent on revealing her winged body to be a 'hoax', wonders whether Fevvers's voice 'had its source, not within her throat but in some ingenious mechanism' (*NC* 43). Similarly, as part of his 'ludic game', Colonel Kearney spreads rumours that 'Fevvers is not a woman at all but a cunningly constructed automaton made up of whalebone, india-rubber and springs' (*NC* 147). However, as Carter acknowledges in *The Sadeian Woman*, Sade's Juliette may give the illusion of agency and mobility, but she operates like a mechanical woman whose 'mind functions like a computer programmed to produce two results for herself – financial profit and libidinal gratification' (*SW* 79). It may be, then, that the corpulent, farting, gorging Fevvers all too closely resembles Vaucanson's defecating duck or Edison's talking doll (Lizzie refers to Fevvers as 'duck' or 'duckie' on several occasions). She may play with the image of the mechanical woman but, time and time again, Fevvers risks falling back into the machinery of this paternal invention – a risk made all too real by Rosencreutz's attempts to sacrifice her to his cult of male virility and the Russian Grand Duke's desire to miniaturise her in a Fabergé egg.

Decadent daughters and monstrous mothers

Although *Nights at the Circus* is often described as an exemplary 'postmodern' or, owing to its emphasis on performance and the circus, 'carnivalesque' text (see Michael, 1998: 216; Morris, 1993: 157), the prevalence of Sadeian and decadent Gothic topographies also situates the novel within a European Gothic tradition.[17] Indeed, while Sage suggests that 'this is a book with hardly any houses at all' (1992: 178), the novel is replete with enclosing and oppressive Gothic interiors — from Ma Nelson's brothel and Madame Schreck's Museum in 'London', to Countess P.'s panopticon penitentiary in 'Siberia'. It is precisely the relentless sense of claustrophobia in this text, argues Armitt, that signals its affinities with the Gothic mode (2000: 181). In fact, while Fevvers has most often been interpreted as a Juliette-like figure (see Keenan, 1997: 39), her blonde hair and repeated returns to dangerous Gothic enclosures highlight her relation to Sade's persecuted Gothic heroine, Justine.

The Gothic interiors in *Nights at the Circus* may belong to the Sadeian and decadent Gothic imagination, but the structure of the novel also has affinities with what Ellen Moers identifies as the female Gothic mode of 'travelling heroism' — a mode concerned with the journey of 'the woman who moves, who acts, who copes with vicissitude and adventure' (1978: 126).[18] Still, while critical attention has tended to centre on Fevvers and the flight of the decadent daughter from the restrictive enclosures of male-authored scripts of femininity, the novel also shares with the female Gothic a focus on the maternal relation. Rather than foregrounding the concerns of the daughter over the mother, the 'dialogic narrative of *Nights at the Circus*', proposes Elaine Jordan, 'is also (effectively) a strong-mother daughter relation, that of Fevvers and Lizzie, fond and ratty by turns' (1992: 128). For, although biologically 'motherless', Fevvers's bird-like hatching 'out of a bloody great egg' delivers her into the 'wholly female world' of Ma Nelson's brothel to become 'the common daughter of half-a-dozen mothers' (*NC* 21). Her subsequent journey through the Gothic spaces of the narrative is mapped out via her encounter with various surrogate mothers — most notably, Ma Nelson and Madame Schreck, but also her ongoing dialogue with her foster mother, the Marxist feminist Lizzie.

Daddy's girls

Ma Nelson's Academy is the primal Gothic space in which Fevvers serves her 'apprenticeship in *being looked at* – at being the object of the eye of the beholder' (*NC* 23). It is here, with the guidance of her first surrogate mother, Ma Nelson, that Fevvers is educated in the art of female performance as a fetishised object for a male gaze. Owing to her 'little feathery buds' she is dressed firstly as Cupid and sits 'in the alcove of the drawing-room in which the ladies introduced themselves to the gentlemen' (*NC* 23); and, secondly, following the onset of menstruation, in the costume of the Winged Victory. Fevvers's upbringing within a 'community of loving whores' has been idealised by feminist readers; but Ma Nelson's brothel establishes an interior architecture that at once evokes and displaces the maternal body. The 'wine-red, figured damask' (*NC* 28) inner wall of Nelson's 'vessel' mimics the womb space. Echoing the Marquis's 'bloody chamber', Baudelaire's 'lonely apartment' and Mother's 'curtained cabinet', the brothel is an appropriation of a maternal Gothic space within which sex is everywhere but biological motherhood is nowhere. It is a place constructed in and through cultural myths about femininity. Fevvers even blames Baudelaire for the 'slow but sure' waning of trade in the brothel:

> 'I put it down to the influence of *Baudelaire*, sir.'
> 'What's this?' cried Walser, amazed enough to drop his professional imperturbability.
> 'The French poet, sir; a poor fellow who loved whores not for the pleasure of it but, as he perceived it, the *horror* of it, as if we was, not working women doing it for money but *damned souls* who did it solely to lure men to their dooms, as if we'd got nothing better to do.' (*NC* 38; emphasis in original)

An 'old, square, red-brick' house, old-fashioned to the extent that 'it had a way of seeming almost too *modern* for its own good', the brothel architecturally represents the 'glittering sterility' of an anti-womb space – even if it is one that is underwritten by a 'sub-text of fertility' thanks to the numerous feline inhabitants, often 'in kitten' (*NC* 39).

The architecture of the brothel is mirrored by Ma Nelson's own self-stylisation. Dressed in the 'full dress uniform' of the eponymous

Admiral, Ma Nelson takes up the position of a 'male impersonator' as she commands 'her ship of battle though sometimes she'd laugh and say, "It was a pirate ship, and went under false colours"' (*NC* 32). Identified as a suffragette, 'a one for "Votes for Women"' (*NC* 38), Nelson is also a cross-dresser. In an act of 'authorial transvestism' (Sage, 1992: 173) that echoes the various citational travesties that constitute *The Passion of New Eve*, Ma Nelson borrows the words of Apollinaire to celebrate Fevvers as 'the pure child of the century that just now is waiting in the wings, the New Age in which no women will be bound down to the ground' (*NC* 25). However, as a male impersonator she participates in a broader economy of the spectacle, reproducing images of the Gothic daughter as a fantasy of the European Gothic imagination. Mary Russo proposes that *Nights at the Circus* 'is unique in its depiction of relationships between women *as* spectacle, *and* women as producers *of* spectacle' (1994: 165; emphasis in original). While the brothel may be a subversive pirate ship in so far as it exploits the fetishisation of the *femme fatale* for economic ends, its pseudo-familial counterculture is underpinned by male-authored definitions of femininity. Although Fevvers claims her training in Nelson's brothel as the key to her later economic independence (or cupidity), its complicity with the commodification of women as spectacles for a male gaze means that her female body has currency only in relation to male sexuality.

Nelson's male impersonation links her to the sterile, phallic mother who presides over a far more dangerous and macabre configuration of the Gothic castle: Madame Schreck and her Museum of Woman Monsters. With its claustrophobic architecture and sinister *mise-en-scène* of female sexuality, Madame Schreck's Museum represents the Gothic centrepiece of the novel. Situated in a square 'with a melancholy garden in the middle full of worn grass and leafless trees' (*NC* 57), this Gothic castle is located in a barren Eden. Catering for those men who are not merely troubled in their bodies, but 'troubled in their ... souls' (*NC* 57), Schreck's museum evokes a horror-inspired, decadent view of female sexuality: 'this place was known as "Down Below", or else, "The Abyss"' (*NC* 61). The 'damask' walls of Ma Nelson's brothel are replaced here by the living, grotesque bodies of Fevvers and the other 'Woman Monsters' who service Schreck's clients:

The girls were all made to stand in stone niches cut out of the slimy walls, except for the Sleeping Beauty, who remained prone, since proneness was her speciality. And there were little curtains in front and, in front of the curtains, a little lamp burning. These were her 'profane altars', as she used to call them. (*NC* 61)

The macabre theatricality and perverse paraphernalia of Schreck's museum reiterate the image of tangled and mutilated bodies structuring the 'Bestial Room' in *The Infernal Desire Machines of Doctor Hoffman*. It is a space forged through the Sadeian Gothic imagination. As Carter describes in *The Sadeian Woman*: 'Sade creates a museum of woman-monsters. He cuts up the bodies of women and reassembles them in the shapes of his own delirium. He renews all the ancient wounds, every one, and makes them bleed again as if they will never stop bleeding' (*SW* 25–6). The display of female bodies in Schreck's dungeon is also reminiscent of Charcot's spectacular display of female hysteria in his 'Museum of Living Pathology'. Situating Carter's text firmly within the visual iconography of discourses of female hysteria, it brings to the fore late-nineteenth-century psychoanalysis in its most Gothic aspect.

With her black dress, 'thick veil' and 'skinny', wizened bosom, Madame Schreck ('Schrecken' in German meaning 'terror' or 'fright') represents the Freudian ideal of post-Oedipal maternity by masquerading as death: 'she had some quality of the uncanny about her, over and above the illusion, so you did think that under those lugubrious garments of hers you might find nothing but some kind of wicked puppet that pulled its own strings' (*NC* 58).[19] Drawn in the Gothic tradition of the monstrous-feminine, she is cast in the role of the 'old hag' or 'Lady Macbeth' who, as Elizabeth A. Fay describes, 'replaces the absent or dead good mother as the evil mother who focuses the Gothic; the monstrous woman whose desire for power allows her to manipulate the patriarchal law that should subdue her' (Fay, 1998: 140–1). She represents the Gothic dark side of Ma Nelson's appropriation of phallic power as 'a woman who acts according to the precepts and also the practice of a man's world and so she does not suffer. Instead, she causes suffering' (*SW* 79).

Concerned only with 'organis[ing] and distribut[ing] images of other women for the visual market', Schreck's own 'disembodied presence', argues Russo, 'suggests the extreme of immateriality and genderless politics; she may, as the narrator suggests, be only a hollow puppet, the body as performance *in extremis*' (Russo, 1994: 166). Toussaint, Madame Schreck's 'manservant', describes how, after her struggle with Fevvers, she is completely disembodied: 'It came to me that there was *nothing left* inside the clothes and, perhaps, there never had been anything [...]. She was weightless as an empty basket and her mittens fell to the floor with a soft plop. A little dust trickled out of the truncated fingers' (*NC* 84–5; emphasis in original). Little more than a 'figure of speech' – an embodiment of the monstrous feminine – Madame Schreck writes herself out of the historic world and turns to dust. She may represent the mother as a 'hole' – but one into which she herself disappears. Although, by representing material excess, Fevvers is cast as Schreck's antithesis, the two represent facets of the same Sadeian economy: the daughter trades on her sexualised body; the surrogate mother denies her maternal body and writes herself out of history. Both, like Juliette, are materialists 'programmed' to pursue financial profit at the expense of their humanity.

Irigaray argues that, in order to re-embody the mother as a speaking subject, it is vital to re-imagine the mother–daughter relationship so that mother and daughter can speak in the presence of one another. It is also necessary, 'if we are not to be accomplices in the murder of the mother, for us to assert that there is a genealogy of women [...] that we already have a history' (1991: 44). Although Madame Schreck represents the monstrous Gothic mother who tries to discipline the Gothic daughter into subjection, *Nights at the Circus* imagines an alternative model for the Gothic mother, and the mother–daughter relationship, in the figure of Lizzie. A 'tiny, wizened gnome-like apparition who might have been any age between thirty and fifty [with] snapping, black eyes, sallow skin [and a] skimpy, decent, black dress [...] white with dandruff' (*NC* 13), Lizzie resembles the 'spectral' surrogate mother Madame Schreck. However, a witchy, 'ex-whore', she is an embodied subject who has already left her mark on the past and is planning for the future.

Daddy's girls

After watching a 'loving' mother pigeon passing 'mute instructions' to her young, Fevvers and Lizzie together realise that Fevvers's flight into womanhood requires that Lizzie take on the role of 'bird-mother': 'this young creature cried out to me, that she would not be what she must become, and, though her pleading moved me until tears blinded my own eyes, I knew that what will be, must be and so – I pushed' (NC 34). Although the text's re-imagining of the mother–daughter relationship is crucial to the daughter's journey of self-discovery, it is also vital to Lizzie's self-positioning. Believing the onset of Fevvers's menstruation and the blossoming of her wings to be 'the Annunciation of [her] menopause' (NC 24), Lizzie historicises herself in relation to the mother–daughter relationship. Russo effectively conceptualises the relationship between Lizzie and Fevvers in terms of an 'intergenerational grotesque', suggesting that it is through their dialectical relationship that 'the "new" becomes a possibility that already existed, a part of the aging body in process rather than the property (like virginity) of a discrete and static place or identity' (Russo, 1994: 179). In Nights at the Circus, the mother–daughter relationship is central not only to the psychosexual development of the Gothic heroine but also to re-imagining the Gothic mother.

Claire Kahane identifies the recuperation of the mother–daughter relationship as a key component of modern Gothic narratives by women: 'for if the older Gothic tradition involved an obscure exploration of female identity through a confrontation with a diffuse spectral mother, in modern Gothic the spectral mother typically becomes an embodied actual figure' (1985: 343). If the disavowal of their bodies positions Nelson and Schreck as diffuse spectral mothers, then Lizzie is very much the 'embodied actual figure' who guides and re-educates Fevvers through the later stages of her journey of self-discovery. When Fevvers and Lizzie leave London and St Petersburg and move into the snow-covered landscape of Siberia – 'a blank sheet of fresh paper' (NC 218) – the text opens up a new imaginary space in which to re-imagine the mother–daughter relationship outside of the heavily codified structures of the Gothic castle. What starts to take place in 'Siberia' is a dialogue between mother and daughter that displaces the emphasis put upon Fevvers's story in the first two sections of the novel. In 'Siberia', Lizzie's Marxist ponderings on feminist futures and identities provide a provocative counterpoint to Fevvers's own musings on her utopian future as a 'woman with wings' who will herald 'the New Age in which no women will be bound down to the ground' (*NC* 25).[20]

Fevvers, the wayward daughter, sees herself as the 'new woman' who will radically transform the social structure, envisaging a moment when 'the old world has turned on its axle so that the new dawn can dawn, then, ah, then! all the women will have wings, the same as I' (*NC* 285). But Lizzie, her feminist foster mother, warns her that: 'It's going to be more complicated than that [...]. This old witch sees storms ahead, my girl. When I look to the future, I see through a glass darkly. You improve your analysis, girl, and *then* we'll discuss it' (*NC* 286; emphasis in original). Lizzie cautions Fevvers, who is 'intoxicated with vision', about the uncompromising faith she has in her emblematic status and attempts to ground her in the economic and social realities of her existence. After all, in *The Sadeian Woman* Carter is unconvinced by the revolutionary promise of Juliette's freedom:

> With apologies to Appollinaire [*sic*], I do not think I want Juliette to renew my world; but, her work of destruction complete, she will, with her own death, have removed a repressive and authoritarian superstructure that has prevented a good deal of the work of renewal. (*SW* 111)

For, in spite of her wings, Fevvers does not truly take flight from the Gothic castle and its imprisoning scripts of femininity. She may temporarily flee from various Gothic enclosures (Rosencreutz's neo-Gothic mansion, Madame Schreck's Museum of Woman Monsters and the Russian Grand Duke's sterile hall), but at the end of the narrative she remains locked in the gaze of her heterosexual lover: 'she felt herself trapped forever in the reflection of Walser's eyes. For one moment, just one moment, Fevvers suffered the worst crisis of her life: "Am I fact? Or am I fiction? Am I what I know I am? Or am I what he thinks I am?"' (*NC* 290).

While Fevvers becomes imprisoned in the architecture of her own fiction, Lizzie explores her freedom as a writing subject. Travelling alongside the Gothic daughter, she has been carrying on her own covert political journey, sending 'news of the struggle in Russia to comrades in exile, written in invisible ink' (*NC* 292) at the request of 'a spry little gent with a 'tache' (*NC* 292) she met in the reading room of the British Museum. Besides this meeting with Marx, Lizzie is also a member of the Wollstonecraft and Godwin debating society, and is thus identified with 'that exemplary transgressive mother', Mary Wollstonecraft (Tauchert, 2008: 6).[21] In the end, then, it is Lizzie who truly dupes Walser as a reader of their stories. Carter's 'Envoi' at the end of *Nights at the Circus* should be read less as the 'sending on her way' of the Gothic daughter than as Lizzie's *envoi de lettres* to 'comrades in exile' via Walser. The novel promotes, in other words, a 'fiction of maternity' (Ward Jouve, 1994: 157) that at once disrupts and secures the Gothic daughter's narrative flight. As Fevvers suggests, her foster mother's story is a 'long history of exile and cunning which [...] will fill up ten times more of [Walser's] notebooks than *my* story ever did' (*NC* 285). Unlike that of James Joyce's artist, Lizzie's is not a story of '*silence*, exile, and cunning' (Joyce, 1988: 251; emphasis added). Freed from the European Gothic's fictions of paternity – the mutilating enclosures of the Sadeian Gothic and the dehumanising iconographies of the decadent Gothic's womb-like havens – the Gothic mother is reinstated above ground, in historical time. The mother is not only, as Ward Jouve suggests, 'the story under the story' (1994: 150). She is the agent of the story.

NOTES

1 In *Powers of Horror*, Kristeva similarly disputes the Freudian thesis to contend that social configurations are established via the repression of maternal authority and origin (1982: 56–7). Ascribing '[f]ear of the archaic mother' to a 'fear of her generative power [...] a dreaded one, that patrilineal filiation has the burden of subduing', she highlights the ways in which primary maternal abjection anticipates the social, cultural and political marginalisation of women (1982: 77).

2 Irigaray illustrates her argument with particular reference to the story of Orestes and Clytemnestra in the *Oresteia*. She argues that the murder of

Clytemnestra, and the fates of her daughters Iphigenia and Electra in death and madness, demonstrate the reaffirmation of patriarchal order and the regulation of femininity: 'The murder of the mother results [...] in the non-punishment of the son, the burial of the madness of women – and the burial of women in madness – and the advent of the image of the virgin goddess, born of the father and obedient to his law in forsaking the mother' (1991: 37–8).

3 Kahane's reading elaborates on Norman Holland and Leona Sherman's influential reading of the Gothic castle as (maternal) body (1977).

4 Although Madame de Franval imagines the father and daughter's matricidal attack, she is not murdered. An ambivalent reunion between mother and daughter is staged at the end of the narrative.

5 Carter's discussion of 'Eugénie de Franval' forms part of the notes that comprise a fifth chapter of *The Sadeian Woman*, entitled 'The Marriage Hearse' (see BL Add MS88899/1/72). This chapter was cut from the published version of the book (see BL Add MS88899/1/74).

6 For a discussion of this mistranslation see Jane Gallop, who points out that the 'English title's "bedroom" leaves out a crucial element in any definition of "boudoir," the distinct gendering of the term. Whatever we think might go on in a boudoir, it is always a woman's room. The 1965 translation of Sade into the sexual revolution took the work's insistent gendering out of the title and covered over what cannot be ignored in the French title, that the book has designs upon women. Sade is making an attempt to bring "philosophy," by which he means a liberating way of thinking, into the boudoir, into the world of women' (2005: 92).

7 Carter concludes the 'Polemical Preface' to *The Sadeian Woman* with an extract from this pamphlet where Sade famously extends his treatise on sexual freedom to women: 'Charming sex, you will be free; just as men do, you shall enjoy all the pleasures that Nature makes your duty, do not withhold yourselves from one. Must the more divine half of mankind be kept in chains by the others? Ah, break those bonds: nature wills it' (*SW* 37).

8 'Hide the cunt' becomes 'hide the woman' (this transposition is not conveyed as clearly in the English translation). Barthes argues that the Sadeian libertines' assaults on the female body amount to turning woman into 'a kind of surgical and functional doll [...] a body *without a front part* (structural horror and flouting), a monstrous bandage, a *thing*' (1976: 123; emphasis in original).

9 The 'sex-murderer' Gilles de Rais receives a specific mention in Carter's notes for 'The Bloody Chamber' (BL Add MS88899/1/83).

10 I also want to return another mother to the text in the form of Colette's short story 'The Tender Shoot'. In the same letter, Carter suggests that 'The Bloody Chamber' 'deliberately alludes to Colette's autobiographical writing; somewhere she speculates about the debauchery of young girls by old men, the terrible sadness of it. [...] The whole "Bloody Chamber" story is a *homage* to Colette, the period, the clothes, the almost cloying fluency of the narrative style – I love Colette but with my eyes open – and the rescue by the mother, of course' (BL Add MS88899/1/84).

11 Suleiman suggests that Carter lifts the scene where Evelyn chases Leilah into the darkness of the city from Robert Desnos's *La Liberté ou l'amour* (1927) (1990: 137).

12 Edison's 'talking doll', made in 1890 using a phonograph mechanism, also provides a context for Ghislaine's doll-like voice and behaviour in *Shadow Dance*.

13 Merja Makinen points out that Carter's demystification of the maternal archetype is complex and contradictory: 'Even if *The Passion of New Eve* makes Mother into a monster, split between radical feminist "consolatory nonsense" and patriarchal misogyny, in the end the mighty female violator's actions are shown to be a source of political enlightenment' (1997: 163).

14 The novel, suggests Carter, is 'set at exactly the moment in European history when things began to change. It's set at that time quite deliberately, and [Fevvers is] the new woman' (Katsavos, 1994: 13).

15 In terms of the novel's avian and vampire iconographies, the allusion to seeing 'through a glass, darkly' points not only to St Paul's comment on the experience of the earthly world (1 Corinthians 13.12) but also to Sheridan Le Fanu's *In a Glass Darkly* (1872), in which 'Carmilla' is collected.

16 See Sage (1994a: 47–8) for further discussion of these images of the winged woman.

17 Although both Day and Sage have noted the extent to which the novel belongs to the eighteenth-century picaresque tradition, I argue that its topography belongs to the Gothic in its European mode. This analysis of Gothic space and the mother–daughter relationship develops an earlier reading in Munford (2002).

18 Moers argues that, in 'Mrs. Radcliffe's hands, the Gothic novel became a feminine substitute for the picaresque, where heroines could enjoy all the

adventures and alarms that masculine heroes had long experienced, far from home, in fiction' (1978: 126).

19 With her wizened bosom, Madame Schreck is a playful parody of the Kleinian 'bad breast'. In her re-visioning of the Oedipal drama Melanie Klein posits the mother's body as central to the child's psychosexual development. Klein argues that the infant's fluctuating experiences of love and hate are projected on to the maternal breast (Klein, 1957). In *The Sadeian Woman*, Carter identifies Eugénie's violation of her mother in *Philosophy in the Bedroom* as an exemplary 'vengeance upon the primal "good" object, the body of the mother' and, specifically, the 'good breast' as the prototypical 'fountain of all nourishment' (*SW* 134).

20 This cross-generational dialogue might be read as one between a post-feminist daughter and a second-wave feminist mother. For more on post-feminism and Carter's Gothic see Munford (2007).

21 Wollstonecraft's more revolutionary turn on the female Gothic mode in *Maria* (1798) re-imagines the Radcliffean paradigm by speaking from the position of the mother who has lost her daughter (see Tauchert, 2002: 115). Confined in an asylum, Maria is, in her own words, 'buried alive' (Wollstonecraft, 1994: 17). In Wollstonecraft's novel the asylum, as a Gothic space of confinement, mirrors the imprisoning limitations of the familial and social structures outside it.

Afterword: The Museum of dust

Dust forms the ceaseless tides of the becoming and dissolution of things. Out of it things are made; into it they dissolve.

(Joseph A. Amato, *Dust: A History of the Small and the Invisible*)

In *Heroes and Villains*, Marianne, the History Professor's daughter, watches 'dispassionately' as the hands of her father's clock go round, 'but she never felt that time was passing for time was frozen around her in this secluded place' (*HV* 1). Shut up in the cold, white tower made of concrete and steel in the Professors' disciplined and well-ordered society, she receives an education in rational thought in her father's study. Although she is taught 'reading, writing and history', and makes her way through her father's 'library of old books', Marianne gazes, distractedly, 'out of the window across the fields to the swamps and brambles and [tries] to imagine a forest of men' (*HV* 7). Lured by the promise of the romantic ruins, inhabited by the savage and captivating Barbarians, Marianne leaves behind her pristine tower and makes her way through the brambles surrounding the father's house until she is carried away into the forest by the beautiful Jewel. She soon finds herself resident in another paternal enclosure, a decaying Gothic ruin surrounded by tall, thorny trees. This time, however, she falls under the cruel and violent instruction of Dr Donally. Fusty, fetid and ornamented with 'death's heads, hourglasses and memento mori, all covered with dust', Donally's study nonetheless contains some of the same books that Marianne remembers from her father's library – 'Teilhard de Chardin,

Lévi-Strauss, Weber, Durkheim and so on, all marked by fire and flood' (*HV* 62). Marianne exchanges one father figure for another: the rational, Enlightenment Professor for the irrational, mythologising magician. Both invent their social structures from the same sources.

I end this book by returning to the novel that Carter — somewhat disingenuously — identifies as the origin of her Gothic endeavours because it provides an illuminating insight into the daughter's enthralment with illusory paternal mythologies. Its dramatisation of the tension between the Enlightenment world of the Professors and the ghostly and dreamlike otherworld of the Barbarians speaks to the interpretative possibilities that Carter identifies in the Gothic's mode of contradiction. But it is also, as Sage argues, 'mocking code for the mental landscape of a late 1960s woman intellectual — the glamour of the guerrilla underground and various vagrant counter-cultural movements' (1994a: 18). Although she is initially fascinated by the romanticism and savagery of the Barbarians, Marianne comes to find in their habitat of unreason a Gothic mirror reflection of the cold and clinical rationalism of the Professors. Partly enthralled by the prospect of playing in the father's Gothic castle, she realises in the end that its monuments of myth (for example, the chapel and the Gothic ruin) must be destroyed. At the end of the novel, Marianne and Jewel burn Donally's myth-making paraphernalia so that all that remains of him is 'dust and ashes' (*HV* 133). Arriving at the seashore, Marianne encounters historical time once again when she discovers a 'monstrous' female figure, made of plasterwork, emerging from the waters that have engulfed the city with a clock held in its arms and supported by its 'forward-jutting stomach' (*HV* 138). In an image that anticipates the end of *The Passion of New Eve*, the close of the novel sees the pregnant Marianne birthing herself into a new mythology in which she will 'be the tiger lady' and rule the Barbarians 'with a rod of iron' (*HV* 150). Although Marianne's matriarchal vision displaces Donally's patriarchal illusion, her mythology is constrained by 'the old habit of mind' (Sage, 1994a: 20). Marianne emerges as 'Eve at the end of the world' (*HV* 124), but an Eve born of the dust of a paternal mythology.

Like the Lady of the House of Love, Carter is a Gothic daughter who has inherited a haunted house full of dust, shadows and echoes. But there is also another 'Museum of dust' that resides in Carter's fiction. Carter's last novel, *Wise Children*, marks something of a departure from the European Gothic bloodline that can be traced through many of her earlier texts. It is, nonetheless, profoundly concerned with questions of inheritance and legitimacy, and with the relationship between fathers and daughters. It is also a novel that returns the Gothic theme of the double in the image of two septuagenarian twin sisters, Dora and Nora Chance, the (alleged) illegitimate daughters of a famous Shakespearean actor, Melchior Hazard. Dora returns to the Gothic attic in Bard Road, the place of her birth, to re-write playfully the family romance – a history 'invented' by Grandma, who 'put it together out of whatever came to hand – a stray pair of orphaned babes, a ragamuffin in a flat cap' (*WC* 35). Full of old clothes, newspapers tied up in bales, faded cuttings and photographs and scrapbooks, the house in Bard Road is a 'Museum of dust' (*WC* 188), cluttered with Grandma Chance's old belongings.

Dora's name may echo that of her Freudian namesake but her garrulous first-person narration gives form to a story that disrupts the family romance. Although the narrative appears to be structured as a quest for paternal origin, this trajectory is persistently interrupted by an uncertainty about maternal origin which, Dora claims, 'founders in a wilderness of unknowability' (*WC* 12). In spite of strong hints that Grandma Chance is in fact Dora and Nora's biological mother, she denies her maternity on the principle that 'mother is as mother does' (*WC* 12) and keeps 'her mystery intact until the end' (*WC* 35). In the unfolding of Dora's family history, the Gothic mirror is re-constructed so that it no longer represents the space into which the Gothic mother vanishes but, rather, returns the double image of the twin sisters 'looking back out of the dust' (*WC* 190). Bard Road is, in the end, populated by mothers. At the end of the narrative, Dora and Nora become foster mothers to another set of twins, planning to turn 'Grandma's old room' into a nursery (*WC* 229). The house on Bard Road may remain intact, but the novel ends with a comic debunking of paternal power. The sacred Melchior Hazard appears in the end as a two-dimensional figure with 'an imitation look [...] like one of those great, big, papier-mâché heads they have in the Notting Hill parade, larger than life, but not lifelike'

(*WC* 230). Nora and Dora ask themselves whether, in fact, he was always just something they dreamed up, something 'to set our lives by, like the old clock in the hall, which is real enough, in itself, but which we've got to wind up to make it go' (*WC* 230). In the end, the father is figured not as a point of (literary) origin but as an image of endless recycling – a 'pulp fiction' crumbling into dust.

Carter's dialogues with the dusty, dirty scripts of her literary forefathers involve simultaneous acts of composition and decomposition. She may, at times, occupy the position of the wayward daughter playing in the father's house but, like Marianne in *Heroes and Villains*, she '[breaks] things to see what they were like inside' (*HV* 4). Carter's intertextual engagements with the sexual and textual violence of a male-authored European Gothic lineage raises unsettling questions about her complicity with an aesthetic structured around the objectification of the female body. Yet, her textual investment in androcentric literary frameworks is not synonymous with a political investment in them. Be it the enthralled evocation of a Baudelairean poetic, or the unflinching recasting of Sade's stylised violence, the alluring literariness of Carter's writing is most often at work as part of a feminist analysis of the 'social fictions' which shape identity and experience. As she argues in 'Notes on the Gothic Mode', the Gothic is primarily an analytic method. Concerned with dismantling its illusory structures, Carter's textual practice does not just vampirically feed off this European Gothic bloodline. Rather, it unmasks and lays bare the machinery of its fantasises and illusions.

Negotiating the European Gothic from within the father's house is a risky endeavour. Its thickly dusted surfaces mean that it is sometimes difficult to see clearly – dust in the eye can distort the field of vision. Carter's 'double allegiance' (Suleiman 1990: 63) to a male-authored, and often misogynist, European Gothic bloodline – her simultaneous commitment to aesthetic practices that 'help to transform reality itself' ('NGM' 133) and her critique of the sexual ideologies underlying those aesthetic practices – is not always comfortable. In *Subversive Intent*, Suleiman argues that 'there is no such thing as a totally tidy theory of playing and modernity – or of anything else, probably. The very search for tidiness and attempt to eliminate loose ends, if carried far enough, leads to the recognition of blurred edges' (1990: 4). This wariness about reconciling loose ends and resolving contradictions is germane to a consideration of Carter's work, which is often cluttered and inconvenient, and on which the critical dust refuses to settle.

Carter's most frequently cited reflection on her textual practice appears at the beginning of 'Notes from the Front Line'. As critically well-worn as this comment might be, this book cannot finish without reiterating it: 'Reading is just as creative an activity as writing and most intellectual development depends upon new readings of old texts. I am all for putting new wine in old bottles, especially if the pressure of the new wine makes the old bottles explode' ('NFL' 69). I would like to end by re-imagining these bottles as dusty bottles, like those stored in the subterranean racks in the Marquis's castle, to which the mother returns in 'The Bloody Chamber'. The semantic peculiarity of dust – signifying absence and presence, decay and replenishment, composition and decomposition – allows Carter's fictions to at once dust down the grubby surfaces of these European Gothic scripts and, at the same time, dust them with renewed meanings.

References

PRIMARY WORKS BY ANGELA CARTER

Works by Angela Carter are arranged in chronological order by date of first publication. I have used square brackets where this is different from the edition cited in the text.

Fiction

Carter, Angela [1966] (1995), *Shadow Dance*, London: Virago.

— [1967] (1981), *The Magic Toyshop*, London: Virago.

— [1968] (1995), *Several Perceptions*, London: Virago.

— [1969] (1981), *Heroes and Villains*, Harmondsworth: Penguin.

— [1971] (1997), *Love*, London: Vintage.

— [1972] (2010), *The Infernal Desire Machines of Doctor Hoffman*, London: Penguin.

— [1974] (1987), *Fireworks*, London: Virago.

— [1977] (1982), *The Passion of New Eve*, London: Virago.

— [1979] (1995), *The Bloody Chamber and Other Stories*, London: Vintage.

— [1984] (1994), *Nights at the Circus*, London: Vintage.

— [1985] (1996), *Black Venus*, London: Vintage.

— [1991] (1992), *Wise Children*, London: Vintage.

— (1993), *American Ghosts and Old World Wonders*, London: Chatto & Windus.

— [1995] (1996), *Burning Your Boats: Collected Short Stories*, Salman Rushdie (intro.), London: Vintage.

References

Editions and translations

Carter, Angela (ed.) (1986), *Wayward Girls and Wicked Women*, London: Virago.

— (1990), *The Virago Book of Fairy Tales*, London: Virago.

— (1992), *The Second Virago Book of Fairy Tales*, London: Virago.

Carter, Angela (trans.) [1977] (2008), *The Fairy Tales of Charles Perrault*, Jack Zipes (intro.), London: Penguin.

— (1982), *Sleeping Beauty and Other Favourite Fairy Tales*, Michael Foreman (illust.), London: Gollancz.

Dramatic works

Carter, Angela [1976] (1997), 'Vampirella', *The Curious Room: Collected Dramatic Works*, Mark Bell (ed.) and Susannah Clapp (intro.), London: Vintage, 3–32.

Selected non-fiction

Carter, Angela [1974] (1996), 'Afterword to *Fireworks*', in *Burning Your Boats: Collected Short Stories*, Salman Rushdie (intro.), London: Vintage, 459–60.

— (1975), 'Notes on the Gothic Mode', *The Iowa Review*, 6:3–4, 132–4

— [1979] (2000), *The Sadeian Woman: An Exercise in Cultural History*, London: Virago.

— (1982), *Nothing Sacred: Selected Writings*, London: Virago.

— (1983), 'Notes from the Frontline', in Michelene Wandor (ed.), *On Gender and Writing*, London: Pandora, 69–77.

— [1985] (1996), 'Preface to *Come unto These Yellow Sands*', *The Curious Room: Collected Dramatic Works*, Mark Bell (ed.) and Susannah Clapp (intro.), London: Vintage, 497–502.

— (1992), *Expletives Deleted: Selected Writings*, London: Chatto & Windus.

— [1997] (1998), *Shaking a Leg: Collected Journalism and Writings*, Joan Smith (intro.), Jenny Uglow (ed.). London: Vintage.

Manuscripts

British Library, Additional MS88899/1/1, Angela Carter Papers, Shadow Dance.

British Library, Additional MS88899/1/34, Angela Carter Papers, The Bloody Chamber and Other Short Stories.

British Library, Additional MS88899/1/70, Angela Carter Papers, The Sadeian Woman.

References

British Library, Additional MS88899/1/72, Angela Carter Papers, The Sadeian Woman.

British Library, Additional MS88899/1/74, Angela Carter Papers, The Sadeian Woman.

British Library, Additional MS88899/1/82, Angela Carter Papers, Miscellaneous fairy tale material.

British Library, Additional MS88899/1/83, Angela Carter Papers, Surrealism and Sexuality.

British Library, Additional MS88899/1/84, Angela Carter Papers, Notes for various works.

SECONDARY WORKS

Acker, Kathy (1997), 'Reading the Lack of the Body: The Writing of the Marquis de Sade', in *Bodies of Work: Essays of Kathy Acker*, London: Serpent's Tail, 66–80.

Altevers, Ninette (1994), 'Gender Matters in *The Sadeian Woman*', *The Review of Contemporary Fiction*, 14:3, 18–23.

Altick, Richard D. (1978), *The Shows of London*, Cambridge, MA: Harvard Unversity Press.

Amato, Joseph A. (2000), *Dust: A History of the Small and the Invisible*, Berkeley: University of California Press.

Apter, Emily (1991), *Feminizing the Fetish: Psychoanalysis and Narrative Obsession in Turn-of-the-Century France*, Ithaca: Cornell University Press.

Aragon, Louis, and André Breton (1928), 'Le Cinquantenaire de l'hystérie', *La Révolution Surréaliste*, 4, 15 March, 20–2.

Armitt, Lucie (1997), 'The Fragile Frames of *The Bloody Chamber*', in Bristow and Broughton (eds), 88–99.

—— (2000), *Contemporary Women's Fiction and the Fantastic*, Basingstoke: Macmillan.

Atwood, Margaret (1994), 'Running With the Tigers', in Sage (ed.), 117–35.

Bacchilega, Cristina (1997), *Postmodern Fairy Tales: Gender and Narrative Strategies*, Philadelphia: University of Pennsylvania Press.

Badmington, Neil (2004), *Alien Chic: Posthumanism and the Other Within*, London: Routledge.

Barchilon, Jacques (2001), 'Remembering Angela Carter', in Roemer and Bacchilega (eds), 26–9.

References

Barnes, Djuna (1961), *Nightwood* [1937], T. S. Eliot (intro.), New York: New Directions.

Barthes, Roland (1971), *Sade, Fourier, Loyola*, Paris: Éditions du seuil.

— (1976), *Sade, Fourier, Loyola*, Richard Miller (trans.), Baltimore: John Hopkins University Press.

Basile, Giambattista (n.d.), 'Sun, Moon, and Talia', in *The Pentamerone* [1634–36], Richard Burton (trans.), E. R. Vincent (intro.), London: Spring, 372–7.

Bataille, Georges (1987), *Story of the Eye* [1928], Joachim Neugroschel (trans.), San Francisco: City Lights.

— (1995), 'Dust' [1929], in Georges Bataille (ed.), *Encyclopaedia Acephalica: Comprising the Critical Dictionary & Related Texts*, Iain White (trans.), London: Atlas Press, 42–3.

— (2006), *Eroticism* [1957], Mary Dalwood (trans.), London: Marion Boyars.

Baudelaire, Charles (1989), *Intimate Journals* [1930], Christopher Isherwood (trans.), T. S. Eliot (intro.), London: Picador.

— (1993), *The Flowers of Evil*, James McGowan (trans.), Jonathan Culler (intro.), Oxford: Oxford University Press.

— (1995a), 'Edgar Allan Poe: His Life and Works', in Baudelaire (1995b), 70–92.

— (1995b), *The Painter of Modern Life and Other Essays*, Jonathan Mayne (trans. and ed.), 2nd edn, London: Phaidon Press.

— (1995c), 'The Painter of Modern Life' [1863], in Baudelaire (1995b), 1–41.

— (1996), *Les Fleurs du mal* [1857 and 1861], Claude Pichois (intro.), 2nd edn, Paris: Gallimard.

— (2002), *On Wine and Hashish* [1851 and 1860], Andrew Brown (trans.), London: Hesperus Press.

Beauvoir, Simone de (1966), 'Must We Burn Sade?' [1951–52], in Sade (1966a), 3–64.

— (1988), *The Second Sex* [1949], H. M. Parshley (trans. and ed.), London: Pan-Picador.

Becker, Susanne (1999), *Gothic Forms of Feminine Fictions*, Manchester: Manchester University Press.

Beckstrand, Lisa (2009), *Deviant Women of the French Revolution and the Rise of Feminism*, Madison, NJ: Fairleigh Dickinson University Press.

Bedford, Les (1977), 'Angela Carter: An Interview', Sheffield University Television.

References

Beizer, Janet (1993), *Ventriloquized Bodies: Narratives of Hysteria in Nineteenth-Century France*, Ithaca: Cornell University Press.

Bellmer, Hans (2005), *The Doll*, Malcolm Green (trans.), London: Atlas Press.

Bellour, Raymond (1993), 'Ideal Hadaly', in Constance Penley (ed.), *Close Encounters: Film, Feminism, and Science Fiction*, Minneapolis: University of Minnesota Press, 107–32.

Belton, Robert J. (1995), *The Beribboned Bomb: The Image of Woman in Male Surrealist Art*, Alberta: University of Calgary Press.

Benedikz, Margret (2002), 'Storming the Sadeian Citadel: Disturbing Gender in Angela Carter's Fiction of Transition', PhD thesis, Stockholm University.

Benjamin, Walter (2006), *The Writer of Modern Life: Essays on Charles Baudelaire*, Howard Eiland et al. (trans.), Michael W. Jennings (ed.), Cambridge, MA: Harvard University Press.

Benson, Stephen (2001), 'Angela Carter and the Literary Märchen: A Review Essay', in Roemer and Bacchilega (eds), 30–58.

Bergson, Henri (2008), *Laughter: An Essay on the Meaning of the Comic* [1900], Rockville: Arc Manor.

Bernheimer, Charles (1989), *Figures of Ill Repute: Representing Prostitution in Nineteenth-Century France*, Cambridge, MA: Harvard University Press.

Bettelheim, Bruno (1991), *The Uses of Enchantment: The Meaning and Importance of Fairy Tales* [1976], Harmondsworth: Penguin.

Birkett, Jennifer (1986), *The Sins of the Fathers: Decadence in France 1870–1914*, London: Quartet.

Bonaparte, Marie (1949), *The Life and Works of Edgar Allan Poe: A Psychoanalytic Interpretation*, John Rodker (trans.), London: Imago.

Bonca, Cornel (1994), 'In Despair of the Old Adams: Angela Carter's *The Infernal Desire Machines of Dr. Hoffman*', *The Review of Contemporary Fiction*, 14:3, 56–62.

Botting, Fred (1996), *Gothic*, London: Routledge.

Brabon, Benjamin A., and Stéphanie Genz (eds) (2007), *Postfeminist Gothic: Critical Interventions in Contemporary Culture*, Basingstoke: Palgrave.

Breton, André (1972), *Manifestoes of Surrealism*, Richard Seaver and Helen R. Lane (trans.), Ann Arbor: University of Michigan Press.

— (1978), *What Is Surrealism? Selected Writings*, Franklin Rosemont (ed.), London: Pluto.

— (1999), *Nadja* [1928], Richard Howard (trans.), London: Penguin.

References

Bristow, Joseph, and Trev Lynn Broughton (eds) (1997), *The Infernal Desires of Angela Carter: Fiction, Femininity, Feminism*, Harlow: Addison Wesley Longman.

Britzolakis, Christina (1995), 'Angela Carter's Fetishism', *Textual Practice*, 9:3, 459–75.

Bronfen, Elisabeth (1992), *Over Her Dead Body: Death, Femininity and the Aesthetic*, Manchester: Manchester University Press.

Burke, Edmund (1990), *A Philosophical Enquiry into the Origin of Our Ideas of the Sublime and Beautiful* [1757], Adam Phillips (ed. and intro.), Oxford: Oxford University Press.

Burt, E. S. (2001), 'Materiality and Autobiography in Baudelaire's "La Pipe"', *MLN*, 116:5, 941–63.

Butler, Judith (1993), *Bodies That Matter: On the Discursive Limits of 'Sex'*, New York: Routledge.

Carter, A. E. (1977), *Charles Baudelaire*, Boston: Twayne-G. K. Hall.

Castle, Terry (1995), *The Female Thermometer: Eighteenth-Century Culture and the Invention of the Uncanny*, New York: Oxford University Press.

Cavallaro, Dani (2011), *The World of Angela Carter: A Critical Investigation*, Jefferson and London: McFarland.

Chainani, Soman (2003), 'Sadeian Tragedy: The Politics of Content Revision in Angela Carter's "Snow Child"', *Marvels & Tales: Journal of Fairy-Tale Studies*, 17:2, 212–35.

Christensen, Peter (1994), 'The Hoffmann Connection: Demystification in Angela Carter's *The Infernal Desire Machines of Doctor Hoffman*', *The Review of Contemporary Fiction*, 14:3, 63–70.

Cixous, Hélène (1976), 'Fiction and its Phantoms: A Reading of Freud's *Das Heimliche*', *New Literary History*, 7, 525–48.

— (1981), 'Castration or Decapitation?', Annette Kuhn (trans.), *Signs: Journal of Women in Culture and Society*, 7:1, 41–55.

— (1993), 'The Laugh of the Medusa' [1975], Keith Cohen and Paula Cohen (trans.), in *Feminisms: An Anthology of Literary Theory and Criticism*, ed. by Robyn R. Warhol and Diane Price Herndl, New Brunswick: Rutgers University Press, 334–49.

— (1996), 'Sorties: Out and Out: Attacks/Ways Out/Forays', in Hélène Cixous and Catherine Clément, *The Newly Born Woman* [1975], Betsy Wing (trans.) and Sandra M. Gilbert (intro.), London: I. B. Tauris, 63–132.

Clark, Robert (1987), 'Angela Carter's Desire Machine', *Women's Studies*, 14:2, 147–61.

References

Clark, Timothy (2000), *The Theory of Inspiration: Composition as a Crisis of Subjectivity in Romantic and Post-Romantic Writing*, Manchester: Manchester University Press.

Clery, E. J. (2000), *Women and Gothic: From Clara Reeve to Mary Shelley*, Tavistock: Northcote House.

Cockburn, Alexander (1974), *Idle Passion: Chess and the Dance of Death*, London: Weidenfeld and Nicolson.

Coleridge, Samuel Taylor (1992), *The Rime of the Ancient Mariner and Other Poems*, New York: Dover.

Conley, Katharine (1996), *Automatic Woman: The Representation of Woman in Surrealism*, Lincoln: University of Nebraska Press.

Cornwell, Neil (1990), *The Literary Fantastic: From Gothic to Postmodernism*, Hemel Hempstead: Harvester Wheatsheaf.

Crofts, Charlotte (2003), *'Anagrams of Desire': Angela Carter's Writing for Radio, Film and Television*, Manchester: Manchester University Press.

Daly, Mary (1973), *Beyond God the Father: Toward a Philosophy of Women's Liberation*, Boston: Beacon Press.

Davenport-Hines, Richard (1998), *Gothic: 400 Years of Excess, Horror, Evil and Ruin*, London: Fourth Estate.

Day, Aidan (1998), *Angela Carter: The Rational Glass*, Manchester: Manchester University Press.

DeLamotte, Eugenia C. (1989), *Perils of the Night: A Feminist Study of Nineteenth-Century Gothic*, New York: Oxford University Press.

Derrida, Jacques (1992), *Given Time 1: Counterfeit Money*, Peggy Kamuf (trans.), Chicago: University of Chicago Press.

Dijkstra, Bram (1986), *Idols of Perversity: Fantasies of Feminine Evil in Fin-de-Siècle Culture*, Oxford: Oxford University Press.

Doane, Mary Ann (1991), *Femme Fatales: Feminism, Film Theory, Psychoanalysis*, New York: Routledge.

Dolar, Mladen (2002), 'If Music Be the Food of Love', in Slavoj Žižek and Mladen Dolar, *Opera's Second Death*, London: Routledge, 1–102.

Duncker, Patricia (1984), 'Re-Imagining the Fairy Tales: Angela Carter's Bloody Chambers', *Literature and History*, 10:1, 3–14.

—— (1996), 'Queer Gothic: Angela Carter and the Lost Narratives of Sexual Subversion', *Critical Survey*, 8:1, 58–68.

Dworkin, Andrea (1981), *Pornography: Men Possessing Women*, London: Women's Press.

Easton, Alison (ed.) (2000), *Angela Carter*, Basingstoke: Macmillan.

References

Fay, Elizabeth A. (1998), *A Feminist Introduction to Romanticism*, Oxford: Blackwell.

Felski, Rita (1995), *The Gender of Modernity*, Cambridge, MA: Harvard University Press.

Fer, Briony (1995), 'Poussière/peinture: Bataille on painting', in Carolyn Bailey Gill (ed.), *Bataille: Writing the Sacred*, London: Routledge, 154–71.

Fernihough, Anne (1997), '"Is She Fact or Is She Fiction?": Angela Carter and the Enigma of Woman', *Textual Practice*, 11:1, 89–107.

Ferrell, Robyn (1991), 'Life-Threatening Life: Angela Carter and the Uncanny', in Alan Cholodenko (ed.), *The Illusion of Life: Essays on Animation*, Sydney: Power Publications/Australian Film Corporation, 131–44.

Fiedler, Leslie A. (1960), *Love and Death in the American Novel*, New York: Criterion.

Fleenor, Juliann E. (1983), 'Introduction', in Fleenor (ed.), 3–28.

Fleenor, Juliann E. (ed.) (1983), *The Female Gothic*, Montréal: Eden Press.

Foster, Hal (1993), *Compulsive Beauty*, Cambridge, MA: MIT Press.

Foucault, Michel (1991), 'What Is an Author?', in Paul Rabinow (ed.), *The Foucault Reader: An Introduction to Foucault's Thought*, London: Penguin, 101–20.

— (1998), *The Will to Knowledge: The History of Sexuality, Volume One* [1976], Robert Hurley (trans.), London: Penguin.

— (2001), *Madness and Civilization: A History of Insanity in the Age of Reason* [1964], Richard Howard (trans.), Oxford: Routledge.

Freud, Sigmund (1959a), 'Medusa's Head' [1922], in James Strachey and Anna Freud (ed. and trans.), *The Standard Edition of the Complete Psychological Works of Sigmund Freud*, 24 vols, London: Hogarth Press, xviii, 273–4.

— (1959b), 'The Question of Lay Analysis' [1926], in James Strachey and Anna Freud (ed. and trans.), *The Standard Edition of the Complete Psychological Works of Sigmund Freud*, 24 vols, London: Hogarth Press, xx, 179–258.

— (1959c), 'On Beginning the Treatment (Further Recommendations on the Technique of Psycho-Analysis I)' [1913], in James Strachey and Anna Freud (ed. and trans.), *The Standard Edition of the Complete Psychological Works of Sigmund Freud*, 24 vols, London: Hogarth Press, xii, 121–44.

— (1990), 'The Uncanny' [1919], in Albert Dickson (ed.) and James Strachey (ed. and trans.), *Art and Literature*, *The Penguin Freud Library*, London: Penguin, 339–76.

References

— (1991), *Introductory Lectures on Psychoanalysis* [1916—17], in Angela Richards (ed.) and James Strachey (ed. and trans.), *The Penguin Freud Library*, London: Penguin.

Freud, Sigmund, and Joseph Breuer (2004), *Studies in Hysteria* [1895], Nicola Luckhurst (ed. and trans.) and Rachel Bowlby (intro.), London: Penguin.

Gallop, Jane (1981), *Intersections: A Reading of Sade with Bataille, Blanchot, and Klossowski*, Lincoln: University of Nebraska Press.

— (1982), *Feminism and Psychoanalysis: The Daughter's Seduction*, Basingstoke: Macmillan.

— (2005), 'The Liberated Woman', *Narrative*, 13:2, 89—104.

Galloway, David (1986), 'Introduction' to Poe (1986a), xvii—lv.

Gamble, Sarah (1997), *Angela Carter: Writing from the Front Line*, Edinburgh: Edinburgh University Press.

— (2006), *Angela Carter: A Writer's Life*, Basingstoke: Palgrave.

Garber, Marjorie, and Nancy J. Vickers (2003), 'Introduction', in Marjorie Garber and Nancy J. Vickers (eds), *The Medusa Reader*, London: Routledge, 1—7.

Garner, Katie (2012), 'Blending the Pre-Raphaelite with the Surreal in Angela Carter's *Shadow Dance* (1966) and *Love* (1971)', in Lawrence Phillips and Sonya Andermahr (eds), *Angela Carter: New Critical Readings*, London: Continuum, 147—61.

Gauthier, Xavière (1971), *Surréalisme et sexualité*, Paris: Gallimard.

Gilbert, Sandra, and Susan Gubar (1979), *The Madwoman in the Attic: The Woman Writer and the Nineteenth-Century Literary Imagination*, New Haven: Yale University Press.

Gilman, Sander L. (1985), *Difference and Pathology: Stereotypes of Sexuality, Race and Madness*, Ithaca: Cornell University Press.

Goldsworthy, Kerryn (1985), 'Angela Carter', *Meanjin*, 44:1, 4—13.

Green, Malcom (2005), 'Introduction', in Bellmer, 7—30.

Grimm, Jacob, and Wilhelm Grimm (1997), 'Little Briar Rose', in *The Complete Fairy Tales*, Padraic Colum (intro.), Ware: Wordsworth, 237—41.

Grossman, Wendy (2005), 'Man Ray's Endgame and Other Modernist Gambits', in Johnnie Gratton and Michael Sheringham (eds), *The Art of the Project: Projects and Experiments in Modern French Culture*, New York: Berghahn Books, 31—50.

Gruss, Susanne (2009), *The Pleasure of the Feminist Text: Reading Michèle Roberts and Angela Carter*, Amsterdam: Rodopi.

References

Haffenden, John (1985), 'Angela Carter', *Novelists in Interview*, London: Methuen, 76–96.

Hale, Terry (2002), 'French and German Gothic: The Beginnings', in Jerrold E. Hogle (ed.), *The Cambridge Companion to Gothic Fiction*, Cambridge: Cambridge University Press, 63–84.

Hall, Daniel (2005), *French and German Gothic Fiction in the Late Eighteenth Century*, Oxford: Peter Lang.

Hanson, Clare (1988), 'Each Other: Images of Otherness in the Short Fiction of Doris Lessing, Jean Rhys and Angela Carter', *Journal of the Short Story in English*, 10, 67–82.

Hayes, Kevin J. (ed.), *The Cambridge Companion to Edgar Allan Poe*, Cambridge: Cambridge University Press.

Heidmann, Ute, and Jean Michel Adam (2007), 'Text Linguistics and Comparative Literature: Towards an Interdisciplinary Approach to Written Tales. Angela Carter's Translations of Perrault', in Donna R. Miller and Monica Turci (eds), *Language and Verbal Art Revisited: Linguistic Approaches to the Study of Literature*, London: Equinox, 181–96.

Heiland, Donna (2004), *Gothic and Gender: An Introduction*, Oxford: Blackwell.

Henstra, Sarah M. (1999), 'The Pressure of New Wine: Performative Reading in Angela Carter's *The Sadeian Woman*', *Textual Practice*, 13:1, 97–117.

Hentges, Jane (2002), 'Painting Pictures of Petrification and Perversion: Angela Carter's Surrealist Eye in *Shadow Dance* and *The Magic Toyshop*', *Études britanniques contemporaines*, 23, 43–53.

Hoeveler, Diane Long (1998), *Gothic Feminism: The Professionalization of Gender from Charlotte Smith to the Brontës*, Liverpool: Liverpool University Press.

Hoffmann, E. T. A. (1982), 'The Sandman' [1816], in *Tales of Hoffmann*, R. J. Hollingdale (ed. and trans.), London: Penguin, 85–125.

Holland, Norman N., and Leona F. Sherman (1977), 'Gothic Possibilities', *New Literary History*, 8:2, 279–94.

Horner, Avril (2002), 'Introduction', in Horner (ed.), 1–16.

Horner, Avril (ed.) (2002), *European Gothic: A Spirited Exchange, 1760–1960*, Manchester: Manchester University Press.

Horner, Avril, and Sue Zlosnik (2008), 'Introduction', in Avril Horner and Sue Zlosnik (eds), *Le Gothic: Influences and Appropriations in Europe and America*, Basingstoke: Palgrave, 1–11.

Hubert, Renée Riese (1988), *Surrealism and the Book*, Berkeley: University of California Press.

Hutcheon, Linda (1989), *The Politics of Postmodernism*, London: Routledge.

References

Huysmans, J.-K. (2001), *The Damned (Là-Bas)* [1891], Terry Hale (trans. and intro.), London: Penguin.

—— (2003), *Against Nature (À rebours)* [1884], Robert Baldick (trans.), Patrick McGuinness (intro. and ed.), London: Penguin.

Huyssen, Andreas (1988), *After the Great Divide: Modernism, Mass Culture, Postmodernism*, Basingstoke, Macmillan.

In the Company of Poets, BBC Radio 4, Sunday 13 March 2011.

Irigaray, Luce (1985a), *Speculum of the Other Woman* [1974], Gillian C. Gill (trans.), Ithaca: Cornell University Press.

—— (1985b) *This Sex Which Is Not One* [1977], Catherine Porter and Carolyn Burke (trans.), Ithaca: Cornell University Press.

—— (1991), 'The Bodily Encounter with the Mother', David Macey (trans.), Margaret Whitford (ed.), *The Irigaray Reader*, Oxford: Blackwell, 34–46.

Jacobus, Mary (1995), *First Things: The Maternal Imaginary in Literature, Art, Psychology*, New York: Routledge.

Jentsch, Ernst (1995), 'On the Psychology of the Uncanny' [1906], Roy Sellars (trans.), *Angelaki*, 2:1, 7–16.

Jordan, Elaine (1990), 'Enthralment: Angela Carter's Speculative Fictions', in Linda Anderson (ed.), *Plotting Change: Contemporary Women's Fiction*, London: Arnold-Hodder, 19–42.

—— (1992), 'The Dangers of Angela Carter', in Isobel Armstrong (ed.), *New Feminist Discourses: Critical Essays on Theories and Texts*, London: Routledge, 119–31.

Joyce, James (1988), *Portrait of the Artist as a Young Man* [1916], London: Paladin-HarperCollins.

Kahane, Claire (1985), 'The Gothic Mirror', in Shirley Nelson Garner, Claire Kahane and Madelon Sprengnether (eds), *The (M)other Tongue: Essays in Feminist Psychoanalytic Interpretation*, Ithaca: Cornell University Press, 334–51.

Kaiser, Mary (1994), 'Fairy Tale as Sexual Allegory: Intertextuality in Angela Carter's *The Bloody Chamber*', *The Review of Contemporary Fiction*, 14:3, 30–5.

Kappeler, Susanne (1986), *The Pornography of Representation*, Minneapolis: University of Minnesota.

Katsavos, Anna (1994), 'An Interview with Angela Carter', *The Review of Contemporary Fiction*, 14:3, 11–17.

Keenan, Sally (1997), 'Angela Carter's *The Sadeian* Woman: Feminism as Treason', in Bristow and Broughton (eds), 132–48.

References

Kenyon, Olga (1992), 'Angela Carter', *The Writer's Imagination: Interviews with Major International Women Novelists*, Bradford: University of Bradford Press, 23–33.

Kilgour, Maggie (1999), *The Rise of the Gothic Novel*, London: Routledge.

Killen, Alice (1967), *Le Roman terrifiant ou roman noir de Walpole à Anne [sic] Radcliffe et son influence sur la littérature française jusqu'en 1840*, Paris: Champion.

Klein, Richard (1993), *Cigarettes are Sublime*. Durham: Duke University Press.

Klein, Melanie (1957), *Envy and Gratitude: A Study of Unconscious Sources*, New York: Basic.

Kokoli, Alexandra M. (2002), '"The Cabinet of Edgar Allan Poe": Towards a Feminist Remodelling of (Meta)History', *In-between: Essays & Studies in Literary Criticism*, 11:1, 55–70.

Kristeva, Julia (1982), *Powers of Horror: An Essay on Abjection* [1980], Leon S. Roudiez (trans.), New York: Columbia University Press.

Kuenzli, Rudolf E. (1991), 'Surrealism and Misogyny', in Mary Ann Caws, Rudolf E. Kuenzli and Gwen Raaberg (eds), *Surrealism and Women*, Cambridge, MA: MIT Press, 17–26.

La Mettrie, Julien Offray de (1996), *Machine Man and Other Writings* [1747], Ann Thomson (ed.), Cambridge: Cambridge University Press.

Lanone, Catherine (2002), 'Verging on the Gothic: Melmoth's Journey to France', in Horner (ed.), 71–83.

Le Brun, Annie (1990), *Sade: A Sudden Abyss*, San Francisco: City Lights Books.

Le Fanu, Sheridan (1977), *In a Glass Darkly* [1872], Devendra P. Varma (ed.), 3 vols, New York: Arno Press.

Lévy, Maurice (1968), *Le Roman 'gothique' anglais, 1764–1824*, Toulouse: Publications de la faculté des lettres et sciences humaines.

— (1984), 'Le Roman gothique: genre anglais', *Europe*, 659, 5–13.

Lewallen, Avis (1988), 'Wayward Girls But Wicked Women?: Female Sexuality in Angela Carter's *The Bloody Chamber*', in Gary Day and Clive Bloom (eds), *Perspectives on Pornography: Sexuality in Film and Literature*, New York: St Martin's Press, 144–58.

Lewis, M. G. (1973), *The Monk* [1796], Howard Anderson (ed.), Oxford: Oxford University Press.

List, Larry (ed.) (2005), *The Imagery of Chess Revisited*, New York: Isamu Noguchi Foundation and Garden Museum/George Braziller.

López, Gemma (2007), *Seductions in Narrative: Subjectivity and Desire in the Works of Angela Carter and Jeanette Winterson*, New York: Cambria Press.

References

Mahon, Alyce (2005), *Surrealism and the Politics of Eros, 1938–1968*, London: Thames and Hudson.

Makinen, Merja (1997), 'Sexual and Textual Aggression in *The Sadeian Woman* and *The Passion of New Eve*', in Bristow and Broughton (eds), 149–65.

—— (2000), 'Angela Carter's *The Bloody Chamber* and the Decolonisation of Female Sexuality', in Easton (ed.), 20–36.

Manley, Kathleen E. B. (2001), 'The Woman in Process in Angela Carter's "The Bloody Chamber"', in Roemer and Bacchilega (eds), 83–93.

Marxism Today (1991), 'Interview' with Angela Carter, July, 48.

Massé, Michelle A. (1992), *In the Name of Love: Women, Masochism and the Gothic*, Ithaca: Cornell University Press.

Matus, Jill (2000), 'Blonde, Black and Hottentot Venus: Context and Critique in Angela Carter's "Black Venus"', in Easton (ed.), 161–72

McNay, Lois (1992), *Foucault and Feminism*, Boston: Northeastern University Press.

Meaney, Gerardine (1993), *(Un)Like Subjects: Women, Theory, Fiction*, London: Routledge.

Meyers, Helene (2001), *Femicidal Fears: Narratives of the Female Gothic Experience*, Albany: SUNY Press.

Michael, Magali Cornier (1996), *Feminism and the Postmodern Impulse: Post-World War II Fiction*, Albany: State University of New York Press.

—— (1998), 'Angela Carter's *Nights at the Circus*: An Engaged Feminism via Subversive Postmodern Strategies', in Tucker (ed.), 206–27.

Mikkonen, Kai (2001), 'The Hoffman(n) Effect and the Sleeping Prince: Fairy Tales in Angela Carter's *The Infernal Desire Machines of Doctor Hoffman*', in Roemer and Bacchilega (eds), 167–86.

Milbank, Alison (1993), 'Introduction', in Radcliffe (1993), ix–xxix.

Miles, Robert (1994), 'Introduction', *Women's Writing*, Special Number: Female Gothic Writing, 1:2, 131–42.

—— (1995), *Ann Radcliffe: The Great Enchantress*, Manchester: Manchester University Press.

—— (2002), *Gothic Writing 1750–1820: A Genealogy*, 2nd edn, Manchester: Manchester University Press.

Moers, Ellen (1974a), 'Female Gothic: The Monster's Mother', *New York Review of Books*, 21 March, 24–8.

—— (1974b), 'Female Gothic: Monsters, Goblins, Freaks', *New York Review of Books*, 4 April, 35–9.

—— (1978), *Literary Women* [1976], London: Women's Press.

References

Morris, Pam (1993), *Literature and Feminism*, Oxford: Blackwell.

Mortimer, John (1984), 'The Sadeian Woman: Angela Carter', in *In Character: Interviews with Some of the Most Influential and Remarkable Men and Women of Our Time*, London: Penguin, 43–7.

Müller, Anja (1997), *Angela Carter: Identity Constructed/Deconstructed*, Heidelberg: Universitätsverlag C. Winter.

Munford, Rebecca (2002), 'Re-vamping the Gothic: Representations of the Gothic Heroine in Angela Carter's *Nights at the Circus*', *ParaDoxa*, 17, 235–56.

—— (2004), 'Re-presenting Charles Baudelaire/Re-presencing Jeanne Duval: Transformations of the Muse in Angela Carter's "Black Venus"', *Forum for Modern Language Studies* 40:1, 1–13.

—— (2006), 'Angela Carter and the Politics of Intertextuality', in Munford (ed.), 1–20.

—— (2007), '"The Desecration of the Temple"; or, "Sexuality as Terrorism"? Angela Carter's (Post)feminist Gothic Heroine', *Gothic Studies*, 9:2, 58–70.

Munford, Rebecca (ed.) (2006), *Re-visiting Angela Carter: Texts, Contexts, Intertexts*, Basingstoke: Palgrave.

Neumeier, Beate (1996), 'Postmodern Gothic: Desire and Reality in Angela Carter's Writing', in Victor Sage and Allan Lloyd Smith (eds), *Modern Gothic: A Reader*, Manchester: Manchester University Press, 141–51.

Paglia, Camille (1990), *Sexual Personae: Art and Decadence from Neferiti to Emily Dickinson*, London: Yale University Press.

Palmer, Paulina (1987), 'From "Coded Mannequin" to Bird Woman: Angela Carter's Magic Flight', in Sue Roe (ed.) *Women Reading Women's Writing*, Brighton: Harvester Press, 179–205.

—— (1999), *Lesbian Gothic: Transgressive Fictions*, New York: Cassell.

Peach, Linden (1998), *Angela Carter*, Basingstoke: Macmillan.

—— (2009), *Angela Carter*, 2nd edn, Basingstoke: Palgrave Macmillan.

Perrault, Charles (1981), 'La Belle au bois dormant', *Contes*, Jean-Pierre Collinet (ed.), Paris: Éditions Gallimard, 131–40.

Phillips, John (2001), *Sade: The Libertine Novels*, London: Pluto.

Pitchford, Nicola (2002), *Tactical Readings: Feminist Postmodernism in the Novels of Kathy Acker and Angela Carter*, Lewisburg: Bucknell University Press.

Poe, Edgar Allan (1986a), *The Fall of the House of Usher and Other Writings*, David Galloway (ed.), London: Penguin.

—— (1986b), 'The Philosophy of Composition' [1846], in Poe (1986), 480–92.

References

— (2008), 'Maelzel's Chess Player' [1836], *The Works of Edgar Allan Poe*, Rockville, MD: Wildside Press, 2008, 83–117.

Polizzotti, Mark (1999), 'Introduction' to Breton (1999), ix–xxvii.

Pollock, Griselda (1988), *Vision and Difference: Femininity, Feminism and the Histories of Art*, London: Routledge.

— (1999), *Differencing the Canon: Feminist Desire and the Writing of Art's Histories*, London: Routledge.

Polonsky, Rachel (2002), 'Poe's Aesthetic Theory', in Hayes (ed.), 42–56.

Praz, Mario (1970), *The Romantic Agony* [1933], Angus Davison (trans.), Oxford: Oxford University Press.

Punter, David (1991), 'Essential Imaginings: The Novels of Angela Carter and Russell Hoban', in James Acheson (ed.), *The British and Irish Novel Since 1960*, Basingstoke: Macmillan, 142–58.

— (1996a), *The Literature of Terror: A History of Gothic Fictions from 1765 to the Present Day. Vol. 1: The Gothic Tradition*, 2nd edn, London: Longman.

— (1996b), *The Literature of Terror: A History of Gothic Fictions from 1765 to the Present Day. Vol. 2: The Modern Gothic*, 2nd edn, London: Longman.

— (1998), *Gothic Pathologies: The Text, the Body and the Law*, Basingstoke: Macmillan.

Punter, David (ed.) (2000), *A Companion to the Gothic*, Oxford: Blackwell.

Quinn, Arthur Hobson (1998), *Edgar Allan Poe: A Critical Biography*, Baltimore: Johns Hopkins University Press.

Quinn, Patrick F. (1957), *The French Face of Edgar Poe*, Carbondale: Southern Illinois University Press.

Radcliffe, Ann (1986), *The Romance of the Forest* [1791], Chloe Chard (ed.), Oxford: Oxford University Press.

— (1993), *A Sicilian Romance* [1790], Alison Milbank (ed.), Oxford: Oxford University Press.

— (1998a), *The Italian* [1797], E. J. Clery (ed.), Oxford: Oxford University Press.

— (1998b), *The Mysteries of Udolpho* [1794], Bonamy Dobrée (ed.) and Terry Castle (intro.) Oxford: Oxford University Press.

— (2000), 'On the Supernatural in Poetry' [1826], in E.J. Clery and Robert Miles (eds), *Gothic Documents: A Sourcebook 1700–1820*, Manchester: Manchester University Press, 163–72.

Robinson, Sally (1991), *Engendering the Subject: Gender and Self-Representation in Contemporary Women's Fiction*, Albany: State University of New York Press.

References

Roe, Sue (1994), 'The Disorder of *Love*: Angela Carter's Surrealist College', in Sage (ed.), 60–97.

Roemer, Danielle M. (2001), 'The Contextualization of the Marquis in Angela Carter's "The Bloody Chamber"', in Roemer and Bacchilega (eds), 107–27.

Roemer, Danielle M., and Cristina Bacchilega (eds) (2001), *Angela Carter and the Fairy Tale*, Detroit: Wayne State University Press.

Royle, Nicholas (2003), *The Uncanny*, Manchester: Manchester University Press.

Russo, Mary (1994), *The Female Grotesque: Risk, Excess and Modernity*, New York: Routledge.

Sade, D. A. F., Marquis de (1965), *Justine, Philosophy in the Bedroom and Other Writings*, Richard Seaver and Austryn Wainhouse (trans. and ed.), New York: Grove Press.

— (1966a), *The 120 Days of Sodom and Other Writings*, Austryn Wainhouse and Richard Seaver (trans. and ed.), New York: Grove Press.

— (1966b), 'Reflections on the Novel' [1800], in Sade (1966a), 91–116

— (1968), *Juliette*, Austryn Wainhouse (trans. and ed.), New York: Grove Press.

— (1969), *Les Infortunes de la vertu* [1787], Paris: Garnier-Flammarion.

— (1969), *Justine, ou les malheurs de la vertu* [1791], Gilbert Lely (intro.), Paris: Union Générale d'Éditions.

— (1976), *Histoire de Juliette, ou les prospérités du vice* [1797], Gilbert Lely (intro.), 3 vols, Paris: Union Générale d'Éditions.

— (1976), *La Philosophie dans le boudoir* [1795], Yvon Belaval (ed.), Paris: Gallimard.

— (1995), *La Nouvelle Justine* [1797], Gilbert Lely (intro.), 2 vols, Paris: Union Générale d'Éditions.

— (2005), 'Eugénie de Franval: a Tragic Tale', in *The Crimes of Love: Heroic and Tragic Tales, Preceded by an Essay on Novels*, David Coward (trans. and ed.), Oxford: Oxford University Press, 239–304.

Sage, Lorna (1977), 'The Savage Sideshow: A Profile of Angela Carter', *New Review*, 4:39–40, 51–7.

— (1992), *Women in the House of Fiction*, Basingstoke: Macmillan.

— (1994a), *Angela Carter*, Plymouth: Northcote House.

— (1994b), 'Introduction', in Lorna Sage (ed.), 1–23.

— (2001), 'Angela Carter: The Fairy Tale', in *Moments of Truth: Twelve Twentieth-Century Women Novelists*, London: Fourth Estate, 221–48.

References

Sage, Lorna (ed.) (1994), *Flesh and the Mirror: Essays on the Art of Angela Carter*, London: Virago.

Schmidt, Ricarda (1989), 'The Journey of the Subject in Angela Carter's Fiction', *Textual Practice*, 3:1, 56–75.

Schor, Naomi (1994), 'This Essentialism Which Is Not One: Coming to Grips with Irigaray', in Carolyn Burke, Naomi Schor and Margaret Whitford (eds), *Engaging with Irigaray: Feminist Philosophy and Modern European Thought*, New York: Columbia University Press, 57–78.

Sellers, Susan (2001), *Myth and Fairy Tale in Contemporary Women's Fiction*, Basingstoke: Palgrave.

Sempruch, Justyna (2005), 'The Sacred May Not Be the Same as the Religious: Angela Carter's "Impressions: The Wrightsman Magdalene" and "Black Venus"', *Women: A Cultural Review*, 16:1, 73–92.

Sheets, Robin Ann (1992), 'Pornography, Fairy Tales and Feminism: Angela Carter's "The Bloody Chamber"', in John C. Fout (ed.), *Forbidden History: The State, Society, and the Regulation of Sexuality in Modern Europe*, Chicago: University of Chicago Press, 335–59.

Shelley, Mary (1985), *Frankenstein: or, The Modern Prometheus* [1818], Maurice Hindle (intro.), London: Penguin.

Shenk, David (2006), *The Immortal Game: A History of Chess*, London: Souvenir Press.

Showalter, Elaine (1985), *The Female Malady: Women, Madness and English Culture, 1830–1980*, New York: Pantheon.

— (1992), *Sexual Anarchy: Gender and Culture at the Fin de Siècle*, London: Virago.

— (1999), *A Literature of Their Own: From Charlotte Brontë to Doris Lessing* [1977], rev. and expand. edn, London: Virago.

Smith, Andrew, and Diana Wallace (eds) (2004), Special issue on the 'Female Gothic', *Gothic Studies*, 6:1.

Smith, Anne (1985), 'Myths and the Erotic', *Women's Review*, 1, 28–9.

Steedman, Carolyn (2001), *Dust*, Manchester: Manchester University Press.

Steele, Valerie (1998), *Paris Fashion: A Cultural History*, Oxford: Berg.

Stoker, Bram (1993), *Dracula* [1897], Maurice Hindle (ed.) London: Penguin.

Suleiman, Susan Rubin (1990), *Subversive Intent: Gender, Politics, and the Avant-Garde*, Cambridge, MA: Harvard University Press.

— (1994), *Risking Who One Is: Encounters with Contemporary Art and Literature*, Cambridge, MA: Harvard University Press.

References

Tauchert, Ashley (2002), *Mary Wollstonecraft: The Accent of the Feminine*, Basingstoke: Palgrave.

— (2008), *Against Transgression*, Oxford: Blackwell.

Tillotson, Victoria P. (1997) 'A Materialist Feminist Reading of Jeanne Duval: Prostitution and Sexual Imperialism from the Mid-Nineteenth Century to the Present Day', in Rosemary Hennessy and Chrys Ingraham (eds), *Materialist Feminism: A Reader in Class, Difference, and Women's Lives*, New York: Routledge, 291–305.

Tonkin, Maggie (2004), 'The "Poetics" of Decomposition: Angela Carter's "The Cabinet of Edgar Allan Poe" and the Reading-Effect', *Women's Studies*, 33, 1–21.

— (2006a), 'Albertine/a the Ambiguous: Angela Carter's Reconfiguration of Marcel Proust's Modernist Muse', in Munford (ed.), 64–86.

— (2006b), 'Musing on Baudelaire: Angela Carter's "Black Venus" and the Poet as Dead Beloved", *Literature Interpretation Theory*, 17, 301–23.

Tucker, Lindsey (ed.) (1998), *Critical Essays on Angela Carter*, New York: G. K. Hall-Simon & Schuster Macmillan.

Villiers de L'Isle Adam, Auguste (1902), *L'Ève future* [1886], Paris: Charpentier.

Wallace, Diana, and Andrew Smith (eds) (2009), *The Female Gothic: New Directions*, Basingstoke: Palgrave.

Walpole, Horace (1996), *The Castle of Otranto: A Gothic Story* [1764], W. S. Lewis (ed.), E. J. Clery (intro.), Oxford: Oxford University Press.

Ward Jouve, Nicole (1980), *Baudelaire: A Fire to Conquer Darkness*, London: Macmillan.

— (1994), '"Mother Is a Figure of Speech …"', in Sage (ed.), 136–70.

Warner, Marina (1994), *From the Beast to the Blonde: On Fairy Tales and Their Tellers*, London: Vintage.

— (2006), *Phantasmagoria: Spirit Visions, Metaphors, and Media into the Twenty-First Century*, Oxford: Oxford University Press.

Watt, James (1999), *Contesting the Gothic: Fiction, Genre and Cultural Conflict, 1764–1832* Cambridge: Cambridge University Press.

Watt, Janet (1979), 'Sade and the Sexual Struggle', *Observer Magazine*, 25 March, 54.

Watts, Helen Cagney (1985), 'An Interview with Angela Carter', *Bête Noire*, 8, 161–76.

Watz [Fruchart], Anna (2006), 'Convulsive Beauty and Compulsive Desire: The Surrealist Pattern of *Shadow Dance*', in Munford (ed.), 21–41.

References

— (2010), 'Angela Carter and Xavière Gauthier's *Surréalisme et Sexualité*', *Contemporary Women's Writing*, 4:2, 100–13.

Waugh, Patricia (1989), *Feminine Fictions: Revisiting the Postmodern*, London: Routledge.

Weekes, Karen (2002), 'Poe's Feminine Ideal', in Hayes (ed.), 148–62.

Weissberger, Barbara F. (2004), *Isabel Rules: Constructing Queenship, Wielding Power*, Minneapolis: University of Minnesota Press.

Wicke, Jennifer (1991), 'Review: Through a Gaze Darkly: Pornography's Academic Market', *Transition*, 54, 68–89.

Williams, Anne (1995), *Art of Darkness: A Poetics of Gothic*, Chicago: University of Chicago Press.

Wisker, Gina (1997), 'Revenge of the Living Doll: Angela Carter's Horror Writing', in Bristow and Broughton (eds), 116–31.

— (2006), 'Behind Locked Doors: Angela Carter, Horror and the Influence of Edgar Allan Poe', in Munford (ed.), 178–98.

Wolff, Cynthia Griffin (1983), 'The Radcliffean Gothic Model: A Form for Feminine Sexuality', in Fleenor (ed.), 207–23.

Wollstonecraft, Mary (1992), *A Vindication of the Rights of Woman* [1792], Miriam Brody (ed.), London: Penguin.

— (1994), *Maria, or The Wrongs of Woman* [1798], Anne K. Mellor (intro.), New York: W. W. Norton.

Wolstenholme, Susan (1993), *Gothic (Re)visions: Writing Women as Readers*, Albany: State University of New York Press.

Wood, Gaby (2002), *Living Dolls: A Magical History of the Quest for Mechanical Life*, London: Faber and Faber.

Wright, Angela (2002), 'European Distinctions of the Idealized Woman: Matthew Lewis's *The Monk* and the Marquis de Sade's *La Nouvelle Justine*', in Horner (ed.), 39–54.

Yalom, Marilyn (2004), *Birth of the Chess Queen: A History*, London: Pandora Press.

Zola, Emile (2002), *Nana* [1880], Henri Mitterand (ed.), Paris: Éditions Gallimard.

Index

Note: 'n.' after a page number indicates the number of a note on that page.

Index

Index

Index

Index

Index

Index